Political Parties and Democracy

Endorsements for *Political Parties and Democracy* (See back cover for additional endorsements)

"To learn about the state of party politics across the world, consult Kay Lawson's sweeping five-volume publication, *Political Parties and Democracy*, a monumental, up-to-date survey of party systems in 45 countries. The set of books should be acquired by all research libraries and should sit on the shelves of all scholars doing comparative research on political parties. It provides a combination of breadth and depth, of comparative and particular analysis. While the strength of this multi-volume set lies in its rich and convenient trove of information about party politics in regions and countries, it also makes important conceptual contributions upon which party scholars may draw."

Kenneth Janda
Professor of Political Science, Northwestern University

"Editing an excellent five-volume set of studies on parties in 46 systematically chosen countries seems an impossible mission. Yet, Kay Lawson attests to the contrary. Teachers on democratic polities, students of comparative politics, and researchers on political parties can find in these volumes a treasure of recent data, analysis, and comprehension. Country chapters address a similar set of questions, and not fewer than 54 country authors answer them with a wise combination of local expertise and sensibility to more general issues of democratic theory. Lawson has been extremely successful in putting forward a common framework—examining the relationship between parties and democracy—that is able to integrate the study of regions as different as the Americas, Europe, Russia, Asia, Africa, Oceania, and the Arab world. At the end, the five volumes restate once again the utmost relevance of parties within an amazing diversity of political contexts, processes, and institutions. If sometimes there are occasions in which a book is a must for its decisive contribution to our knowledge on political parties, this is certainly one of them."

José Ramón Montero
Departamento de Ciencia Política y Relaciones Internacionales
Facultad de Derecho Universidad Autónoma de Madrid

"A pathbreaking collection of top-quality writings on party politics by leading scholars around the world, *Political Parties and Democracy* opens a genuinely new frontier of knowledge, expanding the scope of analysis to the entire globe, combining theory with history, and raising a series of new research questions."

Byung-Kook Kim
Professor, Department of Political Science, Korea University

"This monumental work consists of five volumes with 46 chapters each devoted to the parties of a different nation. Many of the party systems included in the volumes are studied here for the first time in a systematic way with unprecedented levels of knowledge and competence by authors who are native to the respective countries. The chapters are not limited to summary descriptions of the systems they study, but present extremely interesting and original insights. This is crucial for the usefulness and scientific relevance of the chapters dedicated to the more established American, European and, in general, Western democracies' party systems, whose authors manage to present novel views of extensively researched subject areas. Saying that with this work Kay Lawson has set new standards for editorship in the field of political science would be an obvious understatement. *Political Parties and Democracy* is the result of an impressive project that will greatly benefit the scientific community. I am sure that the five volumes it has produced will become fundamental references for the field of political party studies and will take a very prominent place in every party expert's library."

Luciano Bardi
Professor of Political Science, University of Pisa

"This welcome and remarkable collection of original essays covers assessments of political parties in an unusually broad range of countries. Taking into account the critical importance of parties for the operation of democracy, juxtaposed with their weaknesses both as democratic organizations and as agents of state democracy, results in clear and honest assessments of the state of parties today. Bickerton on Canada and Dwyre on the U.S. represent this well-reasoned approach with the confidence that comes from a thorough understanding of their own country's situation."

Mildred A. Schwartz
Professor Emerita at University of Illinois and Visiting Scholar, New York University

"These volumes provide a valuable in-depth and up-to-date analysis of the state of political parties across five continents, written by country experts, and will be an important source for scholars interested in the comparative study of political parties."

Lars Svåsand
Professor of Comparative Politics, University of Bergen, Norway

"Kay Lawson's *Political Parties and Democracy* is a tremendous success in giving readers the most recent information and insights about political parties around the globe. The set includes not only excellent contributions on the party systems that exemplify strong democratic regimes like the United States and the United Kingdom, but careful insights on volatile party systems in newer democracies such as Poland, and on systems still transitioning to democratic rule in places as diverse as Kenya and Morocco. The universal challenges to parties as linkage mechanisms in the early 20th century are everywhere apparent."

Robin Kolodny
Associate Professor of Political Science, Temple University

Political Parties and Democracy

Five Volumes

Kay Lawson, General Editor

Volume I: The Americas

Kay Lawson and Jorge Lanzaro, Volume Editors

Volume II: Europe

Kay Lawson, Volume Editor

Volume III: Post-Soviet and Asian Political Parties

Baogang He, Anatoly Kulik, and Kay Lawson, Volume Editors

Volume IV: Africa and Oceania

Luc Sindjoun, Marian Simms, and Kay Lawson, Volume Editors

Volume V: The Arab World

Saad Eddin Ibrahim and Kay Lawson, Volume Editors

Political Parties in Context
Kay Lawson, Series Editor

Political Parties and Democracy

General Editor, Kay Lawson

Volume V: The Arab World

SAAD EDDIN IBRAHIM AND
KAY LAWSON,
VOLUME EDITORS

Political Parties in Context
Kay Lawson, Series Editor

AN IMPRINT OF ABC-CLIO, LLC
Santa Barbara, California • Denver, Colorado • Oxford, England

Library of Congress Cataloging-in-Publication Data

Political parties and democracy / Kay Lawson, set editor.
p. cm.—(Political parties in context series)
Includes bibliographical references and index.
ISBN 978-0-275-98706-0 (hard copy : alk. paper)—ISBN 978-0-313-08349-5 (ebook)—ISBN 978-0-313-38314-4 (vol. 1 hard copy)—ISBN 978-0-313-38315-1 (vol. 1 ebook)—ISBN 978-0-313-38316-8 (vol. 2 hard copy)—ISBN 978-0-313-38317-5 (vol. 2 ebook)—ISBN 978-0-313-38060-0 (vol. 3 hard copy)—ISBN 978-0-313-38061-7 (vol. 3 ebook)—ISBN 978-0-313-35302-4 (vol. 4 hard copy)—ISBN 978-0-313-35303-1 (vol. 4 ebook)—ISBN 978-0-275-97082-6 (vol. 5 hard copy)—ISBN 978-0-313-08295-5 (vol. 5 ebook) 1. Political parties. 2. Democracy. I. Lawson, Kay.
JF2051.P5678 2010
324.2—dc22 2009047965

ISBN: 978-0-275-98706-0 (set)
EISBN: 978-0-313-08349-5 (set)

14 13 12 11 10 1 2 3 4 5

This book is also available on the World Wide Web as an eBook.
Visit www.abc-clio.com for details.

Praeger
An Imprint of ABC-CLIO, LLC

ABC-CLIO, LLC
130 Cremona Drive, P.O. Box 1911
Santa Barbara, California 93116-1911

This book is printed on acid-free paper ∞

Manufactured in the United States of America

Contents

Political Parties and Democracy: Three Stages of Power

Kay Lawson

Political Parties and Democracy consists of five volumes with 46 chapters, each devoted to the parties of a different nation. The first volume is dedicated to the Americas: Canada and the United States for North America, and Argentina, Bolivia, Brazil, Chile, Mexico, Peru, and Uruguay for Central and South America. Volume II is on European parties: Denmark, France, Germany, Italy, Norway, Spain, and the United Kingdom in the West, and the Czech Republic, Hungary, and Poland in the East. Volume III begins with four chapters on the parties of the post-Soviet nations of Georgia, Moldova, Russia, and Ukraine and continues with the parties of five Asian nations: China, India, Japan, Malaysia, and South Korea. Parties in Africa and Oceania are the subject of Volume IV: Cameroon, Kenya, Namibia, Nigeria, and South Africa, followed by Australia, Fiji, New Zealand, Samoa, and the Solomon Islands. Finally, Volume V is devoted first and foremost to the Arab world, beginning with the parties of Algeria, Egypt, Lebanon, Mauritania, and Morocco and continuing with the parties of two neighboring states in which Arab politics play an important role: Israel and Turkey. All authors are themselves indigenous to the nation they write about. Indigenous[1] co-editors, whose essays introduce each section, have helped recruit the authors and guide the development of their chapters; final editing has been my responsibility as general editor, and the final volume concludes with my Conclusion to the Set.

The purpose of each chapter is to examine the relationship between political parties and democracy, providing the necessary historical, socio-economic, and institutional context as well as the details of contemporary political tensions between the two. To understand this relationship requires a serious effort to understand as well the basic nature of the state. That nature shapes the work of the parties. Whatever mission they give themselves, it is control of the state that they seek. Without that power, programs are mere words on paper or in cyberspace.

Parties are expected to provide the key building blocks of democracy by forming a strong link between citizens and the state. It is a challenge fledging parties commonly accept, because promising to establish a government in keeping with the will of the people is the best way to achieve adequate support and wrest power away from nondemocratic leadership. Even today's most democratic and established parties trace their roots to that primeval calculation and the struggle it entails. Many of the parties studied here are still trapped in that early stage.

Some of the parties formed to wage the battle for democracy have accepted defeat, at least for now, and live on only in puppet-like roles that permit them to share the perquisites but not the substance of power. Others have only recently formed organizations strong enough to have led the way forward from dictatorship and are still working out the new relationship. They came to power waving the banners of democracy, but they are not necessarily bound—or able—to obey its precepts once in power. In some cases, the move to democratic governance has been short-lived and military, religious, or ethnic autocracy has retaken control.

Still other parties, such as the ones scholars in the West have studied hardest and longest, have thrived for many years as more or less genuine agencies of democracy, but are now gradually but perceptibly moving forward to a third stage of power. Serious links to the populace no longer seem to be necessary, as the central organization becomes expert at using the tools of political marketing and the victorious party leaders adopt policies that satisfy their most powerful supporters. Moving steadily away from participatory linkage, parties tend to maintain a degree of responsive linkage, but the answer to the question of to whom they are responsive is not necessarily a reassuringly democratic one.

In short, the development of political parties over the past century is the story of three stages in the pursuit of power: liberation, democratization, and dedemocratization. In every volume of *Political Parties and Democracy* the reader will find parties at all three stages. Sometimes the story of liberation will be part of the recent history that must be understood; in other chapters the unfinished quest for freedom is the only story that can yet be told. Sometimes the tale of post-liberation democratization is very much "a work in progress" (and perhaps a dubious one). Sometimes dedemocratization takes the form of accepting failure under impossible circumstances after the first joys of liberation have been tasted, and sometimes it is a more deliberate effort to escape the bounds of what still hungry leaders consider a too successful democratization. Understanding parties—and their relationship with democracy—means understanding the stage of power their leadership has reached.

Is democracy always dependent on parties, or are there other agencies capable of forcing governments to act on behalf of the entire demos? Perhaps mass movements working via the Internet can be used to hasten liberation, fine tune democratization, and even to forestall dedemocratization. Possibly in the future such movements will not only help the parties take control of the state, but then tame them to live in comfortable league with democracy, offering party leaders sufficient rewards for staying in power democratically and followers better designed instruments for reasonable but effective participation.

However, party democracy, cybertized, is still no more than an interesting dream, and one that goes well beyond the purview of these studies. What one can find in *Political Parties and Democracy* is the actual state of the play of the game.

Introduction to *Political Parties and Democracy: Part I: The Arab World*

Saad Eddin Ibrahim

By the end of 2008, there were some 200 legally registered political parties in the Arab world, in addition to a handful of de facto, albeit nominally banned, parties. Among those Arab countries that allow political parties, the numbers range from 5 in Bahrain to 31 in Jordan. To be sure, most of these parties are quite small and are often family, clan, tribe, or sect based. Indeed, the Freedom House Report (FHR) for that year did not list any of the 21 Arab countries as "fully free" or "democratic." Held to the FHR's rigorous criteria, only seven Arab countries were designated as partly free: Bahrain, Jordan, Kuwait, Lebanon, Mauritania, Morocco, and Yemen.[1]

If political parties are the ways and means of democratic governance, it is clear that in the Arab world such correlations, if they exist at all, are quite weak. And if that is indeed the case, is it then warranted to devote a volume to the subject?

Naturally, the editor and authors of this present volume would answer in the affirmative. For one reason, the whole world has been going through a long era of democratization. The Arab countries of the Middle East and

North Africa have been included in this trend, even as individual countries display marked variations in their political trajectories. Moreover, it is important to remember that the countries of the region are not static. Some countries currently designated as "not free" by FHR, most notably Egypt and Iraq, were for several decades living in conditions acknowledged by that same body to be "democratic" (i.e., before backsliding into nondemocratic regimes). In this environment, the lack of a solid correlation between political pluralism and democratic rule is an anomaly that calls for investigation and reflection.

As part of this reflection, much has been said in western social science about so-called Arab exceptionalism. The reference has generally been used to invoke the persistence of nondemocratic governance in the region at the same time that most of world has been moving steadily toward democracy. Does "exceptionalism" apply to the chapters in this volume as well?

Without getting entangled in an endless, and often fruitless, debate, this present volume has opted to pursue this question empirically. Six Arab nations are represented here: Mauritania, Tunisia, Morocco, Algeria, Egypt, and Lebanon. For the sake of comparison, we have included chapters on Turkey (which is a majority Muslim but not an Arab country) and Israel (neither Muslim nor Arab, but having a minority Arab population and Arab parties) as "Neighboring States."

This volume will not dwell on the definitions of political parties. If there are groups or sociopolitical formations that label themselves or are labeled by significant others as "parties," the authors have taken them into consideration. Many such definitions abound. In 1770, Edmond Burke identified a political party as "an organized assembly of men united for working together for the national interest, according to the particular principle they agreed upon."[2] Later variations have related the function of political parties to the ever-elusive "collective national interest." Thus some 100 years later, Marx would define "party" in exclusively class terms. More recently, "collective interest" has oscillated between ethnonationalistic, class, religious, and sectarian considerations. However, the legal definitions of "political party" in many of the Arab countries—those with laws regulating the matter—have stayed close to the above formulations. Thus, for example, Jordanian law defines a political party as "any organization of citizens who lawfully strive to participate in the political life to enhance their socio-economic-political goals by legitimate means."[3]

Even if we were to accept this as a working definition for the region, the fact remains that six Arab countries do not allow or recognize political parties, namely, Libya, Kuwait, Qatar, United Arab Emirates (UAE), Oman, and Saudi Arabia. This does not mean these nations are free from sociopolitical cleavages along tribal, class, religious, ethnic, and linguistic lines. Rather it means that these disparate groups are not permitted to express themselves publicly, much less by way of sanctioned political parties. The argument for denying such recognition often runs along the lines of "protecting national unity" or sparing the people from seditious divisiveness.

In such an environment, most students of politics or government would agree that, where they do exist in the Arab world, political parties are weak, lacking in both institutional capabilities and internal democracy. Their leadership tends to be autocratic. Moreover, this leadership has a tendency to dwell in power indefinitely. Almost a century ago, the Italian sociologist Roberto Michels noted the so-called Iron Law of Oligarchy in political parties. This "law" refers to the self-perpetuating tendency of the small group of elites at the top of the party. In that sense, political parties—even those in the opposition—become a mirror image of the ruling autocrats. The truth of this reveals itself in the dwindling memberships of Arab political parties, including the ruling ones, in recent decades.

Yet if this is the case, one may wonder why researchers and scholars even bother to study Arab political parties at all. The answer is simple. It is precisely this state of party affairs that merits and compels further diagnosis and proper prognosis.

A HISTORICAL OVERVIEW

Although division and partisanship have existed in Arab societies since pre-Islamic times, "political parties" as such are a relatively new phenomenon. The concepts, structures, and impetus arose from the stormy interaction between the Arab world and the West from the late 18th century on. It was another century before the first political formation called itself a party. Since then, sociopolitical formations that call themselves political parties have revolved around several common axes: national liberation, constitutionalism, social justice, socioeconomic development, religion, and ethnicity. Often, parties tended to revolve around a charismatic leader who dominated the party as well as the national scene in his respective country.

During the early years, if not decades, of Arab political parties, these parties lacked modern procedures and organizational structures, such as formal mission statements, membership records, bylaws, internal elections, leadership, and lines of command and control. When, at a later stage of their evolution, individual societies began to diversify and become more differentiated, so too did the Arab political parties.

During the 19th and early 20th centuries, as European colonialism encroached on one Arab country after another, the initial resistance was carried out by traditional forces and led by either religious or tribal leaders. The first Cairo uprising against Napoleon's French Expedition (1798–1801) originated in and was triggered by the Al-Azhar 'ulema. Thirty years later, when France invaded Algeria, it was a tribal leader,

Emir Abdul-Qader, who led a protracted resistance (1830–1860). This also happened in Libya, where the Italian invasion met resistance from a legendary religious tribal leader, Omar al-Mukhtar. These early responses were generally couched in religious or primordial terms.

However, as European colonial powers subdued indigenous resistance and tightened their grip, they also delineated boundaries around their respective "possessions" and set up modern bureaucracies to serve their designs. In doing so, they unwittingly expedited a process already under way: the emergence of modern classes, namely, a new middle class and a modern working class from which the second wave of resistance to colonialism would ultimately spring.

As standard social science propositions would have it, this was an unintended consequence of the colonial project. However, the important point for the purposes of this volume is that this second wave of resistance was couched in country-based "national movements" and often embodied in the form of modern political parties. It was not accidental that the first of these parties was established by "subjects" who were exposed to modern education in the European metropole and soon wanted to be "citizens" of an "independent country."

Thus, Mustafa Kamel, the founder of the first modern Egyptian party, Al-Hizb Al-Watany (The Patriotic Party), also introduced the slogan "Egypt for the Egyptians." Allal Al Fassi, founder of the first Moroccan modern party, Istiqlal (Independence), would follow suit, using the slogan "Morocco is for the Moroccans" for his party. Ferhat Hashad in Algeria and Habib Bourguiba in Tunisia employed similar rhetoric.[4]

With the exception of Egypt and Morocco, the other Arab countries have become autonomous polities only in the past century—various ancient histories notwithstanding. The boundaries of these late-comers to statehood were mostly a function of the colonial experience. In fact, it was often the resistance movements struggling against foreign encroachment that later evolved into political parties. When they obtained an independence of sorts, those national liberation movements that had not already metamorphosed into political parties now did so, often without giving up the preindependence name. Thus the Egyptian delegation that tried to travel to the Versailles Peace Conference (1918), only to be blocked, was called by the Arabic word for delegation, *al-Wafd*. This name then carried over to the populist party that led the uprising against the British occupation a year later in 1919. Similarly, the earliest Moroccan national liberation movement called itself by the name of its objective, Independence (Istiqlal). The Algerian National Liberation Front simply added the word party later on. The same was true of the Palestine Liberation Organization. Thus the first wave of Arab political parties grew out of the anticolonialist national liberation movements. Their leaders were considered patriotic heroes of independence and the "fathers of the nation."

Here, even in these early days, the distortions of Arab political life began to set in. During the struggle against foreign occupation, "national unity" was urged to foil the colonial tactic of "divide and rule." Splinters and dissidents were considered to be unpatriotic, collaborators, or worse, traitors. This continued in the early years of independence and, in some Arab countries, had the effect of stunting or outright blocking the development of opposition parties.

The result was virtual one-party rule in several Arab countries. These one-party systems took their cues from the like-minded authoritarian and totalitarian systems of fascist Europe and the Communist Soviet Bloc, respectively. Later, no longer wanting to be likened to these ill-famed predecessors, the Arab one-party systems came to be known instead as populist regimes. Initially, populism was a blend of anticolonialism, anti-Zionism, socialism, nationalism, and Islamism. A command economy, a welfare state, and the nationalization of foreign companies were standard practices. The populist mode of governance is not only centered in one-party rule but is also most often associated with a "personality cult." Egypt under Gamal Abd-al Nasser (1952–1970) was a pioneering model. It was later emulated by Libya under Muammar al-Gaddafi (since 1969), Algeria under Houari Boumédiène (1966–1978), Syria under Hafiz al-Assad (1971–2000), Iraq under Saddam Hussein (1979–2003), and Yemen under Ali Abdullah Saleh (since 1974).

However, history shows that within 15 to 20 years the populist regime began to weaken. Sustaining the welfare state was only possible in rich oil economy states like Libya, Algeria, and Iraq or by borrowing domestically and internationally. The endless borrowing became untenable for the populist regimes that were no longer able to manage their debts. This, in turn, opened the door for foreign creditors to interfere in these countries' internal affairs, often under the auspice of economic reform. In the late 1970s and 1980s the reform packages came to be known as the Club of Paris conditions for rescheduling debt, mostly applicable to commercial loans. Some ten years later, the same kind of intervention and conditional ties were applied to interstate loans in what came to be known as the Washington Consensus. This later intervention was orchestrated mainly by the World Bank and the International Monetary Fund, both of which are headquartered in Washington, D.C. In many countries, yielding to these external conditions meant dismantling existing public sector and welfare policies, including subsidies of food and other basic commodities and services. This, in turn, led to occasional food riots and domestic demands for more political participation.

In this politicoeconomic climate, one-party regimes were able to open up the political system to a multiparty formula of one kind or another. At least five countries allowed such political reform on the heels of coerced economic reform or food riots: Egypt, Morocco, Jordan, Tunisia, and Yemen.

COMPETING BUILDING PROCESSES

For much of the 20th century, Arab countries have had to engage in simultaneous processes of consolidating independence, nation building, institution building, economic development, and democracy building.

Not surprisingly, the first two processes took precedence. Even when nation building appeared nearly complete or, more accurately, firmly on track, postindependence leaders continued to advance the argument that "development" was far more pressing than democracy.

During this stage, several countries flirted with quasi-socialist models of a command economy with its attendant promise of rapid development. After some initial success, they ran into economic trouble. Showcase projects would turn into "white elephants," with cost overruns and no or protracted returns. After the first decade, these nations' favorite import-substitution policy—financed by borrowing—led to mounting foreign debts and an inability to service them. Some five decades after "independence," many of these countries had little to show, according to the United Nations Development Program Human Development Reports, especially that of 2004.

DEMOCRACY AS A SCAPEGOAT

Following the establishment of the state of Israel and the first Arab defeat in 1948, the returning armies blamed their defeat on the elected civilian governments at the time. This ushered in an era of military coups d'état. This phase began in Syria in 1949, only a few months after the defeat. Once again, an argument was put forward to postpone democratization. This time, the imperative of vindicating "national honor" trumped democracy and a new cry was heard: "No voice should be louder than that of the Battle for Palestine!" Curiously, countries with military rulers neither won any subsequent wars against Israel, nor did they liberate one inch of Palestine in sixty years. Nevertheless, the same cry continues to echo.

It has been obvious to regional observers for some time that autocratic Arab regimes—whether traditional, military, or police based—have perfected a set of control techniques to consolidate their power. At the same time, they have developed a parallel set of make-believe techniques to give the illusion to their people and the outside world that they are democratizing their respective countries. Arab political parties have been caught up in this charade, sometimes willfully, but more often by default. With the exception of Kuwait and Bahrain, the traditional countries of the Gulf Cooperation Council do not claim, nor do they seek to build, pluralistic governance, of which political parties would be a cornerstone. Likewise, some autocrats, such as Libya's Gaddafi, have not bothered even to pretend to be moving toward democracy. Since his coup d'état in 1969, political parties have been banned in Libya.

This leaves some 13 of 22 Arab countries that have bona fide political parties: Morocco, Mauritania, Algeria, Tunisia, Egypt, Sudan, Jordan, Palestine, Lebanon, Syria, Iraq, Bahrain, and Yemen. Of these, six are analyzed in the chapters in this volume.

THE SECURITY STATE

Though new and still fragile, most Arab states are built around a solid core of security institutions, including the army, the police, and intelligence services. Regardless of their official roles, these institutions often make or break important policies and decisions. Together, and for lack of a better term, they are called the "regime," a possible equivalent of the Western concept of the "establishment." Whoever is the top ruler invariably keeps these institutions under his direct control or under that of his most trusted family and friends. This explains the long tenure of Arab rulers and regimes in the past half century.

A case in point is Libya. Starting as an independent multiparty constitutional monarchy in 1952, it soon felt the influence of prevailing regional pan-Arab ideologies, especially as espoused by Nasser in Egypt. Not directly involved in the wars or defeats with Israel, the pro-Western conservative monarchy drew criticism from young Libyans. In 1968, the junior officers of the newly created army staged a coup d'état. Emulating their counterparts in Egypt, Iraq, and Yemen, they overthrew the king, abolished the monarchy altogether, and declared Libya as a republic. Following the Egyptian model, the young officers declared themselves a Revolutionary Command Council. Very early on, they dissolved all political parties. For several years Libya was ruled by Popular Committees. Foreign military bases, mainly British and American, were closed down, and anticolonial, anti-Zionist, and anti-western rhetoric was in vogue.

ONE-PARTY STATES

In the 20th century, and continuing into the present century, much of the world has been subject to authoritarian and totalitarian style regimes that allow one ruling party and ban all others. Their argument, if they feel they need one, is that their government represents "the entire nation" (in the case of authoritarianism) or "all of the people" (in the case of totalitarianism).

Upon the demise of the Arab liberal age in the mid-1950s at the hands of military coups d'état, the various juntas nevertheless did feel the need for civilian counterparts to give them legitimacy of sorts. They reached out to the European repertoire and found the one-party fascist/authoritarian model. In Egypt it took the name of the Arab Socialist Union; in Tunisia, the Destour (Constitutional) Party; in Syria and Iraq, the Baath (Renaissance) Party; in Algeria, Le Front Liberation Nationale. Under this model, the state machinery, government, and the ruling party would become indistinguishable. This became so entrenched that when, some 20 years later, similar ruling parties were pressured to open up their respective regimes and reintroduce a multiparty system, political realities on the ground hardly changed. The former ruling party retains overwhelming force, enjoying a legitimate or a fraudulent electoral majority that enables it to force legislation that continues to consolidate and perpetuate its own power.

In other words, the one-party state has persisted despite the widespread appearance of pluralism. As of yet, no Arab country that fits the above scenario has developed an opposition party or coalition able to dislodge the former ruling party from power by peaceful electoral means. Algeria and Mauritania are possible exceptions. However, as will be explained in this volume, military-led coups d'état have obstructed would-be democratic transitions, even in these countries.

FAITH-BASED POLITICAL PARTIES

One of the most striking developments in Arab politics in the past three decades has been the rise of faith-based political parties, specifically Islamic parties. To be sure, many such parties have sprung from religious social movements such as the Muslim brotherhood. If we could divide the development of Arab political parties into three phases—with the first being the national-liberation phase and the second being the ideological/populist phase—then the rise of Islamic parties represents the third stage in the overall trajectory of the evolution of Arab political parties. The Moroccan Justice and Development Party is the prototype. Istiqlal (Independence) Party was part of the first stage, and the Popular Forces Party was part of the second stage in that trajectory.

One factor in the explanation of the ascendance of faith-based parties (FBPs) is mass disillusionment with secular parties, whether left, right, or center. Another factor is the Islamic parties' provision of services to the needy, especially in crowded urban slums. Finally, the leaders as well as the rank and file of these FBPs have a reputation of humility, piety, and integrity. These are traits valued in traditional Arab-Muslim culture. FBPs are often run as Leninist parties; they are highly disciplined, hierarchal, and obedient. This fuels apprehensions about the long-term commitment of FBPs to democracy or liberal norms. An FBP leader in Algeria was once quoted to the effect that the Islamists would use democracy to get to power, but once there it would be their divine obligation to remain in office eternally, hence the popular proposition "One Man, One Vote, One Time." Critics often invoke the analogy of the Nazis coming to power through election in the early 1930s.

Although these apprehensions do not seem to have undermined the continuing surge of FBPs, many Islamists themselves have toned down their rhetoric and declared their commitments to some, if not all, of the standard liberal values and practice.

FBPs are one of the unintended consequences of the long-term dominance of autocratic one-party rule in the Arab world. In their quest for total control, these regimes cause a steady contraction of public space. Repressive regimes not only banned political parties, but also severely restricted freedom of assembly and nongovernmental organization. In this environment, the mosque became one of the very few public spaces able to escape the total control of autocratic regimes. Herein lay the roots of many of the faith-based movements that later developed into political parties. In that sense, FBPs had anywhere from a 20- to a 30-year head start over their secular counterparts.

STRUCTURAL WEAKNESSES OF ARAB POLITICAL PARTIES

With the exception of Morocco, Lebanon, Kuwait, and, to a lesser extent, Yemen and Jordan, free media, and hence free debate, are rarely found in the Arab world. The absence of free discourse has crippled all political parties, including the ruling ones. Lack of competitive politics has stunted them. Lack of opportunities to win elections against the ruling party has steadily distanced many citizens from the political process and hence from political parties. Card-carrying membership has steadily declined. A stark example of that is Egypt's Progressive Leftist Party, whose membership exceeded 1 million in the late 1970s. Twenty years later, according to its own newspaper *Elahaly*, the membership had dwindled to about 100,000.

Lack of Internal Democracy

Many of the contemporary Arab political parties have unwittingly devolved into "mirror images" of the one-party regimes they have been otherwise challenging. Their founding fathers stay in power for as many years as the autocrat in office. The same often applies to first-rank deputies and other top aides. The ruling regime often encourages this lethargic tendency among its would-be rivals. In this way, the parties become integral, but nonthreatening, parts of the system. As this lack of internal democracy has become increasingly apparent, it has led, among other factors, to a loss of confidence in political parties on the part of the public.

Weak Institutional Capacity

Lack of internal democracy has been matched by a diminishing institutional capacity and organizational viability. Political parties have become less capable of enforcing bylaws, maintaining membership rosters, establishing provincial and local chapters, securing viable channels of command, communication, and control, and so forth. This weak state of institutional affairs is in part a reflection of the dominant autocratic leadership of the party. Strong institutional capacity would imply a minimum level of autonomy or participatory governance.

Undisciplined Membership

As a result of the two above-mentioned trends, a third naturally follows: lack of discipline. Party directives are not always followed, and enforcement of policy and initiatives becomes increasingly difficult. A lack of discipline is particularly detrimental to activities related to voting along party lines and recruitment and training of new members. The fact that most of the parties under discussion are in the opposition with no prospect to get to or share in power means a scarcity of rewards to offer. Thus there are no incentives for party discipline, loyalty, and achievement.

Limited Autonomous Resources

Aside from the ruling party, which always finds ways of appropriating part of the state resources for its own partisan purposes, other parties are often severely underresourced. When they increase membership dues, they hinder recruiting efforts for new members and run the additional risk of losing older ones. Their ability for propagation and outreach is undermined by having neither media of their own nor access to those that are state-controlled. The same lack is apparent with respect to headquarters, office facilities, and meeting space and is attenuated by legal restrictions on rallies or meetings in public squares. These resources are essential for the sheer survival of the party, much less its ability to thrive. Occasionally, the dominant ruling party may dole out—directly or through a legislative initiative—proportional financial aid to other parties in a move that often serves to expose their weaknesses and vulnerability and to increase their dependence.

Interfacing with Civil Society

Some social scientists have treated political parties as variants of civil society, while others opt to group parties into what is termed political society. Although neither categorization has a particularly greater theoretical or empirical advantage, the pertinent question is how political parties figure in the associational life of various countries. Since de Tocqueville's *Democracy in America,* community and grassroots voluntary associations have been posited to be, if not a requisite, at least a concomitant feature of good democratic governance. In fact, this was what de Tocqueville believed distinguished American from European democracy. Later students of the subject have invariably termed these as "intermediate," "pressure," "interest," "veto," or "countervailing" groups. These groups have been alternatively conceptualized as agents of political socialization whose role is to train individuals in the art and skills of "citizenship." They are thus deemed important for robust democracy.

The Arab world has not been a monolith. There is wide diversity among the 21 Arab countries in terms of size, socioeconomic formations, and political trajectories. This diversity was naturally bound to be reflected in the development of their respective civil societies. The most prominent of these are the professional and occupational associations. Teachers, lawyers, doctors, and engineers have served as functional equivalents of political parties when parties were banned or rendered dysfunctional. Partisan rivalry may rage within these associations to the point of undermining their original functions. However, because such associations are more organically linked to the daily lives of a wider swath of ordinary people, they are more difficult for autocratic regimes to tamper with without causing serious popular backlash.

This functional interchangeability between political parties and civil society organizations has been a saving grace that has allowed minimal levels of pluralism in several Arab countries, especially in the Gulf and the one-party states.

Clan, Tribe, Ethnicity, and Political Parties

For more than two centuries, social science has used a variety of terms to distinguish "modernity" as the movement away from ascriptive or primordial solidarities and toward more organic or achievement-based solidarities. Accordingly, political parties, along with occupational and professional associations, are often seen as embodiments of modernity. They are by nature based on freedom of choice, and as such, these affiliations are not ironclad or caste-like. There are significant opportunities for mobility in and out of such formations. Free voting for a party of one's choice is the mark of such a margin of freedom.

However, in the absence of available, modern forms of expressing and defending interests, individuals may search for and take shelter in primordial forms such as the family, clan, tribe, sect, or ethnicity. Even as they pride themselves on being modern and secular, Arab autocratic regimes, by closing other outlets, have unwittingly caused the revival of those traditional forms of solidarity after several decades of steady decline. The same may be said about the U.S. occupation of Iraq and the fall of the Saddam Hussein's Baathist regime in 2003. In the utter political vacuum that followed, both tribalism and sectarianism were revived, stronger than they had been in the previous century. This was so much the case that the U.S. forces found it expedient to ally and work with the tribes of the western Iraqi province of Anbar.

THE CHAPTERS IN THIS VOLUME

If there is such a thing as a difficult scholarly birth, this volume is certainly an example. It has taken nearly a decade to produce, encountering the same kind of political oppression the parties herein discussed have met. Shortly after its conception by the general editor of the series Kay Lawson and my agreement to serve as volume editor, the Mubarak regime in Egypt began a protracted war of attrition against the director (myself), researchers, and affiliated members of the Ibn Khaldun Center for Democratic Studies. Twenty-eight of us were incarcerated and spent three years between courts and prisons. However, Lawson and I did not give up on the project, corresponding while I was in prison and in exile, replacing authors who dropped out from fear, intimidation, or perhaps sheer impatience and boredom with the long wait. The authors who persisted in the face of all adversities encountered by the project are less than one-third of the original list of contributors. Kay Lawson and I thank them for their valor and perseverance, as well as for the excellence of their final contributions. We also thank Daniel Egel, Bethany Anne Kibler, Roya Soleimani and Moheb Zaki for key assistance in the later stages of this work.

In his chapter "Political Parties in Mauritania: Challenges and Horizons" written before the most recent coup d'état, Mohamed Ould Mohamed Abderrahmane Moine establishes a pattern whereby economic conditions and interethnic turmoil lead to calls for greater political pluralism, which then is mishandled or succumbs to pressures from within or without, leading the people to turn again and again to the military for salvation. Finally, the demographic situation of the country and the lack of an extensive press create a tendency toward fragmentation and work against the creation of a strong political will. These contextual factors have not only set limits to what political parties can achieve in Mauritania, but also to what they strive to achieve. He argues that the main challenge facing political parties is to build genuine representational links between the citizens and the state by way of the power of their elected representatives to solve the overriding problems of the country. In a postscript, he comments on the most recent example of this trend.

Abderrazak Makri's "Democratic Transformation in Algeria: The Role of the Parties" is divided into two parts. The first part reviews the ruling regime's maneuvers, tactics, and goals, illustrating a pattern of intervention on the part of the regime, usually in the efforts to maintain an established favorable balance of power. He follows the trail back to the early years of independent Algeria to show how the military's dominant position during the early years established its political presence and continued dominance within this ruling balancing act. The second part is a sociohistorical analysis of political parties and election. Makri identifies three current or recent trends: the nationalist trend, the Islamist trend, the secular trend. In his conclusion, he sums up the conditions that impede and those that facilitate democratic transformation in Algeria.

Emad El-Din Shahin's "Political Parties in Egypt: Alive, but Not Kicking" starts from the premise that effective political parties are fundamental to democracy. This chapter considers the problem of political parties as a reflection of the wider crisis of the Egyptian political system and its dominant authoritarian dynamics. Shahin uses the disappointing 2005 elections, where turnout was low and results discouraging, as his entry into the Egyptian political arena. He reviews the weak beginnings of democracy and the de-Nasserization era. During this time, Shahin argues, Sadat established a superficial democracy at the same time that he put in place very undemocratic mechanisms to keep the opposition at bay. The next section reviews the obstacles to building effective, democratically salient political parties. Specifically, he analyses the Mubarak regime's manipulation of the multiparty system in order to marginalize, control, undermine, and outright destroy opposition. In the final section, Shahin systematically discusses the relationship between alternative parties, especially the Muslim Brethren, and the regime, paying particular attention to how these alternative parties attempt to establish their legitimacy both within and outside the official political arena. He concludes with the prognosis that "At the present, the status of party life in Egypt is not conductive to promoting a genuine democracy. True democracy requires effective pluralism, which can only thrive in a free environment. Both are clearly lacking."

Mokhtar Benabdallaoui argues in "The Role of Political Parties in Establishing Moroccan Democracy" that the Moroccan monarchy's successful management of the postindependence era kept democracy from developing a deep foothold in the ideologies of Morocco's various parties. Starting with the struggles between the monarchy and nationalist movements over a vision for independent Morocco, this chapter reviews the role and legal status of political parties at various stages of Moroccan political life postindependence. Benabdallaoui outlines a series of conflicts that led to the draining and fragmentation of the national movement and then to a shift in its demands from the call to form a constituent assembly or to participate in rule with the king to acceptance of working under the auspices and supervision of the monarchy. The second half of the chapter reviews a series of recent changes that have been introduced to strengthen the institutionalization—but also the control—of political parties. However, Benabdallaoui reveals a pattern in which parties regularly concede actual power in order to have access to superficial political participation, with ultimate power remaining, to this day, in the hands of the monarchy.

Salaheddine Jourchi's chapter, "Tunisian Political Parties, Democratization, and the Dilemma of the Political Regime," examines the objectives of Tunisian political parties and the reasons that prevented their transformation into effective tools that could integrate Tunisia into the third international democratic wave. He shows how and why pluralism in Tunisia is little more than formal pluralism, ensuring in practice the perpetuation of single-party rule. Here, as in other chapters, we see the pattern by which the extension of formal recognition in fact binds the political parties—once defined by their opposition—to the ruling party. He concludes the chapter by noting that Tunisia has not been able to develop a fully democratic party system nor has it created an influential civil society. He levels blame on the parties, as much as on the ruling regime, for failing both to establish a grassroots network and to develop a program responsive to the nation's needs. He notes that "despite their democratic discourse and their calls for reform," many doubts remain about their sincerity in adopting a democratic project and their ability to change political life.

Antoine Nasri Messarra's chapter, "The Lebanese Partisan Experience and Its Impact on Democracy," explores the institutional structures that governed the development and operation of political parties in Lebanon. He argues that the primary lenses through which Lebanese political parties have been studied—a modernity-based approach, parties as democratizing elements, and the anti-confession approach—are insufficient to understand the nature and function of political parties in Lebanon. As far back as the 1920s, political parties in Lebanon promoted the concepts of democracy, liberation, human rights, nationalism, socialism, and pan-Arabism. According to Messarra, it was not the parties that caused the multinational and regional wars that were waged on Lebanese soil between 1975 and 1990 and in July 2006, but rather the fact that the Lebanese army had been effectively paralyzed by regional pressures. When the army breaks down, society as a whole becomes vulnerable. The chapter concludes by identifying three factors that will be of crucial importance in determining the future relationship between political parties and democracy in Lebanon: (1) political protection of civil society; (2) the strength of private commitment to public action; and (3) the commitment of the parties to responsible management of a diverse society. For their part, Lebanese political parties must strive for significant change in three domains: (1) ideology; (2) responsiveness to civil society; and (3) internal democracy.

At a very late stage in the project we decided to include Turkey and Israel in this volume. Turkey shares a religion with its Arab neighbors. Israel shares neither religion nor language, but rather a long and tormented history of armed conflict over Palestine. Different as the two non-Arab neighbors may be from the Arabs, the two have been reputed to be exceptionally "democratic" in an otherwise nondemocratic region. As such, they provide a necessary counterpoint to the analyses contained herein.

PART I

The Arab World

CHAPTER 1

Political Parties in Egypt: Alive, but Not Kicking

Emad El-Din Shahin

INTRODUCTION

The results of the 2005 parliamentary elections clearly revealed the weakness of party life in Egypt. The ruling party, the National Democratic Party (NDP), proved to be a hollow structure whose survival is predicated primarily on the state's strong backing and electoral irregularities. NDP candidates lost two-thirds of the contested 444 seats, and several of its leading members failed to get re-elected. The results of the elections were similarly discouraging for the legal opposition. The 20 legal opposition parties, which collectively fielded 395 candidates, were able to win only 12 seats (2.5%). A more serious problem was that the elections that followed a period of relative political mobility and mounting expectations for reform and change failed to attract the majority of the Egyptian voters. Only 23% of the registered voters turned out to participate in this presumably momentous national event. The two major winners in the elections were not the legal political parties but the banned Muslim Brothers (MB) and the independent candidates (most of whom later rejoined the NDP, thus giving it the majority it needed in the parliament). The former won 20% of the seats, and the latter captured more than 40%.

The leaders of the legal opposition parties attributed their weak performance to the excessive use of money and intimidation by the government and the use of religion by the MB. In fact, the problems of the legal opposition are much deeper than can be blamed solely on irregularities. These and similar poor results for opposition parties have been a recurring outcome of almost all past parliamentary elections since the adoption of the multiparty system in 1976. They have become a systemic pattern, not an exception, which relates to the wider political dynamics of authoritarianism and the role and functions that are invariably assigned to weak political parties in semiauthoritarian polities.

In democratic systems, the existence of effective political parties is essential for democracy to function properly. Beyond their basic functions of structuring votes and governing, political parties are expected to exercise oversight, provide channels for participation and representation, and aggregate and reconcile competing interests. This process guarantees the strength and vitality of political parties and the overall state of democracy in general. Unfortunately, such dynamics do not exist and hence do not apply to the case of Egypt. Egypt has neither a functioning democracy nor a ruling regime willing to contemplate the possibility of a peaceful transfer of power. The state party has been in power since its establishment in 1978. It was in control for even a longer time but under different names (Egypt Arab Socialist Party, 1976, and the Arab Socialist Union, 1961). Further, the regime does not allow for the full participation of rival, autonomous powers that can effectively offer alternative platforms that might aggregate the interests of society and shake the regime's monopoly over power.

One should therefore go beyond an academic discussion of these party functions and address the specific context at hand. Political parties in Egypt were allowed to emerge only as nonautonomous, controlled actors and were designed to perform certain functions that differ from those in working democracies. They are part of the authoritarian power structures and are tolerated as long as they do not pose a threat to the regime's control. In return for the regime's recognition, financial incentives, and sometimes recruitment into some state structures, opposition parties are expected to help legitimize and maintain the existing structures of authoritarianism. They legitimize the facade of a superficial pluralism by regularly participating in a manipulated electoral system. This relationship has not always been a smooth one, as the regime deliberately keeps the margins of toleration and the windows for dissent in a constant state of flux. These margins are defined by the president, whose role as a final arbitrator, reserving for himself the right to allow the exercise of freedoms supposedly protected under the law, is constantly accentuated and has indeed become indispensable. The regime—parties relationship is sustained through a combination of toleration of dissent, cooptation, legal restrictions, and coercion. It is not surprising that Egypt has 24 legal political parties, yet all are largely ineffective, unpopular, and marginal. None could be considered a serious contender for political power. Meanwhile, the regime has systematically restricted the legalization and even movement of popular actors (organized groups, movements, or individuals) that exhibit a degree of autonomy and can potentially pose a threat to its continued control. Hence, the famous paradox or cliché: "In the Egyptian political arena, the popular parties are illegal, and the legal parties are unpopular." This chapter considers the problem of political parties as a reflection of the wider crisis of the Egyptian political system and its dominant authoritarian dynamics. It will also examine other causes of that crisis that relate to the parties.

HISTORICAL BACKGROUND: A WEAK LEGACY OF PARTY LIFE

A society's historical legacy of a democratic experience (or lack thereof) is important as it positively or negatively affects its political culture. Egypt has a relatively long history of party life, a century old, but this legacy has not always been inspiring. Many of its shortcomings—a weak party life and low levels of political participation (or popular apathy)—have persisted and still characterize today's party dynamics.

Several elements have contributed to the weakness of the party system: the persistent imbalance between the excessive authority of the executive branch and the weak legislature; a high state of polarization and fragmentation between the political parties; their low level of institutionalization; and their lack of clear social and economic programs that address the needs and expectations of the majority of the population. Despite its significant weaknesses, the pre-1952 revolution parliamentary experience had its positive sides. Egyptian political life at that time was relatively vivid and characterized by repeated transfers of power (often due to irregular procedures), the formation of political alliances, and a relative respect for individual and public freedoms. It became evident, however, that toward the end of the first half of the 20th century, Egypt's party life was suffering severe strains.

Shortly after the July 1952 revolution, the Revolutionary Command Council dissolved all political parties, thus bringing to an end all pluralist political life. President Gamal Abdel Nasser was distrustful of the liberal experience and its party dynamics. He always considered political parties to be divisive and to have frustrated popular expectations. He also believed that the Egyptians were not ready for democracy and needed to be resocialized regarding democratic practices. Nasser's understanding of democracy linked public freedoms to the provision of the basic economic and social needs of the people. In practice, he wanted to consolidate power by undermining the sociopolitical forces and building a new support base to ensure the mobilization and full support of the masses behind the new regime. To achieve these goals, he suspended political pluralism, centralized power in the executive and its head, and restricted political participation. The state experimented with different forms of single/state party systems, each lasting only a few years (the Liberation Rally 1953; the National Union 1957; and the Arab Socialist Union, 1961, which ended in 1976).

The single party structures, and particularly Nasser's charisma and overwhelming popularity, mobilized the population in support of the regime's policies but otherwise did not necessarily provide for their participation in the system or their involvement in the decision-making process. The state party was a bureaucratic top-down structure, an instrument of control, and an integral part of the executive that dominated entirely the other branches of the government. Party members dominated the parliament entirely and always rubber stamped the policies and decisions of the regime, and thus the parliament lost its raison d'être. The regime also exercised full control of the associations of the civil society and over the professional unions, subordinating them to the governing party structures.

The policies of the 1952 revolutionary regime had a deep impact on the political culture of the Egyptians and their perceptions of the political system and party life. Nasser's regime institutionalized authoritarianism, the use of extra-legal repressive measures, and the overwhelming power of the state vis-à-vis society. All this shaped the Egyptians' attitudes toward authority and the validity of participation. Many felt the marginalization of their role as citizens and members of the political community. Their participation did not count, as it neither changed policies nor affected the results of the state-manipulated elections. And since dissent was not tolerated, individual or collective organized action against an overpowering state was not only futile but also extremely risky. Many also became deeply skeptical about the potential of the parliament to function as an agent for true representation, policy making, and oversight. In such an atmosphere, eschewing politics and politicians and securing daily socioeconomic survival became more rational choices. Many of these attitudes still shape the political culture of most, if not all, Egyptians.

A multiparty system was restored in the mid-1970s. It was a decision from above, not a product of a thriving civil society or popular pressures. It was simply a grant from President Anwar Sadat who, by introducing major changes to Nasser's political structures, hoped to create his own political system and build a new basis of legitimacy. The decision was also not an outcome of Sadat's deep belief in democracy and democratic values; indeed, he always referred to democracy as capable of having fierce "fangs and claws." Exactly like authoritarianism, it too can "grind" the opposition. He thought that through a controlled pluralism, he could still maintain a strong grip over his opponents; or, as he always liked to call them, "my opposition." The move to a pluralistic system was also necessary in order to give a strong signal to the external actors, particularly the United States, that he was seriously moving away from Nasser's socialist model and embracing a liberal economic and political system.

Sadat laid the foundation for a weak multiparty system, which he could easily manipulate to prevent the emergence of strong contenders to the state party. He orchestrated the process from above and designed the political and legal frameworks within which the parties were permitted to operate. In 1976, he approved the formation of three platforms, centrist, right, and left, within the Arab Socialist Union. Sadat personally picked the heads of this legal opposition. A year later, he granted these platforms the right to evolve into political parties. They became known as the Egypt Arab Socialist Party (the state's party), the Liberal Party, and the leftist Tagamou. In 1978, the New Wafd, the successor of the popular prerevolutionary Wafd Party, was approved. When Sadat felt that the multiparty system was beginning to pose some pressure, particularly after the massive food riots of 1977 and his initiative to engage in peace negotiations with Israel, he decided to restructure the party system and place more restraints on it. He established a "new" state party, the National Democratic Party, to replace the Egypt Arab Socialist Party, and created an alternative opposition party, the Labor Socialist Party, hoping that it would act as a loyal opposition and replace the increasingly critical Wafd and Tagamou parties. To facilitate the creation of the Labor Party, he himself helped found the party and ordered 20 members of his own party to resign and join the newly formed opposition party. Sadat picked Ibrahim Shukri as the leader of the Labor Party. The blatant engineering process and the manipulation of this crucial restorative phase of the multiparty experience stigmatized the legal parties and weakened their credibility as a serious and autonomous opposition. They appeared not to have evolved by popular will or independent socioeconomic forces, but by a top-down decision of the regime.

Sadat also identified the parameters for admission to and exclusion from the political process. He set the conditions and devised the necessary legal constraints to ensure continued state control over the parties. He required the platforms of all political parties not to undermine three issues: national unity, commitment to the socialist achievements of the revolutionary system (July 1952 revolution and his own May 1970 rectification revolution), and social peace. In addition, he denied recognition to parties based on religion, class, region, or profession. He also banned the formation of parties that had existed before the July 1952 revolution. After signing the peace treaty with Israel, Sadat added new conditions: not to oppose the peace treaty with Israel (the Supreme Court later nullified this condition) or the principles of the Islamic Shar'ia [commonly defined as Islamic laws]. Too broad and deliberately vague, these conditions were designed in a way that would enable the regime to easily and arbitrarily interpret and apply them at its convenience.

Their immediate intent was to restrict freedom of expression, which the Egyptian constitution guarantees, and undermine the very idea of a plurality of programs and political stands. These paralyzing restrictions led the New Wafd in 1978 to "freeze" itself and suspend all of its activities. The Leftist Tagamou Party decided to confine its activities within its headquarters, only holding meetings.

To further muzzle the opposition, Sadat designed several "innovative" laws that curtailed the activities of political parties and limited their ability to function effectively. The new laws included the Law of Shame, ostensibly to protect the values of society, and the Law for the Protection of Social Peace. He also manipulated the electoral laws in ways that contradicted regular democratic practices and norms. For example, the elections of the members of the Shura Council and the local structures (municipal and provincial councils) followed a "modified" system of proportional representation that allowed the state party to monopolize all the seats in the local councils, where much of the patronage takes place. In addition, Sadat frequently side-stepped the legislature and resorted to popular referendums whose announced results were clearly the result of fraud.

The Party Formation Law (40/1977) that was promulgated 30 years ago still stands and continues to stifle party life. It predicates the legal approval of a party on the decision of the Parties Committee. This committee also has the authority to end a party. According to the latest 2005 amendment of the Party Formation Law, the committee consists of nine members: the speaker of the Shura Council, the minister of the interior, the minister of state for parliamentary affairs, three former members of judiciary bodies, and three "public figures." The first three are, by position, members of the ruling party; and the other six are appointed by the president, who himself is the head of the ruling party. Thus, the formation of the committee grants the NDP the authority to legalize political parties. Far from being neutral, the opposition and civil society organizations have consistently called for its abolition. Article 6 of the 1977 law gives the Parties Committee the right to turn down any political party if it concludes that the party's program is not distinct from that of already existing parties. Like the committee itself, this is one of the most problematic aspects of the law. While the law, in part, requires the parties to conform, in their polices and platforms, to vague and broad principles, it expects them at the same time to present distinguishable programs. It also gives the right to decide on the nature of a party's program, not to the people, but to a regime-controlled committee. Unsurprisingly, the Parties Committee has continuously used this article to suppress any serious rival to the ruling NDP. Since its formation in 1977 and until 2008, the committee has rejected about 90 parties. So far, it has legalized only five new parties and all except the Ghad Party, described further below, are scarcely known.

In sum, while Nasser disbanded political parties and suppressed political pluralism outright, Sadat maintained a different approach. He allowed the formation of political parties, while expecting them to operate within narrow limits and observe parameters that he had devised. He also expected the opposition parties to be loyal and show him gratitude for allowing them to exist in the first place. When they did not fully comply and expressed harsh criticism of some of his policies, particularly the open door economic policy and the peace process with Israel, Sadat grew impatient, and in 1981 he suspended opposition papers and arrested party leaders. Such repressive measures exacerbated an already charged political situation and contributed to his assassination in October 1981.

Most of the restrictions that impede an effective party life still persist. The opposition parties have been fully aware of these limitations, yet have agreed to participate on the regime's terms, as they were not strong or popular enough to take part in making the rules. They henceforth subjected themselves to an arbitrary process that lacked proper institutionalization and that the regime and its ruling party manipulated. Their propensity to resist and challenge regime manipulations has proven to be very low. They have complied with the regime's restrictions and confined their activities to their headquarters. They wait for the approval of the state security forces before undertaking any activity or publicly engaging their constituency. When the approval has been denied, as is usually the case, they have never defied these arbitrary decisions. On the rare occasions when the legal opposition threatened not to participate or boycott elections, the regime has been able to lure them to rejoin the process and prevent them from keeping their threats. All this cost the political parties, particularly in this formative phase, dearly in terms of credibility and popularity.

POLITICAL PARTIES UNDER MUBARAK: KEEPING THEM ALIVE, BUT NOT KICKING

A characteristic of party life under Hosni Mubarak is the large number of parties that have come into existence since he took power in 1981 and the relative freedom of expression that the opposition or independent newspapers now enjoy. Egypt currently has 24 legal political parties, which are difficult to classify on an ideological basis. With the exception of one or two leftist or socialist parties, most share similar programs and orientations that are not substantively different from that of the state's NDP. As this chapter focuses more on the structural crises of the parties, it classifies them into two groups: the controlled legal parties and the alternative illegal political forces. The legal political parties comprise the five old, and now atrophying, parties that Sadat allowed to exist in 1976–1978: the NDP, the Liberal Party, the Tagamou, the New Wafd, and the Labor Party. Only the NDP and the Tagamou remain functional, while the rest have been either frozen by the state or have become practically dysfunctional because of severe internal disputes or direct state interventions. The other legal parties are marginal, lack popular support, and perhaps with the exception of the Nasserite Party, are not even recognizable by average Egyptians. Their poor electoral performance reflects the limited impact they have on public life. For example, of the 24 legal political parties, 12 have never been represented in the parliament; and in the 2005 parliamentary elections, 17 failed to win a single seat out of the parliament's contested 444 seats. In the last presidential "competitive" elections that 10 candidates contested, 7 of those candidates combined won only 2% of the votes.

Unlike the legal political parties, the alternative political forces enjoy some level of representation and popularity among the various social segments of society and could effectively challenge the policies and control of the regime by mobilizing public protest and mounting a sustained opposition. Within this category are the MB, the Wasat, the Ghad, and the Karama parties. All of these parties, with the exception of the Ghad, have not been legally recognized by the regime. Though varying in influence and effectiveness, they have some social representation and a strong potential as credible opposition to jump start an effective party life. In fact, these could be viewed as original images of the shadow parties that are currently occupying the political arena.

Mubarak has thus managed to keep the multiparty system alive, but ineffective. While keeping the legal opposition weak and discredited, he does not allow the party system to collapse altogether. To do that, he applies several tactics that might seem contradictory but are selected to address specific challenges. Such tactics include the use of carefully designed legal constraints to stifle the existing political parties. He leaves room for the full and legal integration of weak parties, while allowing only partial and not legal integration of the effective political forces in order to keep them engaged and within the system. When a party seems too critical or capable of mounting a threat, the state intervenes to freeze, split, or repress it. To Mubarak's credit, he applies outright repression only after the other means prove unsuccessful.

Mubarak is keen on maintaining the hegemony of the state over party life. He heads the NDP and refuses to heed the demands of the opposition parties, which have called on him to relinquish his chairmanship of the NDP in order to address the imbalance between the state and opposition parties. On several occasions, he admitted that if he did step down, the NDP would become weak, thus implicitly recognizing that what keeps the NDP afloat is the support it receives from the state. Furthermore, the Parties Committee has been reluctant to legalize new parties. With the exception of the old parties that were formed under Sadat, almost all of the legal parties under Mubarak came into existence by order of the Administrative Court, after the Parties Committee had rejected them. The increase in the number of legalized parties has not reflected a similar increase in the vitality and effectiveness of party life. Instead, most of these parties are marginal, with a limited following, and are no match for the hegemonic state party.

On several occasions, when the relationship between the regime and the legalized opposition parties reached an impasse, Mubarak would either introduce new items to revive party life or engage the leaders of the legal opposition in dialogue to keep them busy. For example, following the embarrassing results of the NDP in the 2000 parliamentary elections, Mubarak urged all the political parties to reform themselves, knowing full well that this would be impossible under the existing legal and structural constraints. In 2004, the NDP engaged a number of opposition parties in lengthy dialogue, in which it rejected any discussion of a possible amendment of the constitution. After the opposition conceded to this condition, Mubarak surprisingly decided to amend Article 76 of the constitution to allow for competitive presidential elections. This move further discredited and marginalized the legal opposition. Although it was expected that after years of adjusting to the system the political parties under Mubarak would grow stronger and gain more public support, they in fact grew weaker. Some even argue that the political life in Egypt was much more vivid when there were only six parties, as was true at the end of the 1970s.[1]

STRUCTURAL CHALLENGES TO PARTY BUILDING

We turn now to a closer look at the serious structural challenges Egyptian political parties must face, given the current legal and administrative constraints and the weakness of social and political pluralism in the nation at large.

Legal and Administrative Constraints

Forming a political party is technically allowed, but the legalization of strong, effective parties is practically difficult. Since Mubarak assumed power, party life has functioned under emergency law and other restrictive laws. The emergency law, which gave President Sadat the power to detain all his political opponents in September 1981, gives the regime the power to arrest and detain citizens for long periods of time and to ban demonstrations and meetings. These restrictions confine the activities of the parties to their headquarters and limit the parties' ability to reach out to constituents, communicate their programs, and mobilize public support. Parties are required to obtain the approval of the state security before holding public meetings, distributing party materials, or organizing peaceful demonstrations. Traditionally, granting such approval has been the exception, not the rule. The regime has used the emergency law to detain and try journalists as well as members of unrecognized movements and professional associations, including the Egyptian Human Rights Association. The absence of free association, fear of detention, and high risk associated with political participation have forced people out of the political arena.[2]

The Party Formation Law further curtails the formation of political parties by giving the Parties Committee extensive powers. In addition to legalizing and eliminating parties, the committee has the power to freeze an existing party, ban a party's publication, or veto a party's internal decision. The committee used its authority to freeze several parties that were critical of the regime, such as the cases of the Labor Party and the Ghad, as well as those that have experienced internal leadership rivalry. So far, the committee has frozen seven opposition parties.

Other articles of the Parties Formation Law place strong conditions on the capacity of the parties to mobilize resources. Article 11, for example, prohibits parties from practicing any commercial activity and from investing their money in any project, which further deteriorates the financial capabilities of political parties. Under the current regulations, political parties find it extremely difficult to finance their activities. Additionally, various problems confront the political parties even before they come to exist legally. According to the law, the party must publish its list of founders in two daily newspapers before applying to the Parties Committee. This means that, despite being prohibited from organizing any activity before its legalization, the party has to spend a small fortune on advertisement. Further, the law requires the party to announce in two daily newspapers any donation exceeding £500. Taking into consideration that such announcements would cost up to hundreds of thousands of pounds, parties tend to turn down donations, as the cost of accepting them would exceed their value. Political parties therefore depend solely on the subscriptions of their members (who are limited and dramatically decreasing in number) and the subsidies they receive annually from the regime. For the first 10 years, a legal opposition party receives the amount of £100,000 as a direct subsidy from the regime. The opposition parties also receive a £5,000 grant for each of their elected members in the parliament.

The financial limitations of the parties have obvious effects on the vitality and independence of party life in Egypt. Due to their limited resources, parties cannot exercise patronage, nor are they able to build offices, provide services, or organize events to disseminate their ideas and recruit members. Because many are dependent on the regime's subsidies, they have to moderate their opposition in order to avoid falling out of its financial favor.[3]

Weak Social and Political Pluralism

The existence of political and social pluralism is necessary for political parties to be effective and represent and reconcile the different interests in society. The existence of different political parties, no matter how numerous they are, becomes meaningless if these parties are not a product of autonomous, grassroots social and political organizations.[4] The formation of legal political parties in Egypt does not reflect this dynamic, given that the legal parties are based solely on the consent of the regime. Unlike traditional grassroots political parties, the Egyptian version of a "legal" political party is a top-down structure that starts with a leadership, which then searches for a structure and supporters. Therefore, the parties that claim legality in such a manipulated process often lack public support and legitimacy. Most of them cannot compete with the autonomous "illegal" parties and groups that depend on grassroots support as their source of legitimacy.[5] These outlawed movements increased dramatically in number in 2004 and 2005[6] and represent an added challenge to the popularity and credibility of the legal political parties.[7] Additionally, they reveal the inadequacy of controlled political parties as effective avenues for articulation and political participation. The current laws of associations and political practices further prevent the development of a healthy pluralism by restricting civil society organizations from establishing links with political parties and party activities and prohibiting any political activities on university campuses or factories. Under these circumstances, political parties cannot maintain a presence or organize political activities. Thus, these governmental restrictions dry up the potential of civil society by regulating the behavior of grassroots organizations and depriving legal parties of natural access to a broad constituency in society.[8]

CRISES WITHIN THE PARTIES

Structural problems are not the only challenge facing the Egyptian political parties and hindering their ability to play an effective role in the political process. The parties themselves suffer from clear internal deficits, such as ideological stagnation, lack of internal democracy, and the fragmentation of the party system.

Ideological Stagnation

The ideological orientations of the existing political parties act as a barrier between the party and the average populace in at least two obvious ways. First, the ideologies of most of the legal opposition are outdated and as a result no longer seem appealing. The legal parties have not adjusted their orientations to the rapid changes taking place in society, and continue to present an irrelevant and rigid ideological discourse that fails to relate to the majority of the Egyptian people. Most of the programs of the legal parties tend to be too general, unrealistic, and almost impossible to implement, focusing as they do on "grand" ideological objectives or demands, with inadequate attention to the process, mechanisms, or vehicles needed to achieve them. This tendency almost surely helps explain the low membership of the legal parties, estimated at 2 million members.[9] According to al-Ahram newspaper, 10 political parties have a combined total membership of less than 1,000 members.[10] Recently, the constituency of some parties witnessed a sharp drop. For example, the membership of the left-wing Tagamou Party decreased from over 150,000 in 1976 to around 13,000 in 1998, and the situation is similar in other political parties.[11]

Another ideological reason for the weakness of political parties is the lack of intellectual innovation and syntheses. Most of the existing political parties duplicate ideologies of parties already existing elsewhere in the world, using similar rhetoric and discourse and proposing similar programs and agendas. Therefore, they cannot connect to the average Egyptian who needs an indigenous framework to relate to. For example, the Egyptian left has always followed the "ideology and vision of the international leftists, without being able to present an original Egyptian vision of the core value of the leftist movement, namely social justice."[12] The same problem applies to the liberal parties, which have not yet produced an indigenous liberal model. Many Egyptian liberals are elitist, with an unoriginal and alienating discourse that condones ambiguous and sometimes contradictory stances. They are not autonomous from the regime, and some are even entrenched within the state apparatus, which raises serious questions about their commitment to democratic values. One can easily refer to the case of the "democrats," "liberal-minded intellectuals," and university professors who readily joined the Policies Committee of the NDP in 2000. The liberals have yet to make democracy a primary or relevant value for the Egyptians and effectively mobilize large segments of the population to attain it.

Lack of Internal Democracy

Another major problem hindering the growth and reducing the credibility of most legal opposition parties is their lack of internal democracy. While criticizing the regime for its undemocratic practices and unwillingness to transfer power, most of the parties do not follow acceptable democratic rules and procedures that could provide for their proper institutionalization. The symptoms of the absence of democratic norms are visible in the opposition parties, especially the smaller ones, which have become nepotistic "family parties." The big parties follow similar rules and procedures. All the legal parties are centered on the party *zaim* (chief), who stays for life at the top, appoints his loyal followers to high party positions, and swiftly dismisses intraparty opposition. Similar to the regime's style, all procedures are conducted through a "ceremonial collective" process that gives such arbitrary procedures a democratic face. Mirroring the regime, the legal parties equally suffer from lack of accountability and transparency. Not a single opposition party leader has been held accountable for his party's poor performance, whether dismal election results, failure to recruit members, or inability to resolve internal conflicts. The legal parties do not disclose the exact number of their members or their financial budgets. In brief, the legal parties have not been willing to function as modern, institutionalized structures or exhibit an acceptable level of transparency and accountability.

The continuity of a political party and the growth of its political influence depend heavily on its ability to recruit and prepare new leaders to sustain an effective presence. The party leaders should always be on the lookout for promising young leaders who can maintain the party as a dynamic and appealing force. Clearly, that is not the case with almost all opposition parties. With the exception of the newly established Ghad Party and the unrecognized Wasat and Karama parties, Egyptian political parties are headed by conspicuously old leaders. Some have been at the head of their party for more than 25 years.[13] Many have exceeded the age of 70, and some are in their 80s. These leaders continue to run their respective political parties by using techniques that are similar to those the regime employs to sustain itself at the top: patronage (mainly appointing loyalists to senior party positions), undemocratic procedures, and even intimidation. However, the leaders of the opposition parties often use the restrictive measures of the regime as an excuse for their inability to recruit young leadership. In fact, the authoritarian practices within the legal opposition force out many qualified young members and engender major rifts within the party's ranks. This has been the case with old and new parties, such as the Wafd, the Labor, the Liberals, the Nasserite, the Ghad, al-Wifaq, and Egypt 2000. The MB experienced a similar rift in 1996.

The lack of "fresh," publicly accepted young personalities that could attract people and present innovative ideas has contributed to the stagnation of political parties. This gives the NDP an apparent advantage as Gamal Mubarak, the president's son, young and well educated, is practically running the state party. Another, and perhaps only other, young head of a legal party is Ayman Nour, who has been eliminated as a potentially strong rival to Gamal and is now in prison. The parties of other young and charismatic heads, namely Hamdeen Sabbahi of the Karama and Abul-Ula Madi of the Wasat, have been denied legal status by the regime-controlled Parties Committee.

Fragmentation and Lack of Interparty Cooperation

An eventual consequence of the absence of internal democracy is the frequent splits and fragmentation of opposition parties. These parties are not properly institutionalized structures, as almost all lack effective mechanisms for the resolution of their internal disputes. Typically, problems arise, accumulate, and remain unresolved, leading to major infighting and splits within the party ranks. Moreover, since it is almost impossible to get legalization for a new party, the escalation of the internal disputes often lead to freezing of the entire party by the Parties Committee or to the party's practical death. So far, seven political parties have been frozen by the Parties Committee because of disputes over the party's leadership. These include the Labor, Liberal, Young Egypt, People Democratic, National Reconciliation, Arab Socialist, and Social Justice parties.

With their weak structures and highly personalized decision-making processes, the legal opposition parties cannot adopt effective strategies to advance their goals. The leaders of the opposition have been unable or unwilling to work collectively and challenge the regime's manipulative agenda. Distrustful of one another, they keep intraparty cooperation and coordination at a minimal level. However, some opposition parties have been able to form electoral coalitions that in some cases produced relatively positive results. In the 1984 parliamentary elections, the two historical rivals, the Wafd and the MB, contested the elections on a unified list; and in 1987, the MB entered the elections on the lists of the Liberal and Labor parties. The 2005 electoral coordination of the opposition parties was not successful. In general, the attempts to build coalitions or opposition blocs have been short lived and ineffective.

Several factors have contributed to these failures, such as the historical rivalry between some opposition forces, personal rivalries between their leaders, deep ideological differences, lack of commitment, and internal instability within participating parties. Some members of these coalitions or fronts insisted on the exclusion of the MB, a key opposition force. Following the 2005 elections and the relatively strong performance of the MB, the leftist forces called for forming a coalition, not against the regime that had rigged the elections, but against the MB. The top leaders of different political parties make the important decisions and seem to be focused on the benefits they could secure through collaboration with the regime instead of other parties.[14] On several occasions, they agreed to engage in "national" dialogue with the regime and conceded to its conditions to exclude groups that have popular support, particularly the MB. The limited level of collaboration and coordination between the existing political parties plays into the hands of the ruling NDP. It can also explain the reasons for the recent emergence and growth of alternative movements, such as Kifaya and the other pro-reform groups.

ALTERNATIVE POLITICAL FORCES

Despite the difficulties facing parties in Egypt, certain movements do have some level of social and political representation or some potential to become an effective political force. These include the MB movement, the Ghad Party, the Wasat Party, and the Karama Party.[15] With the exception of the Ghad, the regime has consistently deprived these forces from acquiring legal recognition. Unlike the controlled legal parties, the autonomous political forces are not the clients of the regime, which offer them no patronage. They represent the main ideological or political streams within society: Islamism, liberal nationalism, and Arab nationalism and socialism, and are thereby able to build wide grassroots support.

With the exception of the MB, these are all splinter movements from a larger party or group. For example, the Ghad, the Wasat, and the Karama are offshoots of the Wafd, the MB, and the Nasserite Party, respectively. Each is led by young, charismatic leaders who, given certain arrangements, could revive party life and even challenge the candidacy of Mubarak. Not only are they products of the generational gap within the legal parties, but they have also emerged in protest against the organizational inflexibility or weakness of their mother movements. Some have mainstream orientations that attempt to appeal to larger segments in society and a proactive or defiant attitude that could augment their popularity and potential to challenge the regime. Further, most of these forces have relatively good relations with one another, surprisingly with the exception of the MB and the Wasat, and with newly emerging protest movements. They all support legal integration of the MB in the political process. The Karama Party joined the MB-led coalition, the National Coalition for Reform. Members from the MB, the Wasat, and the Karama helped found the Kifaya movement, which succeeded in articulating a popular protest to the extension of Mubarak to a fifth term. It is also believed that a large number of young MB votes went to Ayman Nour during his contest for the presidency.

The response of the regime to these forces has not been uniform. In general, the regime has been reluctant to integrate fully the forces that have actual popular presence. At the same time, however, it is difficult to crush these groups and movements without endangering stability. Therefore, its response has varied from some form of partial integration that tolerates some of their activities to periodic repression that prevents them from evolving into a full-fledged force. It is clear that their ideological orientation, Islamic, liberal, or pan-Arab, has not been a key factor in determining which approach to apply. The regime certainly views them all as a threat because of their potential for gaining popular support. The regime's margin of toleration starts to narrow when these forces challenge the demarcated boundaries of a tolerable opposition, come close to posing a threat to its control, or shake its grip over power. The next section focuses on two of these forces, the MB and the Ghad, which maintained an assertive approach toward the regime. It also deals briefly with the Wasat and Karama parties that have not been willing to defy the regime's restrictions and opted to fight their battles through the courts.

The Muslim Brothers

The Society of the Muslim Brothers is one of the oldest and most highly institutionalized political forces in Egypt. Despite a ban on the movement since 1954, it fulfills the description of a real political party: a nationwide organizational structure that survived the founder's lifetime and has a vision, an ideology, and grassroots support. The last parliamentary elections of 2005 revealed the MB to be the main opposition force and a key player in Egyptian political life. Its members captured 20% of the seats, an unprecedented performance for an opposition force since Egypt became a republic in 1952. However, at the same time it is difficult to determine accurately the ability or willingness of the MB to dislodge the regime or the exact levels of its popularity among the overall population.[16] Concerns about the MB revolve around its high organizational and mobilization skills, its influence in comparison to the other opposition, and the lack of clarity regarding its future plans.

The regime has always combined toleration with repression in its relationship with the MB. This approach has served several purposes. Under Sadat, the MB was tolerated as part of his de-Nasserization process and later to perform a moderating effect of the emerging radical Islamic groups. The latter objective continued under Mubarak until the mid-1990s, when the state appeared to be winning its battle against the violent Islamic groups. Mubarak then cracked down on the movement to trim its growing influence. The period from 1995 to 2000 became known as the "bone-crushing" phase, during which several leaders and members of the movement stood before six military tribunals and 79 of its leading members received jail sentences. Subsequent periodic arrests and crackdowns continued in order to prevent the movement from growing into an uncontrollable threat to the regime's hegemony. However, the regime has so far stopped short of completely crushing the movement, tolerating its presence in the parliament and in society. This presence allows the regime to showcase its toleration of opposition, while at the same time maintaining absolute political power. The regime also realizes that the elimination of this moderate movement will not necessarily guarantee political stability, as radical, violent groups are likely to emerge to fill the vacuum. Further, the presence of this active Islamic movement in society pushes the secular opposition and intellectuals to stay loyal to the regime that shares their secular orientation. The same relationship provides a pretext for the regime to maintain the extralegal processes and suppressive measures to impede the "Islamic threat." Finally, the regime uses the increasing influence of the MB and its potential "threat" to fend off the external pressures for democratic changes and present itself as the West's plausible ally.

The MB 2005 electoral successes did not come easily. In comparison to the legal opposition, the MB has been much more exposed to the regime's repression and restrictions. Unlike the legal opposition, however, it is willing to challenge the regime's harassment, reassert its presence in society, and consequently pay the price for its defiance. The MB fully realizes the comprehensive nature of its movement and the general objectives it seeks to accomplish. It is an activist movement with a comprehensive reform message, combining multidimensional spheres that give the movement a reasonable space to maneuver within even when its activities are severely constrained at one dimension. It has adopted a gradualist bottom-up approach for change that seeks to resocialize society along Islamic lines (the individual, family, society, and then the state). The brotherhood had sustained repeated phases of brutal regime repression. All this has generated a particular political orientation for the movement that is characterized by caution, gradualism, slow adaptation, and fear of experimentation and failure. In the movement's view, failure will reflect not simply on the leadership of the group at a particular moment, but on the entire movement as a precursor and exemplar for others. It can even affect the fortunes of political Islam as an alternative to the postindependence foreign-inspired secular models. Therefore, preserving the survival and structural coherence of the movement has always been a top priority. It is an objective that for long has dominated the brotherhood's political calculations and levels of interaction in the political process and enabled the movement to exhibit a pragmatic attitude whenever the circumstances warrant.

Over the past few years the MB undertook major transformations at the level of orientation and strategy. Its recent documents and the statements of some of its leaders began to reflect commitment to the civic nature of political authority, notwithstanding its adherence to the principles of the Shari'a: respect for the basic values and instruments of democracy; respect for public freedoms; acceptance of pluralism; transfer of power through clean and free elections; sovereignty of the people; separation of powers; rejecting the use of violence and adopting gradual and legal means to achieve reform; acceptance of citizenship as the basis for rights and responsibilities for Muslims and non-Muslims; and support of human rights, including those of women and Copts.[17] The MB adopted an assertive strategy in its relationship with the regime and a pragmatic orientation in the reform agenda it proposed. This change became quite noticeable in early 2005, when the movement insisted on reasserting its presence in the political process, defied the regime's bans on its demonstrations, and even threatened acts of "civil disobedience." It also cooperated with other political forces that did not share its ideological perspectives and jointly formed reform-oriented fronts.

A real challenge facing the MB is generating a societal consensus over its integration into the system and articulating its future plans. The two seem to be closely intertwined. At the moment, the MB is not seriously pushing to be legalized as a political party, particularly under the current legal constraints that stifle political parties. Its existence as a comprehensive movement, not a party regulated by the state laws, gives it more maneuverability and appeal, despite the regime's periodic repression. So far the MB has been able to survive that repression and eventually increase its credibility and legitimacy as a serious and effective opposition. Meanwhile, the movement has expressed willingness to be part of a pluralistic political system and has linked its reform demands to the wider demands of the pro-change movements.

The MB has also revisited some of its positions vis-à-vis the West. It has recently begun sending messages to the West in an attempt to improve its image. The Second Deputy of the General Guide Khayrat Al-Shater addressed the West in an article in the Guardian titled, "No Need to Fear Us," in which he reconfirmed his movement's respect for "the rights of all religious and political groups."[18] In a later interview with the MB official Web site, he asserted that the movement is not promoting an anti-Western agenda.[19] These messages have been harshly criticized by the Egyptian regime, which considers the MB's move toward a centrist position a serious threat.

With regard to its future plans, the MB seems to be ambiguous and needs to be clearer on some issues. A major issue that needs clarification is the relationship between the Islamic state it intends to establish and the civic nature of authority to which it has declared commitment. A challenging question immediately arises: Is the implementation of the Shari'a as a way of life and a frame of reference reversible? In other words, how would the MB respond to a situation where it came to power through democratic means and established a state with Islamic foundations, but was then voted out of power by a secular party that implements a secular program that gives only lip service to Islam? Is it not the duty of a Muslim to uphold and defend the Shari'a? The MB also needs to be clear on issues such as the status of secular parties in an Islamic state (freedom of expression and advocacy) and the extent of respect and protection of the individual's private sphere in this Islamic state. It is also noteworthy that despite the moderate statements of the movement's leaders regarding citizenship, the Copts, and women, these viewpoints need to be adequately developed and embedded in the movement's official documents.

The Ghad Party

The swift rise and fall of the Ghad Party is a sad testimony to the regime's perception of pluralism and its tactics in dealing with a promising legal opposition. Thanks to its charismatic young leader Ayman Nour and its liberal orientation, the Ghad appeared to represent a new generation of political opposition that could replace the aging Wafd Party and attract a considerable following. To many, it was expected to present a middle way between the ruling NDP and the MB. Perhaps for that reason, the regime brought the career of the new party to a sudden and brutal end.

The legalization of the Ghad in October 2004 came at a time of remarkable political vitality in the country and amid popular pressures for political reform and reviving political life. Nour was able to attract six members of the parliament and a few independent representatives as founding members of his new party, enabling the Ghad to lead the opposition in the parliament. In his rush to establish the party, Nour did not apply rigorous recruitment criteria. Thus, the party founders also included several prominent public figures, in addition to people of differing political backgrounds. At one point, the number of the party's founders exceeded that of its members (over five thousand founders to four thousand members!). This oversight later created serious rifts within the party.

Following the official recognition of the Ghad, Nour was elected as party head in a democratic process; and, for the first time in Egypt's party practices, his tenure was limited to two terms. Nour announced his party's plan to vigorously contest the upcoming parliamentary elections and end the hegemony of the ruling NDP. The party that he said would provide a platform for liberal youth attracted segments of the young generation—young and medium-size businessmen—and some former members of the liberal Wafd Party. The dynamic and articulate Nour worked tirelessly to build the party structures in several provinces. He also defied the regime's constraints that restricted the political activities of parties and their ability to engage the population. The Ghad also linked its program to the demands of the emerging pro-reform movements that called for amending the constitution and introducing fundamental changes to the power structures. The speedy emergence of the Ghad and Nour stirred up and revitalized the country's stagnant party life.

However, in January 2005, only three months after the party became legal and active, the regime arrested Nour on charges of forging powers of attorney to help found his party. Many believe the charges were politically motivated, aimed at ending Nour's career and putting checks on the growth of his party. A month later Mubarak announced his approval of amending Article 76 of the constitution so as to allow the country to have multicandidate presidential elections for the first time. Nour continued with his defiance and declared from prison his intention to run for the presidency. The regime seemingly bowed to internal and external pressures and released Nour on bail in March. Still not convicted, Nour was able to run against the president. Throughout his campaign, he focused on his bitter tragedy and intensified his criticism of the regime. He challenged Mubarak to an hour-long televised debate to expose the regime's corruption and present his program. Nour's strongest point in his presidential campaign was his plan. If he won, he promised to act as an interim president for two years, during which major institutional reforms would take place, a new constitution would be written to establish a new democratic system, and new free parliamentary and presidential elections would be held. Out of 10 presidential hopefuls, Nour came second after Mubarak, capturing almost 8% of the votes. Three months later, Nour was arrested again, tried, and sentenced to five years in jail. If Nour's pending appeal is rejected by the Cassation Court, his political career will be adversely affected as he will become politically disenfranchised. Following Nour's incarceration, the party experienced a devastating split that has affected its momentum and the promise it had generated.

The case of the Ghad Party reveals the regime's low level of toleration of serious challengers to its stranglehold on power, regardless of whether its political rivals adhere to an Islamic ideology or a liberal one. It also exposes the various repressive tactics that the regime uses to undermine the status of legal parties. With his dynamic personality, ambitions to institutionalize his party, willingness to defy the set limits for political action, and ability to reach to the public, Nour presented a threat not necessarily to Mubarak, but more seriously to his son Gamal, who is practically leading the state party and is being groomed to become the next president. The Ghad proposed a liberal program similar to that of the governing NDP. The youthful Nour was of the same generation as Gamal and the group associated with him, but he was by far more charismatic and resourceful. Had the Ghad been allowed to fulfill its promising growth, Nour could probably have become a serious contender for power in the 2011 presidential elections. The regime used all the means at hand to preempt this possibility. When the usual legal constraints did not seem to work, it removed Nour from the scene and directly intervened to break up his party. The Ghad and Nour have raised the ceiling for opposition, escalated the confrontation with the regime, and invited the regime's wrath.

The Wasat Party: A Civic Party with an Islamic Framework

The origins of the Wasat date to the mid-1990s, when a group of young members of the MB spilt because of differences in orientations and in protest to internal organizational rigidity within the movement. They formed a party and applied three times, in 1996, 1998, and 2004, to the regime-dominated Party Formation Committee. Each time, the party's request was denied. The founders pursued their case through the judicial channels, which have also repeatedly denied them recognition. The standard reason was that the party's program is not distinguished from those of already existing political parties. The significance of the Wasat Party lies in its attempt to form a civic party with a mainstream Islamic orientation. It is distinguished from the MB as it separates political functions and religious proselytizing (*da'wa*).

In fact, the Wasat's program does present a new orientation. It is a civic political party with an Islamic reference that attempts to appeal to broad segments of the Egyptian population. It presents Islam as a cultural framework that can assimilate the religious aspirations of Muslim Egyptians and the natural cultural affiliations of the country's Copts. (In fact, several founding members of the party were Copts.) According to its program, the party's vision of Islam is based on three fundamental pillars: citizenship that provides equal rights for Muslims and non-Muslims; the right of all citizens to assume all positions; and coexistence with other cultures on the basis of respect of cultural specificities—justice and equality, interdependence, and mutual interests. The Wasat has reconfirmed its unequivocal commitment to peaceful and legal change and to the fundamental democratic principles: the sovereignty of the people; separation of powers; transfer of power; citizenship; freedom of belief; political and intellectual pluralism; full equality between men and women; freedom of expression; and respect of human rights. The Wasat also seeks through democratic means to implement the principles of the Shari'a, through a selective and modernist process that while achieving the objective of the Shari'a would lead to the development and progress of society.[20] In terms of organizational structures and popularity, the Wasat is not a match for the MB. It is still a nascent and evolving entity, but with a strong potential. The Wasat leadership is young, active, and articulate. It has established good ties with the existing political forces and managed to present a moderate and programmatic Islamic orientation.

The Al-Karama Party

The Karama (Dignity) Party is an offshoot of the officially recognized Nasserite Party. As in the case of the Wasat, a younger generation under the leadership of Hamdeen Sabbahy split from the Nasserite Party in protest to the management style and orientation of the party's older leaders. They established al-Karama Party and sought official recognition in 2004. The regime has repeatedly denied the party official approval. The party publishes a weekly newspaper and its leader, Sabbahy, managed to win a seat in the 2005 parliamentary elections. Although the extent of the popularity of al-Karama is not exactly known, the party represents a trend—Nasserite, socialist, and Arab nationalist—that has some appeal in society. Its emphasis on social justice, independent development, and the rights of the workers and poorer classes would certainly attract segments in society that have been adversely affected by the structural adjustment that has been taking place in Egypt.

CONCLUSIONS

At transitional junctures in the move from authoritarianism, political parties are essential agents for democratic change. Civil society organizations and spontaneous protest movements are quite significant in this process but are not enough to single handedly challenge a regime's power. Parties are more equipped for aggregating demands, structuring votes, and coming to power. However, in Egypt the legal political parties are weak, divided, and ineffective. The weakness of party life is a reflection of a wider structural problem and of the authoritarian dynamics that control the political process. Initially, the country had a weak legacy of party life, characterized by the continued dominance of the executive branch, polarization between dominant parties and weak ones (the Wafd versus the minority parties and currently the NDP versus the weak parties), and a low level of institutionalized party structures. Party life deteriorated even further under the single-party regime that forced people's conformity and mobilization at the expense of their effective political participation in the political process. The single-party system marginalized the role of the parliament, suppressed pluralism and dissent, and eroded people's confidence in party life.

Sadat allowed a multiparty system to emerge in the mid-1970s. He adopted political pluralism as part of the process of de-Nasserization, building a new support base and legitimacy and ensuring the support of the West. Sadat envisioned a loyal, marginal, and controlled opposition that would showcase Egypt's new "democratic" system. He therefore developed restrictive legal frameworks to ensure that the opposition would not get out of line. When the opposition became critical of some of his policies, he applied the "claws" of democracy, as he used to say, to the feeble bodies of the newly emerging political parties. Sadat's formative phase of political pluralism was in fact a "deforming" one that stifled party life and limited the growth and effectiveness of the legal opposition. It has had far reaching consequences on Egypt's party dynamics.

The same legal constraints are still in place and continue to stifle party life under Mubarak, who has added restrictions for civil society organizations, syndicates, and the press. A quick look at the distribution of power within the state structures reveals the limited avenues available for the legal opposition. Mubarak heads the executive and at the same time he is the head of the ruling party, the NDP. His son Gamal practically controls the NDP. The current cabinet is dominated by the NDP. Also, the NDP is in control of the parliament. Despite all the talk about pluralism and the increase in the number of parties, Mubarak has maintained the hegemony of the ruling NDP over party life. This is expected to continue as the NDP is the only vehicle through which his son can come to power, provided that he secures the approval of the military, which has been traditionally the only vehicle for coming to power and continues to safeguard the post-1952 regimes. While keeping the opposition parties weak and marginal, Mubarak is also keen on keeping the multiparty system alive. Its existence legalizes the authoritarian nature of his regime and is equally necessary to legalize the succession process.

The political parties themselves are also to be blamed for their weak state. The legal opposition has consented to take part in a pluralistic experience that has not been properly institutionalized and has been subject to clear manipulations. They perform the roles the regime expects from them in return for securing its patronage or avoiding its wrath. They have also failed to institutionalize their party structures, follow internal democratic procedures, attract and train young leadership, and cooperate with one another. Their moment of truth came in 2004 and 2005, when spontaneous pro-reform movements emerged as alternative avenues for articulation and protest.

The alternative political forces, officially unrecognized, reveal further indications of the weakness of the legal opposition. They have an actual presence in society, some level of support, and enjoy credibility, as they have not been the product of regime patronage. They include actors with different ideological orientations: the MB, the liberal Ghad, centrist Wasat, and the pan-Arab Karama. Because these groups represent genuine political orientations in society and are consequently equipped to jump start serious multiparty politics, the regime has consistently denied them legal recognition. The only one that escaped the legal constraints, the Ghad, became an exemplar of the regime's ability to bring a serious contender to a quick demise and still maintain a superficial pluralism.

At present, the status of party life in Egypt is not conductive to promoting a genuine democracy. True democracy requires effective pluralism, which can only thrive in a free environment. Both are clearly lacking. The legalized political parties have accepted the regime's cooptation and have given up their basic roles as a serious opposition to an authoritarian regime and as vehicles for popular participation, recruitment of new cadres, structuring votes, and promoting change. The regime has succeeded in marginalizing and when necessary crushing the alternative political forces. This apparent failure of the political parties prolongs the life of authoritarianism and sheds serious doubts on the future of democracy in Egypt.

SUPPLEMENTARY BIBLIOGRAPHY

Adel Latif, Omayma. "Egyptian Electoral Politics: New Rules, Old Game." *Review of African Political Economy* 28 (June 2001).

Baker, Raymond. *Sadat and After: The Struggle for Egypt's Political Soul.* Cambridge: Harvard University Press, 1990.

El Amrani, Issandr. "Controlled Reform in Egypt: Neither Reformist nor Controlled." *Middle East Report Online* (December 15, 2005).

El-Ghobashy, Mona. "Egypt's Paradoxical Elections." *Middle East Report* 238 (Spring 2006).

Fahmy, Ninette. *The Politics of Egypt: State-Society Relationship.* Curzon: Routledge, 2002.

Ibrahim, Saad Eddin. *Egypt, Islam, and Democracy: Critical Essays.* Cairo: American University in Cairo Press, 2002.

Kassem, Maye. *Egyptian Politics: The Dynamics of Authoritarian Rule.* Boulder, Colo.: Lynne Rienner, 2004.

"Reforming Egypt: In Search of a Strategy." *International Crisis Group, Middle East/North Africa Report* 46 (October 2005).

Stacher, Joshua. "Parties Over: The Demise of Egypt's Opposition Parties." *British Journal of Middle Eastern Studies* 31 (November 2004).

Tadros, Mariz. "Egypt's Election All about Image, Almost." *Middle East Report Online* (September 6, 2005).

CHAPTER 2

The Lebanese Partisan Experience and Its Impact on Democracy

Antoine Nasri Messarra

INTRODUCTION

To many Arabs, the Lebanese partisan experience is synonymous with war, disintegration, and disunity. In fact, however, since as far back as the 1920s, political parties in Lebanon have promoted the concepts of democracy, liberation, human rights, nationalism, socialism, and pan-Arabism. It is not the parties that caused the multinational and regional wars that were waged on Lebanese soil between 1975 and 1990 and in July 2006, but rather the fact that the Lebanese army had been effectively paralyzed by regional pressures. When the army breaks down, society as a whole becomes vulnerable. The result in Lebanon was that the political parties became the executors and victims of war simultaneously. Lebanon epitomizes all issues of concern to the Arab world, issues that have been a source of calamity for Lebanon. Maintaining and developing a functioning party system capable of managing diversity democratically has been all but impossible in recent years. Despite the fact that the years of warfare have generated a new readiness on the part of many to establish the rule of law and rationality, there are still confession-based forces affiliated with external powers that are at the same time dependent and domineering. These forces have detached themselves from whatever remains of their grassroots base, becoming increasingly dependent on support from external actors. This chapter will explore the institutional structures that govern the development and operation of political parties, discuss the historical events that have shaped that development, and then conclude with a discussion of the future of democracy and political parties in Lebanon.

APPROACHES TO THE STUDY OF THE PARTISAN PHENOMENON IN LEBANON

Parties are political institutions that seek to reach power and practice it in accordance with their beliefs or programs. In general, political parties have been studied based on three main perspectives: parties as modernity-based (secular rather than confessional), parties as democratizing agents, and parties as confessional and therefore inadequate as instruments of democracy. As will be seen in the following brief descriptions and critiques of each, none of these approaches fully encompasses the complexity of the partisan phenomenon in Lebanon.

A Modernity-Based Approach

This approach views political parties as necessarily situated within a modern framework, in contrast to tribal, kinship, and confessional structures. Confidence in the modernity of the partisan phenomenon is deeply rooted and long-standing in Lebanese political culture. Yet, at the same time, confessional affiliation is no less legitimate than party affiliation, and both may threaten individual and collective freedoms.

According to this approach, the "confessionalization" of political parties does not accord with the notion of modernity, as political parties based on religion may exploit sectarian sentiments for the purpose of mobilization. Even political parties that used to consider themselves secular or nationalist have drifted toward sectarian mobilization as an effective medium for attaining de facto power during the wars in Lebanon and the Arab region. This has not been the case with most of the representatives of religious denominations.

Parties as Democratizing Agents

Parties have emerged "when the public was introduced into political life," according to Maurice Duverger.[1] However, two prominent authors, Moisie Ostrogorski and Roberto Michels, warned against the nondemocratic risks of parties. Ostrogorski fears authoritarianism and seeks protection in order to avoid the risk of party rule. He suggested, in 1903, the accreditation of the formula of mobile organizations engaging in ad hoc activities to bring people together for a specific purpose, instead of a political party that continuously seeks to recruit its members into a permanent mold. Citizens who disagree on one issue may reconcile on another issue. The goal is to avoid the circumstantial and combat the institutionalization of public opinion, keeping citizens mobile.[2] On the other hand, in describing oligarchic orientations within political parties, Michels states: "The social revolution will not change anything in the internal structure of the people. The victory of socialists shall not be the victory of socialism; the latter shall retreat at the moment when its proponents succeed."[3]

Anticonfessions Approach

This third approach describes the Lebanese political system as sectarian, reactionary, and confessional because of its pragmatic and normative structure. This approach does not contribute to a thorough understanding of the partisan phenomenon in Lebanon. Writers and media professionals who have scrutinized political parties in Lebanon have been oblivious to the study of the function of parties in promoting unity and efficacy and of the link between parties, the state, and the electoral system in a society based on participatory rule. Lebanese party life is a laboratory for those searching for a general and comparative theory on parties in regimes that are not based on absolute competition. The Lebanese experience contains discrepant efficacy levels, and these variances call for further study of Lebanese political parties.

The new political literature on the end of ideology and history and the notion of civil society expresses fear of the rule of political parties. Party structures carrying traits of modernity may appear to be shiny instruments, but, in fact, they perpetuate a primitive conflict. This, therefore, necessitates that Lebanon must adopt a less absolute approach toward political parties as instruments of modernization and democracy. What is needed is a relative and open approach that does not seek to explain parties solely in terms of other structures such as religious institutions, parliamentary blocs, or professional, economic, and social associations. These institutions can be effective representatives and can play a parallel role in Lebanese political life.

The retreat of political commitment within political parties across the world, the changes in the behavior of citizens, and the impact of nonparty organizations on the electorate justify a revival of such an approach. In his 1954 dissertation on "Current Political Forces in Lebanon" the former minister of justice in Lebanon, Bahige Tabbarah, offered a balanced design, treating separately "Religious sects and minority conglomerations" (chapter 1), "Fiefdoms and political figures" (chapter 2), and "Political parties" (chapter 3).[4] Here too we need ways to identify parties that, although they may use modern machinery, work simply to perpetuate ancient conflicts, as well as parties that are merely combinations of figures. After all the experiences during the many years following Tabbarah's work, we have yet to develop a way to study Lebanese political parties and other forces that is based on reality.

It is not enough to say that organizations based on religious sects or personal fiefdoms are not really parties at all, as some have done in an effort to obviate the sociopolitical problem of proposing a law for political parties. The problem is sociological as well as legal, as is made clear in the following two illustrations.

Salem Al Gisr, in his cynical and profound description of the different candidates in the Lebanese elections, draws a picture of the party candidate as follows:

> The most prominent thing in the candidate is his tongue. It is enough to posit[ion] this candidate before two persons and he will lecture them on the party principles, policies, and beliefs and why this party should reach power. . . . In his [the candidate's] opinion, Lebanon is always subject to risk if it does not follow party planning. Yet, ironically, he does not hesitate, notwithstanding his party beliefs, to reach agreements with other political parties, with different principles, to obtain a seat in parliament. He follows Haj Hussein Al Oweini in saying "this is something and that is another." He allies temporarily to disagree later or to blame his failure on his allies.
>
> Unfortunately for him, most of the party supporters are below legal age for elections and those who are of age have family links and friends whom they cannot easily give up. Thus, his calculations do not add up to reality and [after electoral defeat] the party candidate becomes satisfied with the title of "former candidate," which in the future allows him to carry the title of "ambassador" or "director."[5]

Similarly, in the play "Comrade Sij'ân,"[6] Jalal Khouri describes the behavior of a Lebanese country man, a Marxist from a Lebanese village where kinship and family loyalties and interests put on Marxist and communist attire in a normatively primitive context. Comrade Sij'ân represents a pattern in the Lebanese political parties where the party becomes a cover for local traditional solidarity, and in some cases, a cover for one family against another as each entrenches itself within its borders and engages in acts of violent and intense animosity with the other.

LEGAL FRAMEWORK OF POLITICAL PARTIES

The legal framework of political parties in Lebanon poses three problems for anyone seeking to differentiate between parties and associations. First, is the formation of political parties subject to the same rules and regulations governing associations? Second, what is the state's legislative orientation in the regulation of parties? Third, what is the framework that governs the confessional system in Lebanon, which is also an active agent in the public arena? The sections below examine each of these questions in turn.

Parties and Associations

Rules and regulations governing associations apply to political parties in accordance with the international conventions on human rights and the Lebanese law on associations issued on August 13, 1909. Article 1 of the 1909 Associations Law is a literal replica of the Waldeck-Rousseau Law issued in France in 1901, which governs associations, including political parties. However, it stipulates that the Ministry of the Interior be informed of the formation of the association (Article 2) by depositing the association's articles of incorporation and founders' resumes at the ministry. Founders receive a receipt upon submission of these documents (Article 6), but there is no time limit for delivery of the receipt. The French State Consultative Council states that the receipt is not considered an administrative decree,[7] and that administrative courts should monitor the delivery of the notification of the formation of the association.[8] There are some problematic issues concerning the legal age for forming an association (20 years), as some consider 18 years of age adequate.

In 1992, the government issued cabinet decrees to dissolve 127 associations that were co-founded with political parties. Some of these decrees appeared to be vindictive, but the decision to revoke the license was formally based on whether the organizations had not undertaken any activities or been involved in "clandestine" work. Some associations went to court to fight the decision, while others did object to the decision[9] because of the pressure posed by the Syrian military presence in Lebanon. Then, the Ministry of the Interior laid restrictions upon receipt of associations' foundation documents, particularly focusing on those associations engaged in human rights. They judged that human rights issues are political and thus associations that focused on them required licenses. In 1983, a legislative decree was issued, and later annulled, that substantially limited the freedom of association. Furthermore, the Ministry of the Interior issued General Decree 499/9 dated December 12, 1996, urging associations to limit their activities to the goals indicated in their articles of incorporation and to adhere to the dates of the election of their administrative bodies so the ministry could exert control over elections. These arrangements were considered a flagrant violation of the deliberations of the administrative courts that forbid interference in the affairs of associations except in cases explicitly defined by the law.[10]

The International Charter of Civil and Political Rights of 1966, which was put into force in 1976, constitutes the general framework for the freedom of association that supersedes national legislation. The report presented by Lebanon to the United Nations in 1996[11] stipulates that associations do not need to be licensed, but because of "risks to the security, the notification on the formation of the association is not automatically released." The Preamble of the Lebanese constitution, amended on September 21, 1990, stipulates that Lebanon adheres to international human rights legislation, but that courts have subsequent absolute jurisdiction to interpret international and local legislation.[12]

Among the most salient event related to the freedom of association in Lebanon was the issuance of the state's consultative council decree that was based on a legal claim by the "Association for the Defense of Rights and Freedoms—ADL," headed by lawyer and member of parliament Ghassan Mekhaibar. This annulled the notification issued in 1996 by the Ministry of the Interior that claimed it constituted a violation of the principle of freedom of association and the law of 1909. Ghassan Mekhaibar described this decree as "of great importance and one of the most crucial decisions issued by the State Consultative Council and an honor to the entire Lebanese judiciary."[13] Among the prominent judicial decrees in defense of the freedom of association is the verdict of the court of first instance in Beirut, which considers the leadership of the Phalangists Party illegitimate.[14]

In sum, the ability of associations to form has been limited by the state in the past in order to "prevent risks to security," and there is nothing to guarantee that this will not continue to be so. In recent years there have been important judicial rulings enhancing the freedom of association. We turn now to how the parties—a very special form of association—have fared in this regard.

The State Regulation of Political Parties

As noted, parties are subject to the laws governing associations. Officially, the state does not "regulate" parties and safeguards the principle of freedom of association. However, new electoral laws have been passed in 1996, 2000, and 2008, including a bill specifically addressed to the parties. The situation at the present writing can be summarized as follows[15]:

1. From the perspective of the freedom of association, there is no distinction in the freedom of incorporation between a party and any other association. The Lebanese cabinet, in conformity with the general system of rights, has stated this at its historic session dated August 8, 2005, when Minister Khaled Kabbani affirmed the principle of absolute freedom of association.
2. The state does not organize the affairs of civil society. Otherwise, society would not be called civil nor would it be independent from governmental institutions. The government regulates government departments to serve the people but does not "regulate" syndicates, associations, or political parties. Instead, these civil organizations regulate themselves. The government issues legislation to guarantee the exercise of freedom.
3. The Arab tendency to assert basic freedoms and link them to law relies on customary law, not on an abstract concept of right or on a system of rights that is more comprehensive. Here is the sticking point. In Arab societies there is formal recognition of basic freedoms, but at the same time ubiquitous legislation that overregulates to the extent that rights disappear. The objective of customary law is to safeguard and assert basic laws, not to limit them. However, many Arab constitutions have linked basic laws with their

legal frameworks instead of safeguarding them. This is evidence of the supremacy of customary law, which the ruler may enact as he wishes (witness the rule of Saddam Hussein in Iraq), and at the expense of rights.

4. A dominant mentality limits politics to competition for power and influence as opposed to a broader understanding of politics as the administration of public affairs. If an association for the protection of children or an association for environmental education nominates one of its members to the parliamentary elections or collects signatures to put forward a bill, does that make it an association or a political party? The dividing line between an association and a political party is the entry of the association into the electoral arena. This transformation is something the association itself decides on the basis of its programs, strategies, and dynamics of development; it is not simply a dividing line between what is political in influence and power and what is not political.

Some states have resorted to "regulating" parties for ad hoc purposes related to parliamentary nomination as well as for public purposes related to transparency and financing electoral programs.

Religious Affairs Sector

The distinction between the political party system and the religious confessional system is often difficult to ascertain or maintain in Lebanon. The religious affairs sector of society is composed of separate and primarily autonomous entities in the context of the confessional system. However, each denomination is independent in running its affairs and does not have to coordinate relations with other confessions or religious sects at the national level. The Lebanese system reflects the absence of a theoretical and practical framework that organizes the relationship between the state and confessions. Furthermore, the confessionalization of the regime has been exacerbated by the establishment of representational councils for denominations without coordination among them and without a clear definition of jurisdiction. Moreover, there are no clearly drawn borders for religious affairs or the independence of confessions in running their affairs, which opens the door to the politicization of religion within the context of political rivalry.[16]

Organizations for Islamic and Durzi confessional councils emerged in the 1960s without clear jurisdiction. Instead of helping to contain sectarian conflicts, they contributed to a deepening of the concept of religious jurisdiction, spreading it to all public affairs. This occurred in the absence of an official and joint referential authority among these councils to curb the risks of confessional independence. The legal organization of these councils lacked a general theory of the constitutional situation of confessions in Lebanon as well as the needs they were supposed to fulfill. Such ambiguities led to the failure of these councils in their ability to effectively monitor and regulate the affairs of the Lebanese confessions. Because the concept of religious affairs has never been clearly defined and different religions have separate elected bodies, the legal organization of Durzi, Sunni, and Shiite councils have become independent representative councils that are not related to one another and are concerned with public issues that may be the jurisdiction of other official bodies.

The Islamic and Durzi councils, which are subject to legal organization, have adapted to the system of confessional participation in government. Their different regulations have stipulated that current and former ministers, deputies, director generals, governors, and members of professional associations form their councils. The Durzi, Sunni, and Shiite confessional councils are connected to the government apparatus that appoints their staff and allocates their budget and are official entities whose employees are considered state employees and are appointed by decree upon the suggestion of the head of each council. Laws regulating Shariah courts apply to these employees.

On the other hand, Christian confessional councils are not affiliated with the state apparatus and do not enjoy the internal cohesiveness that the legal legitimacy provides to Islamic and Durzi councils. The difference in organization and the referential authority among Islamic and Durzi councils on one hand, and Christian councils on the other, reflects the absence of a general organization in which confessions function within the state, rather than outside or against it. Confessional councils do not limit their activities to the management of their own affairs and are concerned with general religious and national affairs.

The jurisdiction of sects in the Lebanese system is defined in Articles 9, 10, and 19 of the constitution, which regulates the 18 recognized confessions on a case-by-case basis. These jurisdictions include personal status (Article 9) and educational services offered by religious institutions (Article 10). Also, Article 19 permits the heads of the confessions to refer to the constitutional council in some exclusive matters. They have the right to debate freely about the right of confession, the balance between them, and to defend their interests through entities that represent them or claim that they do. On the other hand, the participation of religious denominations in government is subject to Article 95 of the constitution, which prevents the use of religion to obtain higher representation in the seats than the percentage fixed by electoral law.

The difficulty of fixing the line between religious organization and political entity was recognized as far back as March 13, 1936, when Decree 60 addressed the organization of religious sects, setting up a system disregarded by subsequent legislation and political practice. It established a system subject to the supervision of a central authority that applied to all confessions—Christian, Muslim, and Durzi—but also took into account the specific characteristics of each sect and sought to establish an open, neutral environment allowing individuals to refuse affiliation with any of the sects or to abandon their original sect of affiliation. However, three years later, Decree 53, issued March 30, 1939, stipulated that the 1936 decree would no longer apply to Muslims because Islamic jurisprudence does not recognize civil systems in personal status matters. It was decided that the organization of confessional councils, without legal coordination among them, within the framework of state institutions, would cause confusion in matters of representation and the exercise of roles. The councils that seek the direct representation of sects are not concerned exclusively with their interests and work independently from one another. On the other hand, the parliamentary council that seeks to combine political representation with confessional representation in enforcing the principle of a unified electoral body avoids any discussion of religious or sectarian affairs in absolute terms and does not exercise any control over them. While the parliamentary council is a forum for meeting, the confessional councils, in their isolated organization and without a joint organization that binds them together, form independent and separate arenas while the spiritual leaders that are circumstantially brought together seek to reduce risks and contain conflicts.[17]

In sum, the confusion created in the 1930s persists to this day, making it impossible to distinguish the exact legal rights of such groups, separately or collectively, to participate in electoral politics and call themselves political parties. The result is ad hoc and biased regulation, from one election to the next.

HISTORICAL DEVELOPMENT OF PARTIES IN LEBANON

There have been three stages of partisan politics in Lebanon since World War II: the stage of peace and fragmentation (1943–1975), the stage of wars (1975–1989), and the postwar stage (1990–present).

Prewar Politics in Lebanon

Prior to the establishment of the Lebanese state in 1920, partisan politics nonetheless existed under the Ma'ni monarchy and then later under the Shihabi monarchy. The two competing parties were the Qaissi Party and the Yamani Party. At a later stage, the duality Qaissi/Yamani became Junblati/Yazbaki, the first under the Qaissi Junblati family and the second under the Arsalans.[18] Once the French mandate system was established, new political elites emerged particularly within the Christian sects, and specifically the Maronites. Two main factors gave prominence to the new political leadership: the French policy that encouraged leaders who were close to French orientations and the transfer of the political decision-making center from the Jabal to the capital city of Beirut. The main locus of Lebanese politics under the mandate revolved around the position of the political leadership toward the mandate system, particularly in the aftermath of the decision of the high commissioner to suspend the constitution of 1932. Two blocs were formed within the parliament, based on the alliances between influential political leaders within the Christian and Islamic sects. During these early years (prior to 1943), there were two types of parties: the radical parties that questioned not only the form of the political system but also the raison d'être of the state as an established entity and national parties that participated in political life within the political games of the established political order. Three Armenian parties (Dashnak, Hunchakian Handchaq, and Ramgavar) also participated in parliamentary elections. Of note is the Dashnak, which helped its candidates obtain parliamentary seats. However, these parties attracted Armenians only and their programs often addressed interest issues unrelated to the internal situation in Lebanon. Other small political parties participated in political life, but they were local, such as Al Nedaa Al Qawmi (the National Appeal Party) under Adnan Al Hakim in Beirut and the Nasserite parties in Saida and Tripoli.

Criteria used to distinguish parties of the left and right do not necessarily reflect distinctions between the left and the right. It is not for nothing that the journalist Edward Said used to say that if Marx had lived in Lebanon, he would have become an abhorrent bourgeois It was already apparent that in Lebanon the dilemma posed by national parties was that they raised critical issues of change that clashed with the social structure of the Lebanese society, the reality of the state, Arab schisms, and Arab despotic orders. What was largely absent in the parties was democracy. All conflicting and controversial issues were raised for debate except the issue of democratic political competition and democratic practices within political parties.

The Stage of Peace and Pluralism (1943–1975)

During the period of peace in Lebanon, party representation in parliament witnessed a staggering increase, rising from 20% in the early 1950s to 30% in the 1972 parliament. In 1992 there was a slight decline to 27%, but new parties entered parliament and other parties left, particularly the parties with Christian bases that boycotted elections.

By this time political parties in Lebanon could be described as what Maurice Duverger called "*petits partis*," meaning parties that enjoy limited numerical representation in parliament and are not capable of playing an important role in support or opposition. Two types of small parties can be distinguished. These are the parties of personalities and the parties of permanent minorities.

The apogee of partisan politics in Lebanon was reached during the five or six years that preceded the outbreak of the 1975 war. This era witnessed an unprecedented amount of intense party activity. The segment of the population most involved in political parties were youths from secondary schools and universities. The student movement in Lebanese universities mirrored the situation of partisan politics in Lebanon in the first half of the 1970s, and the presence of the Palestinian armed resistance had an impact on party activism, particularly within the ranks of the political forces that opposed the armed Palestinian presence in Lebanon.

Parties made positive contributions in political activism so long as peace prevailed. They activated and modernized political life by giving prominence to new political elites. In the mid-1970s, Lebanon reached the highest level of nonsectarian political activism since its independence. It also reached the highest level of daily interaction among different social groups in political life, housing, schools, and universities.

Most notably, the Phalangist Party was distinguished during this period by the sound management of its organizational "machinery," particularly during elections. More than other parties, it sought to nurture a modern and organized political party with a set of core tenets. The most important achievement of the Phalangist Party was the generation of new political elites within the Christian sects, particularly among the Maronites.

The War Period (1975–1990[19])

The political parties in Lebanon began to arm themselves to protect their constituencies against the presence of the armed Palestinian Liberation Organization (PLO). The turning point in this militarization of the parties was in 1973, following an armed confrontation between the Lebanese army and the PLO, and the parties effectively became militias as the war broke out in 1975 following hostilities between Christian and Muslim/PLO forces.[20] During the war years, political parties constituted the main executive tool of the war machinery. However, it is not possible to understand armed conflict in Lebanon or the role of parties in it without understanding regional conflicts, particularly the Arab-Israeli conflict.

Most of the political parties that participated in the armed conflict witnessed internal divisions that were violently resolved. Acts of violence that took place among parties who theoretically shared the same cause were detrimental to the parties and society in general. In particular, they harmed the very social base that the parties claimed to defend.

The war years witnessed the rise of new political parties and the demise of others. The most significant change took place within the Shiite sect upon the emergence of Hizbullah as the main political and military power competing with the Amal movement that existed before the eruption of the wars. Hizbullah, which was not officially founded as a political party until 1985, emerged as a militia in response to the Israeli invasion of Lebanon in 1982. Armed, funded, and trained by the Iranian government, Hizbullah became the dominant party among the Shiite communities by the end of the 1980s after a protracted struggle against Amal, the other Shiite party.[21]

During this period other parties ceased to exist for military or political reasons, including Al Murabitun, with its Sunni base, and in recent stages, the Guards of the Cedar Trees, with its Christian base. Other parties became inactive but resumed activity after the war, such as the Labor Communist Party with its Christian base, in addition to several local Nasserite parties.

The Postwar Period: 1989 to the Present

The Ta'if Accords were signed in 1989, permitting the official end of the war the following year. This agreement legitimized the continued presence in Lebanon of the Syrian army, which had entered Lebanon as a peace-keeping force during the civil war in 1976 to protect the Christians at the behest of Lebanon, but sided with the PLO soon after its arrival. The stage following these accords was characterized by oppression, penetration, imprisonment, and the uprooting of political parties. It is also known for the generation and armament of artificial organizations by the Syrian-Lebanese intelligence apparatus supported by selective judicial authorities. This was manifested when Michel Aoun, later the leader of the Free Patriotic Party founded in 2005, was sent into exile in 1990, through the imprisonment of the commander of the Lebanese forces, Samir Geagea in 1994, and with the July 2006 war, which was an Israeli-Syrian-Iranian confrontation. This war highlighted Hizbullah's free hand in declaring war and peace while ignoring the repercussions of such decisions.

This oppressive trend is the result of years of mobilization among a large minority within the Lebanese Shiite sect, in support of pro-Syrian regime leadership. However, such practices are not in accordance with the Lebanese partisan heritage of the 1920s, nor the provisions of the National Reconciliation document of November 5, 1989. The latter agreement, which was the outcome of the Ta'if Accords and reasserted Lebanese control over southern Lebanon, legitimized the continued presence of the Syrian army in Lebanon and reduced the political influence of the Maronite Christian community, which is now a taboo subject for the Syrian regime. However, the parties have confronted the challenge of their rehabilitation as political forces that play a positive and active role in society and in political life. The major challenge lies in securing a systematic mechanism for the shift from a military or militia state to a partisan, democratic state within or outside the party. Political parties appear to be incapable of renewing their base through attracting a new generation of youth. They are still trying to cope with the radical and profound transformations in the region, and in the whole world, since the establishment of political parties in Lebanon half a century ago, including the Arab-Israeli conflict, the state of Arab regimes, the end of the Cold War, and the disintegration of the Soviet Union.

The main criterion for the failure or success of partisan political forces is genuine democratic practice in party work. The battle for positive change is a battle to provide roots for democracy in party activism on all levels, from the bottom to the top leadership. Recent history has not made this task a simple one in Lebanon. During the 1992, 1996, and 2004 elections, regulations in the Lebanese-Syrian intelligence centers were designed to exclude certain political trends and install majorities that favor the continued presence of the Syrian army in Lebanon. The distribution of seats within parliament after the 2005 elections is shown in Tables 2.1 through 2.4, but it should be kept in mind that the interventions by the military have enhanced the penetration of the chosen parties and incapacitated the parliament as a regularizing and permanent institution of dialogue.[22]

LOOKING AHEAD

Three factors will be of crucial importance in determining the future relationship between political parties and democracy in Lebanon: political protection of civil society, the strength of private commitment to public action, and the commitment of the parties to responsible management of a diverse society.

Protecting Civil Society

Lebanese civil society, consisting of voluntary associations not directly related to government authority, is of great vitality due to their social structure and freedom of association. This freedom is unique in comparison to other Arab regimes. The Lebanese civil society—which has resisted the war system, its armed parties, and the de facto forces—fears penetration by a central authority that opposes freedoms if there are no political forces that defend and protect civil society and integrate its aspirations and expectations into law and legislation. The endeavors to transform notifications for the establishment of associations into licenses and the intervention of the central authority in the affairs of syndicates, as well as the surveillance of mass media, particularly audio visual media, point to the need to rely on political forces for the protection of civil society and its activities.

This must include protection of religious associations. In a situation where the rule of law is shaken, confessions may play a positive role in the protection of freedom due to their social legitimacy. However, several

Table 2.1 Classification and Size of Party Blocs and Alliances in Parliament in the Aftermath of the May–June Elections of 2005

Alliance or bloc	*Representatives (out of 128 seats)*
Future Movement (Saad El Hariri)	36
Progressive Socialist Party (Walid Junblat)	15
Liberation and Development (Nabih Berry)	15
Hope Movement (Hizbullah)	14
Qornet Shehwan	14
Independents	5
Lebanese Forces	6
Phalangist	2
Deputy Solange Gemaye	1
Free Patriotic Movement	14
Elie Skaff Bloc	5
Tripoli Bloc	3
Al Matn Bloc	2
Syrian Social Nationalist Party	2
Democratic Renewal Party	1
Democratic Left	1
Baath Party	1
Independent	5

Source: Julia Choucair, "Lebanon: Finding a Path from Deadlock to Democracy." Democracy and Rule of Law Project. Carnegie Endowment for International Peace: Carnegie Papers. Number 64, January 2006. http://www.carnegieendowment.org/files/CP64.Choucair.FINAL1.pdf

religious figures were assassinated during the war years and de facto forces have sought to circumvent the organization of joint spiritual summits.

Strengthening Private Commitment to Public Action

Lebanese society suffers today from an abstinence from politics in general. A new citizenry is emerging that needs to be nurtured, as a result of common suffering. But the pain of the postwar phase, the continued pressuring of the regional situation, and the agonizing memory of the violations by armed parties and militias have understandably led to widespread abstinence from politics and lack of interest in the public sphere. The appeal for commitment to issues of public affairs is an urgent need for reconstruction, and this is not limited to material structures. It is a need for sustainable development and the democratic path in general. Political parties and forces, in addition to the voluntary organizations, universities, social organizations, and mass media, are the frameworks that attract public debate and commitment to public interest, and this is a key role for them to play in strengthening Lebanese democracy.

Table 2.2 Parliamentary Majority through Parliamentary Blocs in the Aftermath of May–June 2005 Elections

	Deputies (out of 128)
Bristol Gathering	
Future Movement	36
Democratic Gathering	15
Qornet Shehwan	14
Tripoli Bloc	3
Democratic Left	1
Democratic Renewal	1
Independents	2
Alliance of Hizbullah, Amal Movement, the National Party, Baath, and Phalangists	
Liberation and Development Bloc	15
Al Wafaa Resistance Bloc	14
Syrian National Socialist party	2
Phalangists	1
Baath	1
Free Patriotic Party	14

Source: Rita Sharara, "Map of Parliamentary Blocs and Alliances in June 2005," *An-Nahar*, June 21, 2005.

Partisan Commitment to Responsible Management of a Diverse Society

There is a new understanding in Lebanon of the ways parties might serve as active elements in negotiations and in containing conflicts. However, the wars have shaken the parties' relationships with one another, their structures, and their potential constituencies. Nonetheless, the crisis

Table 2.3 Name and Size of Partisan Blocs and Alliances in June 2005

Future Movement (Saad El Hariri)	36
Liberation and Development (Nabih Berry)	15
Resistance Bloc—Hizbullah	14
Nationalist Party	2
Phalangists Party	3
Baath Party	1
Free Patriotic Party	14
Progressive Socialist Party (Walid Jumblat)	15
Lebanese Forces Bloc	6
Reformist Phalangists Bloc	3
Qornet Shehwan Bloc	5
Tripoli Bloc	5

Source: Rita Sharara, "Map of Parliamentary Blocs and Alliances in June 2005," *An-Nahar*, June 21, 2005.

Table 2.4 Distribution of Deputies According to Blocs during the Parliamentary Consultations on June 30, 2005

Bloc	Deputies
Liberation and Development (Nabih Berry)	15
Future Movement (Saad El Hariri)	32
Progressive Socialist Party (Walid Junblat)	18
Al Wafaa for Resistance	14
Popular Bloc (Elias Skaff)	4
Lebanese Forces	6
Tripoli Bloc	4
Reformist Phalangists Bloc	2
Democratic Renewal	1
Democratic Left	1
Armenian Deputies Bloc	2
Baath Party	1
Syrian National Socialist Party	2
Phalangists Party	1
Free Patriotic Bloc	14
Independent	9

Source: Rita Sharara, "Map of Parliamentary Blocs and Alliances in June 2005," *An-Nahar*, June 21, 2005.

of partisan structures is an international one. The experiences of party rule in the world, the development of critical thinking on citizenship as a result of education, the accelerated pace of history since the 1980s, the end of grand ideologies, and in particular the implementation of projects and plans in favor of citizenship, human rights, and democratic culture all reflect the nature, form, and degree of citizens' commitment.

However, party organizations, political programs, and mobilization ideologies have—from this point forward—an expiration date. The trend is now moving toward profound transformations in mentalities, conflicts, and solutions. But it is hard for political parties around the world to live through these transformations without drowning in opportunism, and in the Middle East this is of course compounded by the absence of peace. Eventually, the parties must abandon politics based on the bitter experiences of nationhood and fundamentalism.

Lebanon has a rich experience in managing diversity. It is hard for its parties to forget that their historic origins have always been linked to issues of identity and dualities (small Lebanon and big Lebanon, Lebanese-ism and Arabism, progressive and reactionary). Undoubtedly, these issues express a historic state but lack usefulness in putting in place a system for democratic management of diversity as the Lebanese people experience it today. The general population has a thirst for communication and exchange based on common interests, as opposed to dwelling on historical disparities in identities, remote origins, and primordial affiliations.

Nonetheless, parties play a crucial role in achieving permanent public peace and placing nations on the democratic path. Will political parties in Lebanon take on increasingly sectarian characteristics, which would transform Lebanon into an arena of conflicts over origins, identities, and affiliations that can only be solved by a radical solution? Or will they alternatively indulge in dialectic, continual, and mobile relationships that would be consistent with the expectations and aspirations of Lebanese citizens?

CONCLUSIONS

It is no longer possible to ask people anywhere in the world to commit themselves for life to a political organization or rigid beliefs. Today, citizens are committed to short-term policies or at most to a medium-term project with a set of definite political goals. As a result of the development in education, and in some countries, the development of democratic culture, the commitment of citizens is no longer comprehensive or absolute. It is fraught with reservations. People are now aware that the risk that politics may deviate from its path is part and parcel of politics, democratic or otherwise. The virtue of caution is the virtue of citizenship par excellence and is exercised through governments and all agencies including parties that have or seek power.

The more political practice distances itself from the exploitation of authority and the more it comes closer to public affairs, the more commitment is linked to the credibility of the leaders, transparency, and interaction. The revelation of scandals in a president's or a crown prince's or a minister's private life reflects a well-established public conviction that whoever is in a position of public affairs must expect objectivity and sacrifice of immediate and individual interests. Mass media and rulers have used this phenomenon to incite the people or take revenge on adversaries. However, this kind of surveillance also reflects a transformation in the understanding of what politics means, moving away from conceiving it as merely the crass exploitation of authority toward a new insistence on the sober management of public affairs. Commitment and reconciliation between parties and their grass roots now requires higher levels of credibility. Democratic ethics are concomitant to legitimacy.

At a workshop on political parties held March 11, 1995, the late Joseph Moghaizel, former minister and deputy and head of the parliamentary committee for human rights, one of the founders of the Democratic Party and the founder of the Lebanese human rights association, spoke as follows:

> It is now time to cast a fresh look at our political life and discuss the renewal of parties. Lebanon's political future will remain uncertain if there is no reform that changes discourse into reality. During the war, all parties lost the role expected of them. The more urgent issue now concerns youth

> and the future of democracy in the country. . . . The absence of a majority in parliament makes deviation easy for those who are capable of that. It is possible to exert pressure on some individuals or groups to push them in one direction or the other. . . . A question is now raised on how to activate political life in Lebanon based on popular representation.[23]

The parliamentary majority formed by combining parliamentary parties and blocs that emerged after the evacuation of the Syrian military forces from Lebanon, the elections of 2004, the assassination of Prime Minister Rafik al-Hariri and his companions on February 14, 2005, the series of assassinations (George Hawy, Samir Kassir, Jobran Tweini) and assassination attempts (Marwan Hamadeh, Mai Shediak, and Elias El Mor) in 2005, and the massive anti-Syria protest in the spring in Beirut on March 14, 2005, all demonstrate the political turmoil from which Lebanon must move forward, even as the Lebanese-Syrian intelligence system seeks to hold it back. As Nabil Khalifeh wrote about Hizbullah:

> The challenge is Lebanese and realistic. Its gist is: Regardless of its capacities, political, military, and demographic abilities, does Hizbullah believe it is alone capable to impose—using its individual power—a special situation in the whole of Lebanon, something that the super powers could not do? In other words, Can the party (or even the confession) control the other confessions in Lebanon by playing solo, or does it have to reach an understanding and cooperate with other forces to form the required consensus as a base for a common life in Lebanon?[24]

Certainly not all signs are positive. The authoritarian structure to be imposed on new parties appears in the draft of the text regarding internal regulations for a political party:

1. (Name of the President), given his location and historic role, is an ex-officio member of all party committees and councils.
2. (Name of the President) has the right to appeal any decision taken by the party.
3. (Name of the President) has the right to attend any of the party meetings on any level and preside over the meeting upon his arrival.
4. (Name of the President) has the right to appoint members in the Senate.

To struggle against this effort to maintain authoritarian control, Lebanese political parties must strive for significant change in three domains:

1. *Ideology.* The clause in the preamble of the Lebanese constitution stating that "Lebanon is the ultimate homeland of all its children" requires a critical review of the foundation of several Lebanese parties that were formed around identities, affiliations, Lebanese-ism, and Arabism. Parties must move away from the discussion over identities toward a discussion of public policies.

2. *Response to civil society.* Parties, including opposition parties, have become part of the power mechanism and mostly seek to reproduce relations of power and influence instead of focusing on the concerns of the people and issues of civil society. There is nothing wrong with populist parties that adopt daily life issues and socioeconomic rights that are linked to the quality of people's lives, including education, health, housing, the environment, and the four most important requisites: school, house, hospital, and consumer goods.[25]
3. *Internal democracy.* Partisan life is an arena for controversy over public issues. This requires the development of parties' internal democracy and communications between and among parties far beyond what we see at present. The lack of public debates within parties is evidenced by the establishment of youth, women, students, and syndicate divisions, each of which repeat and reiterate what the leader says, responding to clientelistic motivations. Many youths have been introduced into parties in order to applaud the leader rather than to give the party access to, and knowledge of, the different age and professional groups in society in order to fulfill their needs.

Parties' internal democracy and their contribution to the development of democracy are linked to the culture of human rights instead of relations of power and influence. It is also linked to the development of public awareness of free citizens who are aware of their daily and legitimate rights.

The Lebanese experience prior to the war years (1975–1990), the aggressive and fraternal occupations by foreign forces, and the incessant transgressions by the Lebanese-Syrian intelligence organization all demonstrate the importance of the link between democratic and effective partisan life and professional associations that enjoy autonomy from parties in exercising their economic and social functions. In Lebanon, the challenge is great, but so is the promise.

CHAPTER 3

Political Parties in Mauritania: Challenges and Horizons

Mohamed Ould Mohamed Abderrahmane Moine

INTRODUCTION

Mauritania is a small Arab country whose population does not exceed three million, distributed among four major ethnic groups. Based on unofficial estimates made in 1958 during the time of the French administration, the first, and by far the largest, ethnic group is that which derives from Arab origin. This group is divided internally into two smaller groups: the white Arabs and the black Arabs who hail from the population formerly enslaved by white Arabs, known as the Harateen. The three other ethnic groups are the Fulan, who together comprise 11% of the population, the Suninkis, who comprise 3%, and the Wolof, who comprise 1.1%.

Mauritania has witnessed three eras of political opening in its recent history, beginning during the last decades of the French occupation of the country, when the stage was set for independence, achieved in November 28, 1960. A single-party system was established under the leadership of President Mokhtar Ould Daddah and lasted until the establishment of the military coup of 1978. The second era of political opening began in 1984 when Maaouya Ould Taya deposed the military government and began the return to civilian rule. After the fall of the Berlin Wall in 1989 and the beginning of political mobility in Sub-Saharan Africa, Mauritania witnessed considerable progress toward democratization, particularly between 1992 and 2005 when multiple parties were permitted to exist. However, the experiment came to a halt as the political regime, still under the rule of Ould Taya, was unable to establish mechanisms for the effective exchange of political power and another military coup took place in 2005. This time the military moved speedily toward the reestablishment of civilian government, which took place in March 2007. However, this third era of political opening ended abruptly with another military coup on August 6, 2008.

This chapter will consider the nature and role of political parties during these three eras when steps were taken toward democratization. However, this is a story that must be told in context. To understand the relationship between parties and democracy in Mauritania, it is also important to understand the other forces at work during these periods: the role played by endemic problems such as poverty and ethnic and language conflicts; the complications engendered by the pursuit of power by leaders little concerned with parties except as agencies serving their own ambitions; and the effects of the policies of foreign governments and international conflicts on Mauritania. Thus, each section will not only describe the parties but also summarize and explain the complex interaction of these other factors and show how they have set serious limits to what can be achieved by the parties as well as influenced what the parties have been *interested* in achieving.

THE FIRST WAVE OF DEMOCRACY

Political parties were formed in Mauritania during the last two decades of the French occupation following the French legislative elections of 1945, the same year that witnessed France's reorganization of its overseas regions, the establishment of the district of Mauritania, and the enactment of subsequent rights of parliamentary representation.

During this stage two political parties rose to the fore: the Reconciliation Party and the Mauritanian Progressive Party. The Reconciliation Party was founded by deputy Ahmed Ould Horma, who proved able to attract a large number of youth and leaders such as Mohamed Fal Ould Amir, the prince of Al Tararza; Zakaria Sise, head of the Kidimagha; and his deputy Diawra Ghani. Ould Horma also had the support of the French branch of the Socialist International, particularly Leopold Senghor, the deputy of Southern Senegal (and later the president of Senegal). This wide appeal allowed the party to enjoy influence in the villages and small towns until it was disbanded after 1956 when it demanded that Mauritania be annexed to the newly independent Morocco.

The Mauritanian Progressive Party was supported by the traditional structure of tribal chieftains and Sufi orders that permeated it and was able to win overwhelming victories in the 1951 and 1956 elections with the support of the French occupation forces. During that time, Sidi Al Mokhtar Enjay, the first speaker of the Mauritanian Parliament, and the young lawyer Mokhtar Ould Daddah rose to the forefront of the political scene.

In the first elections held in preindependent Mauritania in 1951, the Reconciliation Party's choice of the indigenous Ould Horma as its candidate (over his competitor of French origin, Ivon Rasaq, who had long worked as a senior official in the administration of Mauritania) brought victory to the party and to its socialist members.[1]

Developments in the aging French empire following World War II eventually led to the autonomy[2] of the French colonies, followed soon thereafter by full independence facilitated by the administrative reforms introduced by the French, such as the Framework of Authorities, known as the Law of Gaston in 1956, and the laws in 1957 that sought to implement a federal system of administration based on the decentralization of authority and jurisdiction. In the wake of these reforms, the tide turned in favor of the Progressive Party, the party that was closest to the French administration. After independence in November 1960, this party found itself in control of an independent state, an independence that had been acquired not as an outcome of a strong national struggle in which the desert people of Mauritania aspired to freedom from the colonizer, but largely as a result of France's desire to rid itself of a poor colony that was not worth retaining. Sidi Al Mokhtar Enjay, former deputy in the French Fourth Republic, became speaker of parliament and the young lawyer Mokhtar Ould Daddah became prime minister, accountable to a multiparty parliament.

However, the return of General Charles de Gaulle to power in 1958 and his control over the terms of the new constitution in the creation of the French Fifth Republic had seriously undermined the power of the African parliaments. In successive years African parliaments were weak, as African presidents monopolized power, following the example of Paris, their main economic and military guardian, which had itself adopted the same approach to governance, albeit to a lesser degree.

In the case of Mauritania this meant the victory of the head of the executive authority and aborted the embryonic experiment in parliamentary rule. Shortly after Mauritania achieved independence on November 28, 1960, Roundtable negotiations[3] that included all political parties were held. These negotiations led to political unanimity, bringing together all political forces into one party. An important additional motive for moving to a single-party state was the need to secure support and solidarity against the demands of Morocco to annex Mauritania.[4]

In order to expand his party base, Ould Daddah entered into a series of dialogues with small parties such as the Mauritanian Youth Organization, the Renaissance Party, and the Islamic Union at the Aleg conference of 1958, and the Roundtable discussions in Nouakchott in 1960–1961. These meetings resulted in the birth of the Al Tagamu' Party and later of the leftist Mauritanian People's Party, which came to dominate the political arena. Such was the status of party politics until the July 10, 1978, military coup. This first coup came as a result of a lack of genuine political pluralism coupled with the deteriorating situation in the Saharan war.[5]

THE SECOND WAVE OF DEMOCRACY

Although direct military rule ended in December 1984, when Muawya Ould Taya staged a bloodless coup d'état and became chief of state, Mauritania remained heavily under military control and in a state of chronic instability for the next decade and a half. A wide range of economic and social hardships, particularly those associated with and stemming from the ethnic conflict between the Arab and the Polari groups, reached its peak in 1989 with a tragic and open struggle in the south, resulting in thousands of casualties and refugees.[6] The governments of Mauritania and Senegal exacerbated the problem by resorting to a painful transfer policy, mandating the forceful evacuation of migrants and sometimes of racial and ethnic groups that had their origins in other countries.

The security concerns of the military also led to its undertaking a campaign of ethnic cleansing in the military and security institutions during the winter of 1990–1991.[7] This campaign was primarily due to the military's concerns about the reactions to the large-scale suppression of the Polari people that came in the aftermath of the failed coup staged by the Polari officers in October 1987, an attempt that clearly had a racial character.

Compounding this turmoil were the difficulties associated with the absence of badly needed economic reforms. In addition, Mauritania's negotiating position with its Western partners in the structural adjustment cooperation agreements was undermined by the pro-Baghdad stance of the Nouakchott government during the 1991 Gulf War, resulting in an unannounced Western-imposed embargo against Mauritania.

Under these circumstances, voices were raised calling for greater political opening. Change was becoming inevitable. In the spring of 1991, Ould Taya attended the African-French conference held in France at La Beaule. There he heard the calls for greater political freedoms as well as French President François Mitterrand's support for democratic reforms. Ould Taya responded positively, albeit in carefully measured steps. He issued pardons for a number of political prisoners and allowed exiled political figures to return home. Within a few weeks there was not a single prisoner of conscience in prison. This was followed by a presidential decree organizing the profession of written journalism and a draft constitution law that was presented for referendum in July 1991. A new agenda for presidential, parliamentary, and municipal elections was also scheduled for consideration. And once again, political parties, illegal but nonetheless active during the military period, were legalized.

The Union of Democratic Forces Party (UDF) was the main inheritor of an earlier coalition, the United Democratic Front for Change. It was a strong alliance of a group of influential personalities and political and social movements that demanded political power and sought to put an end to the ethnic problems of the Mauritanian society. It was characterized by a high degree of resilience and openness, which helped it expand its popular base in a short period of time, despite the complicated ethnic situation at the end of the 1980s. The principal parties joining this coalition were:

1. The National Democratic Party: A progressive leftist party with communist leanings, working closely with the Mauritanian Trade Union, an organization that exerted social pressure through demonstrations calling for the restoration of normal constitutional life, which had stopped after the military takeover in 1978.
2. The Free Party: A socially enlightened movement that sought to combat racism and slavery. It was established by former slaves and other Harateen or children of former slaves.[8]

   These first two movements had long been participants in one way or another in several governments without enjoying legal recognition. They were always represented in the state organs, particularly in education and professional syndicates.
3. Al Umma Party: A banned Islamic group that was ideologically similar to the Muslim Brotherhood.
4. The Initiative of the Democratic Union: A club that called for democracy and the settlement of all pending problems, particularly the rights legacy.
5. The Independent Democrats Movement: A students' movement with strong influence in university circles. This movement can be considered the nucleus of the Conscience and Resistance Organization, which later played an important role in overthrowing the rule of Ould Taya. It organized several strikes in Mauritanian educational institutions.
6. The Alliance for a New Mauritania: A movement that demanded political rights for the Polari people. It is closely related to the front for the liberation of Mauritanian blacks, who suffered oppression as a result of the ethnic conflict in the country.

In addition to the above organizations, several important political figures organized in a challenging move against the army such as Al Hadramy Ould Khetry, a former minister and the first to demand that Arabic be considered an official language; Mohamed Ould Babah, the last minister of defense under Mokhtar Ould Daddah; Hamdy Ould Meknas, the last minister of foreign affairs under civilian rule; Moulay Mohamed Ould Moulay Ismail, a former minister of finance under the civil regime; and a host of intellectuals, writers, and artists such as Yakoub Dialou, head of the Bar Association, movie director Mohamed Houndou, and the artist Al Malouma Bent al Meidah.

As the presidential elections of January 1992 approached, Ahmed Ould Daddah, the half brother of former president Mokhtar Ould Daddah, first minister of economic affairs and founder of the Central Bank of Mauritania, returned from his voluntary exile and found no difficulty in securing the UDF's nomination for the presidency, relying on his personal charisma and large popularity in the cities. The appearance of Ahmed Ould Daddah resulted in the further expansion of the base of the UDF. Intraparty preparations for the elections took place within a more peaceful atmosphere as the party's candidate enjoyed the support of businessmen and traders who had for a long time been complaining about the oligarchic privileges granted by Ould Taya to his close circles at the expense of other major financial centers. By supporting Ahmed Ould Daddah, they were expressing their dissatisfaction with the class of nouveaux riches.

The Democratic Social Republican Party (hereafter the Republican Party) was the second most important party during this era. It had been established in haste by Ould Taya in 1984 and he remained leader of the party after his election as president in 1992. Despite the presence of numerous political groups and centers of power, the real support for this party came from the tribal chieftains who acted as the social mediators between the state and citizens in rural areas, providing goods and services to those in need. The majority of important figures in the party's political bureau had played the same role of social mediation for all successive regimes starting from the French administration to the single party and from the military regime to the semidemocratic rule eventually established by Ould Taya.[9]

Social mediating—or clientelistic—parties are in effect patronage networks that derive their influence from the facilities and privileges granted to them by the ruler. They are unclassified social institutions that exercise their tribal influence through the dissemination of the culture of submissiveness among the poorer groups who need the support and care of these patrons in the local social fabric. The role of these institutions is limited in the small towns and is nonexistent in the large cities, but is decisive in the rural areas. The demise of the middle class and the exacerbation of poverty gave the ruling politicians of this unclassified sector the ability to operate independently of the parliamentary institution since the majority of deputies hailed from poor and rural provinces and were elected on the bases of narrow local and tribal criteria.

In addition to the patronage networks, the Republican Party could draw upon a large base of employees who embodied all the meanings of bureaucracy and associated nepotism and opportunism, providing a rich base of educated individuals ready to defend the status quo and justify its existence at any cost. Thus the Republican Party became the party of ministers, *walis* and senior state officials, in addition to tribal chieftains and leaders of Sufi orders.

This party also benefited from the support of Baathists and Nasserites and all Arab progressive figures who looked upon the Arabization policy adopted by Ould Taya as a mode of resistance to French cultural hegemony. This explains why the historic leader and member of the National Command of the Arab Socialist Baath Party Mohamed Yehdih

Ould Bridleil, who had just been released from the prison of Ould Taya, supported the latter and joined his party.[10] Given the strength of the two main parties, the UDF and the Republican Party, smaller political organizations and parties such as the Unionist Party for Democracy and Unity, the Popular Front, the Baathi Vanguard Party, the Nasserite Popular Alliance Party, Salvaging Slaves Movement, and many others remained weak and derived what limited power they had from their alliance with one of the two main political blocs. Other opposition parties boycotted the legislative elections but took part in municipal elections in early 1994.

As has been true throughout their history, the ability (and sometimes the desire) of the parties to move toward greater democratization was strongly influenced by the nature of the problems faced (and sometimes created) by the government. The more urgent problems revolved around how to deal with the legacy of military rule, particularly since the beginning of the Ould Taya era. While on the one hand the Union of Democratic Forces wanted to expose past legal transgressions, punish culprits, and compensate victims, leaders of the Republican Party avoided this discussion and asserted that the violations would simply not be repeated. Any attempt to reopen these files ran the risk of destabilizing the military institution and consequently the whole country. The fact is, however, that the demand to reveal transgressions related to ethnic liquidation within the barracks led to the consolidation of the army and made Ould Taya appear as the only defender of that silent institution. The demand for investigations shifted to foreign tribunals particularly in countries that had signed the Universal Declaration of Human Rights that grants the foreign judge some authority to inspect human rights violations.[11]

Similarly, the practice of slavery remained a controversial issue between opposition and majority parties. The latter believe that slavery is the result of poverty and used a strategy of obscuring the practice enhanced by the fact that a number of Harateen (former slaves) have occupied senior positions in the state such as Prime Minister Asgheer Weld Mubarak and Minister Beigel Ould Hamid and others.[12]

During the final years of Ould Taya's rule, the government became ever more powerful and ever more disdainful of the rights of parliament. Indeed, during these years only two bills of those passed originated in parliament itself; all the rest were government-introduced bills.[13] The two exceptions were a bill passed in February 1993, which pardoned all human rights crimes and violations in military and para military institutions during the military rule of the country, and a law passed in November 1996, which allowed custom exemptions on private cars imported by deputies and senators. Parliamentary deputies did not reject any of the laws presented to them by the government with the exception of the 1997 amendment of the budget law, which curtailed financial allocations to parliament.[14] The archives of the two chambers confirm the absence of any genuine legislative status for parliament, which became merely an institutional formality. Indeed the regime treated parliament as though it were merely an arm of the executive branch of the state.

The continued setback of political rights and the exacerbation of the crisis in the country led to the atrophy and disintegration of opposition political parties. The Union of Democratic Forces witnessed internal conflicts that led to schisms. A branch spun off and established the Labor Party for Change under the leadership of the Harateen Masoud Weld Boulkheir. Another group spun off and formed the National Movement for Democracy then the Union of Forces of Progress Party and many joined the ruling Republican Party.

Despite the structural weakness of the opposition parties, the regime still harassed them, arrested their leaders, and even dissolved some of them. This started with the Union of Forces of Democracy, followed by the Labor Party for Change and the Vanguard Party.

This smothering atmosphere was accompanied by widespread corruption[15] and the failure of development plans. The Mauritanian currency witnessed a remarkable decline, with the rate of inflation reaching 200% in 2004. Corruption was not confined to the internal front but also reached foreign partners, such as the scandal of the faulty figures presented by Mauritania to the International Monetary Fund in 2003–2004, which almost prevented Mauritania from enjoying concessions of the eight industrial states exempting the poorest and indebted countries from repayment of debts.[16]

In addition to the difficulties created for Mauritania and the development of a stable party system by these internal machinations, foreign governments also had a powerful impact on internal politics. Among underdeveloped nations, the small African states remain the most vulnerable to foreign influence. These states' annual budgets largely depend on external aid, and they have old and historic links and defense agreements with European states for their protection against one another. If it had not been for the strategic agreements with France, Mauritania would not have been able to resist the Moroccan plot to annex it or the increasing Algerian influence in the country.

Within this context, relations with Paris deteriorated in the last few years of Ould Taya's rule, and the government had made attempts to approach the United States. The atmosphere of internal stalemate caused by the legacy of the military regime and its inability to adjust to its international rights commitments resulted in the rise of strong pressure groups in the West seeking to overthrow Ould Taya. These pressure groups were the main supporters of the Mauritanian parties that called for democracy.

Partly to counter this development, the regime began to establish relations with Israel in order to become close to U.S. strategic circles concerned with the Arab region.[17] This rapprochement came at a high price on the internal and external fronts, placing the regime in confrontation with the Islamic religious community, including clergymen and scholars of religious schools. This conflict reached its climax in 2000 when a senior Mauritanian clergymen passed a *fatwa* (religious decree) declaring relations with Israel religiously forbidden. Furthermore, despite Tel Aviv's desire to support Ould Taya, the Israeli machinery in the West could not present him as an enlightened leader or an acceptable partner to the United States.

However, an opportunity to polish Ould Taya's image presented itself in the war against Islamic terrorism in the aftermath of 9/11. Almost immediately the regime took measures that did not seem grave in the beginning but that generated critical repercussions. For example, security cooperation with U.S. circles began by arresting some Mauritanians who were accused of affiliation to Al Qaeda, and other developments and preliminary inquiries took place that were characterized by physical violence. Citizens were handed over to the Americans without much incriminating evidence. In fact, at present writing many of them are still in the prison at Guantanamo.[18]

With the second term of President Ould Taya coming to an end, the regime adopted a policy of exaggerating the hazard of Islamists[19] and presenting them as imminent threats. The president himself wrote articles for the French press on terrorism and the need for dialogue among civilizations.

This policy of creating an internal common enemy in an attempt to find an external ally reached its climax in May 2003 when the minister of religious guidance proposed a draft law allowing the state to appoint and expel imams and close some mosques that were deemed "harmful."[20] This state policy affected a number of imams and preachers as well as representatives of Arab charity organizations and the Mauritanian branch of the Mohamed Ben Saud Saudi University, which had to close despite its Saudi nationality. The campaign expanded to include notable scientists and ulemas. The escalating campaign against political Islam led to an unprecedented situation of frustration and stalemate, which paved the material and psychological grounds for the attempted coup d'état in June 2003.

The military institution's monopoly over power had encouraged many of the young people of the 1980s to join the military college in order to reach power. But the political reforms of the 1990s, although timid and hesitant, had nevertheless led to the marginalization of the army and its departure from the political scene, thereby ending its control over civil society. However, the continued absence of democratic life prompted the establishment of communication between some of the military elites and the traditional political forces, such as the tribal and regional chieftains. The army was soon transformed into competing tribal and local factions, while the regime fell in the arms of tribalism and turned to the army to defend it.

Coordination was established between youth officers hailing from the densely populated and resource deprived eastern states influenced by the nationalist and Islamist trends as second generation Arabophones and some intellectuals and targeted clergymen. This cooperation soon generated an unprecedented revolution. In the early hours of June 8, the artillery forces opened their doors to allow Soviet T55 tanks—an old gift from Iraq—to head toward the presidential palace and control the area. President Ould Taya fled following a minor act of resistance, during which the general commander of the army was killed. The police were neutralized and the leaders of the coup soon took full control of the radio and television stations.

The fact that Ould Taya was not arrested allowed him to continue to contact commanders of the internal areas who scurried over to rescue him. After a fierce resistance during which prisons were opened and scientists and clergymen liberated, the pro-president forces were able to regain control of the situation and the leaders of the coup fled the country.

Upon regaining power Ould Taya put the prisoners of conscience who had been released back in jail along with scores of officers and soldiers, many of whom had not taken part in the armed mutiny but had strong tribal or family links to the commanders of the June 8 leaders. New elections were scheduled for November 2003.

It was soon clear that the government was determined to ignore the desire of the political parties to carry out elections[21] under international supervision. Increasing frustration led several parties and important figures representing different trends to support the nomination of Mohamed Khouna Ould Haidallah who, in addition to being a former president, was an officer who enjoyed the respect of the majority of army officers. Additionally, he had the support of Ahmed Ould Daddah, leader of the alliance of democratic forces formed after the dissolution of the Union of Democratic Forces, and the blessings of Massoud Ould Boulkheir, leader of the Popular Progressive Alliance.

Although all the nominees were convinced that the casting of ballots would never by itself lead to the overthrow of the oligarchic regime that controlled the state and the judiciary, the goal behind their public involvement was the desire to embarrass the regime and push it to commit grave political mistakes that would help sustain the state of frustration and even convince the military and security circles of the need to abandon supporting it.

The security crackdown that followed the military mutiny permitted Ould Taya to arrest Ould Haidallah (who was close to the Islamists) just 24 hours before Election Day, although he was promptly released because arresting a candidate could have led, according to Mauritanian law, to cancellation of the entire election process. But as soon as the election results were announced, Haidallah was immediately rearrested and returned to prison. He was subsequently tried, together with a number of rights advocates and cultural and political figures, on charges of conspiring to overthrow the president.

News of the trial caused a wide-scale international outcry. The rush of renowned African and European lawyers to join the defense panel and the broad media coverage inflicted great harm on Ould Taya's relations with many foreign capitals. Among the numerous charges levied against his opponents, the one that drew widespread public attention was the charge of obtaining funds from foreign countries like Libya and Burkina Faso, whose relations with Nouakchott had reached the state of boycott and explicit antagonism.

Not surprisingly Ould Taya's relations with Arab countries worsened as Mauritania moved to strengthen relations with Israel. Its ties with neighboring African countries were also weakened when Nouakchott abandoned the Economic Commission for West Asian States (ECWAS). These policies led to Ould Taya's isolation and worked in the interests of his adversaries, who found support and refuge in those countries that now felt little warmth toward his regime.

Additionally, rather than allowing the opposition some breathing room to let off steam, Ould Taya arrested and put on trial a number of officers and soldiers who took part in the coup attempt. No sooner had the first round of arrests ended when the regime announced in August 2004 that it had aborted a new coup attempt; thus began another cycle of massive arrests that included scores of officers and soldiers, many of whom were senior staff.

This painful political atmosphere continued into March 2005 with numerous trials taking place that included a large number of opposition figures. Although the court tried to avoid execution sentences, deep schisms still emerged between the eastern tribes and the regime, whose leaders came from the sparsely populated northern tribes of Mauritania.

The escalation of the political crisis following the succession of failed coup attempts and the failure of the regime to introduce measures to diffuse the accumulating frustrations and engaging, effectively, the various opposition groups, led the Algerian Salafi group Dawa and Combat (which later developed into the base for the jihadist movement affiliated with Al Qaeda in the Maghreb) to decide the time was ripe to take action. On June 4, 2005, this Salafi group—irked particularly by Ould Taya's insistence on playing the role of police in the African Sahara region though eminently unqualified to do so—took up arms against the regime. On June 4, 2005, the Salafi group inflicted, without much loss, a painful defeat on the Mauritanian army, when it succeeded in neutralizing the Al Maghity force on the Mauritanian, Mali, and Algerian borders. The return of the Mauritanian army to this region was a message of warning and an expression of Nouakchott's interest in playing some role in the war against Islamist terrorism, which settled in the triangle on the borders after the Islamist network was expelled from Sudan and Afghanistan. Although the human and material losses could not be described as severe because of the small size of the Al Maghity base, Nouakchott considered the incident a gift that confirmed the deteriorating situation and gave the regime's harsh security crackdown on opposition groups new justification. It provided an ideal opportunity to join the U.S. war against terrorism.

However, despite the concerns of Washington, D.C., over pockets of desert-based extremist groups[22] and its sponsorship of the Sahel initiative in the combat against terrorism and the creation of an Africa command for that purpose, it was reluctant to cooperate with the dictatorial regime of Ould Taya, which was politically and economically isolated. But Nouakchott's determination to chase the Salafi group encouraged the United States to participate in and give its approval to the military conference of the African Sahel countries held in Nouakchott on July 2, 2005. It even exercised pressures on Mali and Niger to allow the Mauritanian army to pursue and chase out the Salafi groups in their territories. Thus encouraged, Ould Taya launched a campaign to purge Ezwad, the region north of Mali and Niger inhabited by the Arabs and Towareg, using limited resources and a regiment of the 4,000 troops that formed the core of the Mauritanian military forces.[23] However, the opposition parties as well as a majority of officers were dissatisfied with that move on the grounds that the campaign would depopulate the western region, which contained the country's main infrastructural and economic projects, thus offering a golden opportunity for the Cavaliers of Change, a militant group that was receiving arms from external powers, to try to take power there.

The state and the media it controlled were thus unable to translate the Ezwad campaign and the ongoing events into a popular cause, one producing social and political solidarity as the nation faced a foreign threat. Instead, the oppressive situation in this totalitarian state, the absence of dialogue and social interaction, as well as the accelerating events led to increasing dissatisfaction even within the ruling military camp that began to call for internal dialogue, political reconciliation, and unity of the internal front.

Within this turbulent climate, Ahmed Ould Sidi Baba, leader of the Alliance for Democracy and Unity, a small political party that is linked to the Republican Party, called for a national seminar on June 25–28, 2004, to discuss urgently needed reforms. Most political organizations and parties participated except for the Popular Progressive Alliance, which boycotted the debate. Despite the media significance of the initiative, it failed politically due to the absence of any signs of seriousness on the part of the ruling party, which had minimal representation in the meetings and did not take part in the subcommittees or accept the notion of pardoning prisoners of conscience. The meeting concluded by issuing recommendations, and the government was left free to implement those recommendations that suited it.

This obvious absence of a political will to undertake audacious reform measures reinforced the state of political despondence. Finally, the Mauritanian people turned once more to the military for salvation from a stumbling and dictatorial regime.

THE THIRD WAVE OF DEMOCRATIZATION

The military coup of August 3, 2005, was actually the first step in renewing an effort to bring democratization to Mauritanian. It was carried out by Colonel Mohamed Ould Abdelaziz, the young commander of the special presidential private guards.[24] After freezing the nation's constitutional institutions, Ould Abdelaziz then asked the more senior Colonel Eli Ould Mohamed Fal, director of national security, to preside over a newly established military Council for Justice and Democracy, a body that included commanders of all the military zones and units. Members of the council had agreed on a transitional agenda inspired by the petitions that were submitted by the coordinating agency of the opposition parties demanding, for example, international monitoring of elections and rejection of the nomination of members of the transitional authority to the new government.[25] In effect, the army was ideologically and pragmatically promoting the demands of the opposition parties.

The leaders of the new coup faced external and internal difficulties that would not have been surmountable if it had not been for the support offered by political parties and other organizations.[26] A unique situation of political unanimity arose around the transitional program, which helped restore trust between citizens and the state.

There was, however, less agreement about the political process to be followed. The military refused the demand of the political parties that candidates in elections not be allowed to run as independents but rather must be affiliated to a particular political party as a condition for eligibility. This demand was motivated by the desire to combat tribalism and strengthen party politics, but after the junta's rejection of the idea, the parties decided not to dwell on the subject in an attempt to show goodwill and enhance the spirit of trust between the transitional authority and the political structures. In truth, the parties and all other political actors had by that time reached a point of deep exhaustion after the long years of Ould Taya's autocratic rule and wished to enjoy a political truce that would allow them to prepare for the upcoming elections. Parliamentary and municipal elections were held on November 19 and December 3, 2006, and the presidential election, resulting in a second ballot election of Sidi Ould Cheikh Abdallahi, was held on March 22, 2007. It was the first multicandidate election in the country's postindependence history.

Nonetheless, from the beginning there were signs the junta was not about to permit the establishment of a full-fledged democracy. In fact, despite the logical merit of the junta's counter-argument that the Constitution upholds the right of every citizen to run for office, regardless of whether he belongs to a political party, subsequent events confirmed that the military had been in fact plotting to weaken parliament by encouraging patrons from among tribal chieftains, clergymen, and bureaucrats to run for elections without party affiliations in order to prevent the formation of a majority from any party and allow the formation of a government without parliamentary accountability.

Thus independent nominations were the vehicle used by the military to abort the potential power of any effective legislative authority. As independents ran in large numbers, no one political bloc was able to achieve an absolute majority in parliament. Consequently, the outcome was the forging of a parliamentary majority constituting of a coalition of parties close to the military power and the independents who had traditional loyalties and were ready to work with any government chosen by the president from outside the well-known political party base.[27]

The communication and alliance between a president free of any party affiliation and deputies who had no ideological commitments was the safety valve, permitting the military to play an effective autonomous role in Mauritanian political life, seriously reducing the opportunity of the parties to play a significant role in putting Mauritania back on the track of democratization. Furthermore, many of the small parties now formed were not themselves committed to the democratic process.

The demise of the middle class as a result of the retreat of the social welfare role of the state and its continued adoption of the structural adjustment policies led to the erosion of the middle class, which had always been the carrier of the values of democracy. The prevalence of poverty, which further reduced the influence of the educated classes and the intelligentsia, was accompanied by the rise of a class of rent-seeking opportunists who benefited from the privileges they acquired through their connections with the ruling elites. Within this context, several small parties were established by intelligence organs and civil society organizations and newspapers, all in order to weaken and destroy the newly born political and media structures.

Mauritanian Political Parties, 2007–2008

The ballots provide the only objective dividing line between political parties. Using the official list thus created, each of the contending parties will be described according to the political status they were able to enjoy in the legislative, municipal, and presidential elections. The difficulties that challenge the growth and success of each party will also be analyzed.

The Republican Party for Democracy and Renewal

The Republican Party for Democracy and Renewal is another name for the Republic Democratic and Social Party, which managed the country during the rule of former president Ould Taya. This party shares the despotic past of the overthrown regime and continues to play the same role in the current regime. It acts as a base affiliated to the regime that may be manipulated in any political or social move. The fall of Ould Taya's regime, the party's denial of having taken any role during that period, and its harassment by the administration in the days that followed the fall of Ould Taya led to an unprecedented situation of political hemorrhage. The party now receives financial support from the state and several of its members have been included in the government. As a result, it has been supporting the current regime in compliance with the orders of the military.

This party won only 7 of the 95 seats in the 2006 parliament, losing most of the municipalities that it used to control. It is clear that the party has largely been deserted by the majority of politicians and local figures who preferred to run for elections independently. The party has been characterized by submissiveness to and dependency on the ruler, whoever that person may be. This condition of submissiveness finds its roots in the prevailing totalitarian culture built on the notion of obedience to the winner and the need to follow the ruler, even if he is a tyrant, so long as he does not openly declare apostasy. This engrained notion in Islamic societies, particularly Sunni societies, has taken shape over centuries and is supported by the rural and newly urbanized classes. In the Mauritanian case, the tribe as a social and political system is the ideal framework for such a regressive idea to flourish. It reflects the failure of the state-nation in the Arab societies where the tribe is transformed into a tool for monitoring people in the interests of the state.

The Alliance for Democracy and Unity

The Alliance for Democracy and Unity is a branch of the Republican Party. It was established by Ahmed Ould Sidi Baba, chief of the tribe of Al Samaseed, which has financial influence although small numerically. It is no coincidence that this is the same tribe to which former president Muawya Ould Taya belongs. The party played a major role in enhancing formal pluralism and has participated in several coalition governments during the rule of the previous president. It has also attracted individuals who were dissatisfied with the Republican Party.

The failure of the party leader to enter parliament did not stop it from winning three seats in parliament due to the system of proportional representation. The leader of the party tried hard to integrate his party into a new party, which supporters of the current president seek to establish.

The Union for Democracy and Progress

The Union for Democracy and Progress was established by the Hamdy Weld Meknas as a moderate alternative and soon began to revolve around the Republican Party. In the transitional stage, it won three seats in parliament with the support of the current president. This is the only party in the country that is led by a woman, Naha Bent Meknas, daughter of the former leader of the party.

The Popular Front Party

The Popular Front Party won one seat in parliament in 2006 and is led by former prisoner of conscience Al Shabieh Al Sheikh Maael Enein. Like the Unionist Party and the Union for Democracy and Unity, the Popular Front has not been able to break the circle of personal influence of the party leader and is thus considered to be more a club than a party in the sociological sense of the term.

The Alliance of Democratic Forces

The Alliance of Democratic Forces is the main inheritor of the political legacy of Mokhtar Ould Daddah and the political inheritor of the Alliance of Democratic Forces, which was banned by Ould Taya following its demand to investigate the burying of nuclear waste in Mauritanian territories. During the political truce in the first few months of the military rule, this party was able to build itself and benefit from the collapse of its historic adversary, the Republican Party. Thereafter, it occupied the top position in the National Assembly by maintaining 17 members in the 2006 parliament out of a total of 95. This is the highest representation obtained by any Mauritanian political party during the legislative elections. It also controlled most of the municipalities such as the central municipality of Nouakchott and the municipality of Kiffa, the second-largest city in Mauritania, and the municipalities of Rosso and Boutelmeit.[28]

Ahmed Ould Daddah, the party leader, was nominated for the presidential elections for the third time and reached the second round of elections[29] against the candidate of the military and independents, Sidi Ould Cheikh Abdallahi, the eventual winner who profited from the lack of participation on the part of all opposition parties. The Popular Progressive Party left the elections race following the second round of elections given the solidarity of the forces of change in the Mauritanian society who endeavored to send the military back to the barracks.

This surprising position, mainly attributed to the lack of chemistry between the two competing leaders in the opposition camp, allowed the victory of the current president who is supported by the conservative forces and those affiliated to the military's transitional authority.

The Popular Progressive Alliance

The Popular Progressive Alliance is an alliance between the Free Organization, mentioned above, and some affiliates to the Nasserite Party, which until recently was one of the most leftist parties. It has a long political legacy of struggle against slavery and in defense of the Arab identity in the country. The party was able to create two successive surprises during the election agenda of 2006–2007.

The first was its control over a number of important municipalities, giving it six parliamentary seats, and the second was its decisive control over the second round of elections by concluding a sudden deal with the conservative candidate Sidi Ould Cheikh Abdallahi.[30] According to this deal, Masoud Ould Boulkheir, who had obtained 9% in the first round of elections, was elected speaker of the National Assembly and his party was allowed to take part in the current government with four other ministers.[31] This is the largest share any party has had in the present government.

The fact that the Alliance abandoned the mechanism of spontaneous solidarity between opposition parties also led to confusion among the camp supporting the current president, which resulted in the formation of a semitechnocratic government in which the majority of organizations supported that camp in the first term of the presidential elections.[32]

The Union of Progressive Forces

The Union of Progressive Forces was born when members of the National Democratic Movement spun off from the Union of Democratic Forces Party, one of the oldest Mauritanian organizations and inheritor of the Renaissance Party and the Proletariat Party with communist tendencies. Leaders of this party are particularly attractive to the non-Arab population of the Mauritanian south because of their daring stance toward the Wadi Al Nahr crisis during the Mauritania–Senegal border war of 1989–1991.

The party took second rank in the parliamentary elections by winning 9 of the 95 National Assembly seats.[33] Sound election engineering helped achieve this result, as the party paid special attention to the constituencies that could lend it support in the second round of elections and in implementing the mechanisms of solidarity between opposition parties agreed upon by the coalition of Forces of Change. Despite the low score (5%) obtained by Mohamed Ould Mawloud in the presidential elections, the party continued to attract and receive the respect of the younger generations because of the absence of contradictions in their political stances. However, some factors contributed to weakening the party. These included the adoption of an antagonistic policy toward clergymen and tribal chieftains without considering the impact this could have on rural areas and its alliance with trade unions.

The Hatem Party

The Hatem Party was born during the final days of political turmoil under Ould Taya. It is a new party established by former army officers who had been imprisoned following the numerous coup attempts. Some of them experienced exile in desert areas north of Mali and Burkina Faso. The party leader Saleh Ould Henena enjoys remarkable popularity in the poorer neighborhoods of the city of Nouakchott and other internal cities. The party benefited from close alliance with locally well-known Islamists and middle-ground reformists, as well as from the agreement of solidarity between the political forces constituting the coalition of Forces of Change. Its close alliance with the Islamists caused some to consider the party a political facade of the Mauritanian Islamist trend, a not implausible claim given that Mauritanian Islamists are forbidden to participate in politics by a law promulgated under the regime of Ould Taya.

The party's semiopen confrontation with the military council kept it out of favor with the state. It was officially recognized quite late and even then the state used it as bait to prevent influential forces in various places from joining it. Its leaders enjoy revolutionary legitimacy and a great deal of charisma, sufficient to allow it, despite limited resources, to influence the outcome in several municipalities in Nouakchott and elsewhere and to win three seats in parliament. This is considered a remarkable achievement for a small poor party that is regularly besieged politically. Lieutenant General Saleh Weld Hanana[34] won 7% of the vote in the presidential elections, enhancing his position as a significant figure for young people.

The Middle Ground Reformers

The Middle Ground Reformers, not a party but a political movement with some of the characteristics of a political party and so deserving a brief mention here, is a group of Islamists in Mauritania who have adopted a spirit of moderation in defending themselves against the charges of extremism that the regime of Ould Taya tried to attach to them. In reality, Islamists in Mauritania are closer to the Egyptian Muslim Brothers, despite their declared links with Turkish semisecular Islamists. They accept the republican legacy in its entirety as well as concepts related to secular authorities and the distinction between beliefs and management on one hand and the state on the other. They adhere to the concept of Islam as a state and a religion. They have daring positions and views about antislavery and the rights of women and, despite state harassment, the organization has been able to win four parliamentary seats and has had full control over several municipalities in the country.[35]

The Conscience and Resistance Organization

The Conscience and Resistance Organization played a significant role in exposing oppression in several well-known cases during the regime of Ould Taya. Its activities helped create political and media tension and facilitated the coordination between the military and the antiregime political parties. During the transitional stage, it played a prominent role in electing the current president. It created common negotiating grounds as a mediator between the Popular Progressive Alliance Party and the independent candidate Sidi Ould Cheikh Abdallahi. It is an organization that operates amid intellectuals and does not preclude the affiliation of its members to political parties so long as they are of leftist orientation. The limited number of members in this organization does not allow it to perform public activities, at least in the foreseeable future, despite its remarkable media engagements and the fact that it makes effective use of modern information technology, particularly the Internet.

The FLAM Movement

The African Liberation Forces of Mauritania (FLAM) Movement has demanded the promotion of the Mauritanian non-Arab black interests, particularly the Polaris, and the return of southern blacks to the land from which they fled or were expelled in the 1989 conflict with Senegal (see pp. 66–67). It has also called for teaching and promoting non-Arab languages in schools. As a semiseparatist movement, it is seen by many as out of step with the general decline of influence of internal nationalist movements and the growing readiness of Mauritanians to reach satisfactory and moderate solutions to racial issues. The end of the conflict with Senegal, the internal schisms within the movement, and the legal ban imposed by the state prevented it from playing its expected role as a principal agent representing the interests of the Polari group in the recent elections. However, some analysts attribute the prominence of candidate Sar Ibrahima in the latest presidential elections to the support he received from the historical leaders of this movement.[36] In general, it is difficult to predict the future of the movement and much depends on how the rights legacy will be resolved. This includes the rights of the victims of oppression against the Polari group, particularly during the rule of Ould Taya.

CHALLENGES FACING MAURITANIAN POLITICAL PARTIES AS AGENCIES OF DEMOCRATIZATION

Overall, the main challenge facing Mauritanian political parties is how to create genuine representational links between the citizens and the state and use the power of their elected representatives to solve the overriding problems of the country: ethnic and cultural prejudices, the psychological and social distortions created by the successive totalitarian governments, the impact of conflicts with other states, particularly Senegal and Morocco, and the need to achieve a more equitable and efficient allocation of financial and human resources. As has already been evident in this chapter, these problems are closely interrelated.

Ethnic and cultural conflicts have involved serious violations of human rights, the cultural and linguistic hegemony of those in power, and the difficulty of figuring out how the different ethnic and cultural actors in the Mauritanian society can share the internal political space available to them. Language and ethnicity have divided Mauritanians in complicated ways. Although as already noted, most Mauritanians are ethnically Arab, this group is itself divided into white and black (Harateen). Fulanis (11%), Suninkis (3%), and Wolof (1.1%) comprise the remainder of the population. Thus there are four main national languages in Mauritania in addition to French, which occupies a prominent position in the public sector.[37] Language conflicts have contributed to the rise of ethnic conflicts. The demand of the Arabs to teach Arabic and recognize it as the administrative language has always provoked non-Arabs and pushed them to teach their children their own local languages. This conflict reached its peak in 1980 when the Institute for National Languages was established and sought to promote writing in the Polari, Walfi, and Sonenki languages. It was closed in 1989.[38]

Meanwhile, French is and long has been the language used in the government departments and the official state transactions and is often the preferred language of black non-Arab groups for intergroup communication. Although the overwhelming majority of the nation's population speaks Hassania (the local name given to the Arabic language in Mauritania), the law stipulating the teaching of Arabic in schools has resulted in bloody confrontations in mixed schools, neighborhoods, and cities.

During the French occupation the non-Arab black minority largely settled in the fertile land near the Senegalese border, where its members benefited from the building of schools and housing of teachers more than did white nomadic Arabs following the Bedouin lifestyle in that area. When border conflicts broke out between Wolof-dominated Senegal and Mauritania in 1989, international tensions were compounded by the internal tensions between Arabs and non-Arabs. Thousands of black Mauritanians in the border area either fled into Senegal or were expelled into that nation and Mali; Senegal reciprocated by expelling Arab citizens and destroying their shops and homes. As the two nations moved toward peace, land was redistributed under the terms of agreements reached by the two national governments, agreements that were not accepted by all of the victims. Eventually joint ministerial committees were formed under French patronage and the remaining files of complaints have now been reduced to a few thousand cases of migrants who demand an organized return to their land under international auspices. Political organizations have reached a semiunanimous agreement to reopen the issue and hand over the land.

But the issue involves more than land. The legacy of the ethnic cleansing undertaken by the Mauritanian army under the leadership of Ould Taya during 1990–1991 left yet deeper scars. To this day no one knows how many were killed, or how, or where they were buried. Not surprisingly, the army does not wish to open an investigation of this subject. Different strategies have been proposed. Some call for a literal application of the law (this is the demand of the opposition parties, the alliance of the democratic forces, and the union of forces of progress), the building of a political reconciliation based on court judgments, and an official apology in the name of the state with indemnity to the victims (this is the position of the Republican Party and the Al Tagamu' Party). Experiences of other newly democratic states favor a position that neither punishes culprits nor pardons them. In any case, despite the passage of more than a decade, these events are considered the main obstacle that hinders a final reconciliation among ethnic and language groups in Mauritania.

Within the same context, numerous pressure groups demand laws to ban slavery and punish it. The Harateen of slave origins favor the enactment of positive discrimination laws that expand the quota for slaves in government positions and take into account the large educational and economic gap between this class and others.

Material Difficulties Faced by the Parties and the Problem of Fragmentation

In addition to the complex issues dividing the Mauritanian electorate, Mauritanian political parties face other problems all their own, and here we look at two: fragmentation and funding.

The large geographic size of the country and the distribution of population as well as the lack of licenses to local free radio stations add to the responsibility of parties to educate the people. Given the rise in awareness about the danger of current party fragmentation, it is legitimate to imagine that the need to unite a number of small and middle-sized parties will result in the creation of new larger parties, once they are again able to function normally. This new awareness was apparent during and after the most recent elections. The Democratic Renewal, the Popular Front, and the Tamam Party agreed to unify their ranks into one national party. Previous candidates for the presidency, Dahan Ould Ahmed Mahmoud, Mohamed Ould Sheikhna, and Osman Ben El Sheikh al Maaly, who (together) had obtained more than 5.1% of the votes, have decided to liaise with the Alternative, Democratic Renewal, and Democratic Middle Grounds parties to create a new structure.[39] The Grouping for Democracy and Unity, the Unity for Democracy and Progress, the Republican for Democracy, and the Renewal parties were also seeking to form a new political entity prior to the 2008 coup.

It is clear that the desire to combine party responsibilities includes a financial dimension. The absence of financial resources that forced parties' reliance on the personal support of the party leader or some of the politbureau members was the reason why the majority of Mauritanian parties disappeared from the political scene in the transitional stage. Party fragmentation explains the decline and dispersion of parties' financial resources. It is also responsible for the rise of the unclassified sector's politicians, such as tribal chieftains and social mediators, who are not capable of creating organizational links that ensure maximum use of political freedom to create a genuine legislative life based on differences in opinion and not on ethnic or tribal differences. These are the natural frameworks within which the traditional structures that are not capable of assimilation in the same nation and the different political schools can interact. The state forbade parties and political organizations from receiving foreign funds but provided guarantees of state funding, applying specific criteria of representation in parliament and the municipal councils. During the parliamentary election campaign the state also agreed to grant financial assistance to the parties' media departments, a decision especially helpful to opposition parties. However, the largest amount of public funds granted to parties reached $400,000 annually, and the executive authority refused to enact laws organizing audiovisual media in ways to enhance democratic gains.[40] Parties were also subject to regular auditing by the public accounts agency as they also continued to depend on the individual donations of supporters.

CONCLUDING REMARKS

The above review shows that despite all the difficulties faced by political parties in Mauritania, they have nevertheless had an enlightening and effective role in significant political developments that took place in the nation in the years prior to the most recent coup. It appeared that the military, after decades in which they monopolized power, had finally been persuaded of the inevitability of introducing major reforms into political life. This was particularly apparent in the role of the parties in parliament, where several significant advances have been seen:

1. The opposition political parties were able to push for a law criminalizing slavery practices and the adoption of a financial policy that combats this abominable practice.
2. The parties were able to open the human rights file in a reconciliatory manner that satisfied most of the victims of repression, after the president publicly apologized to the victims of human rights in the name of the state. At the same time, parliamentary debates convinced the ruling majority of the need to open the door for the return of Mauritanians who migrated in 1980 in the aftermath of the conflict between Mauritania and Senegal.
3. There were rising voices in the National Assembly and the Senate demanding the severing of relations with Israel and a final, just, and comprehensive solution for the Arab Israeli conflict. The trend within the National Assembly seemed to be shifting toward giving the government a chance to examine this matter further in order to ensure that no harm was inflicted on Mauritanian interests.

The vociferous parliamentary discussions around these and other issues gave the impression of the beginnings of a real legislative life, capable of producing strong organizational links between parties and citizens. The government's apparent recognition and acceptance of election results and the participation of opposition parties in the government created a common ground of understanding between political actors on major issues of concern. This common understanding and the spirit of tolerance and institutionalized bridges between political parties, on the one hand, and between them and the ruling elected institutions, on the other, combined to make observers optimistic about political stability in the country in the foreseeable future.

Other nonpolitical factors also gave grounds for optimism. Mauritania had finally broken out of the circle of indebtedness to the West, having benefited from the decision of the eight industrial countries to forgive repayment of the loans given to Mauritania. This decision allowed the treasury to save one-third of the national budget, which had previously gone to service those loans.

In addition, the prices of raw materials reached a remarkable 270% in 2006. In the next four years the government will launch the industry of phosphoric acids and phosphorous products in addition to doubling the production of oil, which started in 2006.

All in all, the improvement of the economic situation, the positive political climate, and the vitality of the elected institutions suggest the strong possibility that, if consolidated, they would inevitably strengthen political parties and nurture the burgeoning Mauritanian democratic institutions.

EPILOGUE

On August 6, 2008, Mauritania suffered another military coup, once again setting back its progress toward the consolidation of a democratic state. The coup, which removed President Abdallahi who had been president for just over a year, was carried out by a group of high-ranking military officers, many of whom had supported Abdallahi's initial bid for the presidency. In its wake, a military council, led by General Abdel Aziz, a key participant despite being a strong supporter of Abdallahi in the past, was established to assume the responsibilities of the presidency until elections could be held. Despite harsh criticism and demands from the international community that President Abdallahi be released and reinstated, the coup received strong support from the parliament, with 67 of 95 deputies and 39 of 56 senators declaring their support. The text released by the deputies supporting the coup declared that "The changes of August 6 are the logical and indisputable result of President Sidi Ould Cheikh Abdallahi's behaviour to stall the republic's institutions."[41] A national consultative meeting was held at the end of December shortly after the release of Abdallahi and a presidential election was proposed for May 30, 2009. Although this meeting was attended by the leaders of many political parties, lawmakers, heads of civil society, religious leaders, and diplomats from 70 countries, it was boycotted by Abdallahi and the National Front for the Defense of Democracy, a coalition of parties, unions, and humanitarian groups opposed to the coup.[42]

CHAPTER 4

The Role of Political Parties in Establishing Moroccan Democracy

Mokhtar Benabdallaoui

INTRODUCTION

After independence was achieved in 1956, the installation of a democratic regime in Morocco was a priority for only one small party; the Shura and Independence Party. Its leader, Belhacen El Ouzani, who studied in Switzerland, preached a parliamentary system based on the legitimacy of the popular vote and equipped with a strict separation of powers. This vision irritated the two large political actors on the scene: the monarchy, jealous of preserving its historical prerogatives, and the Independence Party, which could not resist the temptation of the single-party system. This small party embarrassed everyone and no one spoke out as its militants were physically neutralized by the Independence (Istiqlal) Party's militia in massacres but are, nonetheless, a well-known part of Morocco's modern history.

The left wing of the Independence Party rose up against the authority of the traditional elite of the party and founded its own party, but this new party was much more interested in establishing a socialist regime than in serving the cause of democracy.

The question of democracy is new in Morocco and was first raised as a main political challenge only during the last decade of the past century when the monarchy became convinced it could not reign forever without sharing power, and the traditional parties concluded the popular vote was the only means for them to participate in the ruling of the country.

EARLY DEVELOPMENT OF THE PRESENT MOROCCAN POLITICAL SYSTEM

Moroccan political development in the three decades after independence falls into three stages, each stage defined by the type of constitution, the objectives of political parties toward the state and the institution of the monarchy, and the balance of power and influence between the various political alliances and coalitions. The first stage began with the independence of Morocco, continued through two failed military coups (1971 and 1972), and extended until the declaration of emergency rule in the mid-1970s. Politically, this period can be described as the era of conflict between the monarchy and the various political parties that had emanated from the national independence movement. Although both belligerents pretended they were defending the cause of democracy, the struggle for power was the main challenge.

The second stage started after the two military coups and was marked by an agreement to return to the rule of institutions and recognition of the need for national unity. The king now understood he could no longer trust his army more than political parties. Finally, the third stage was one of preparation for a smooth transfer of power within the monarchy. Hassan II knew the transfer of power was very delicate and that he could not lean solely on the administration. To preserve the monarchy, he needed real political parties involved to balance other forces during this critical phase.

The Stage of Political Conflict: 1958–1975

The political system Morocco inherited on the eve of independence was doomed to be plagued by a conflict between two sources of legitimacy: the religious and historical legitimacy of the monarchy that wanted to maintain its vast powers, and the legal and political legitimacy of political parties who demanded a constitutional system with balanced governing institutions. The conflict took place on three levels. On the constitutional level, the vibrant political forces called for the creation of a constituent assembly, an institution that the monarchy feared would infringe upon its historically pervasive role in Moroccan political life.[1] Political parties, emerging from the national independence movement, struggled with the monarchy, on the one hand, and among themselves, on the other.[2] Internally, they struggled to determine who would be the main political actors in the postindependence stage. The conflict within the Independence Party and subsequent division that followed under El Mahdi Benbarka[3] and Abdullah Ibrahim[4] gave the palace the opportunity to pit the parties of the national movement against one another. The monarchy did this by forming the 1958 government, which included both the leftist wing of the party under

Abdullah Ibrahim as well as Allal Al Fassi, the traditional leader of the Independence Party. The conflict was not confined to the Independence Party, but also continued with the Shura and Independence Party, the second pole of the national movement, whose leaders were subject to wide-scale liquidation. Despite its elitist nature, the Shura and Independence Party was the only party with a clear political vision for the postindependence era. However, it could not easily penetrate the political scene and found itself challenged by the Independence Party, a party seeking to monopolize the political scene and the palace, which was upset with the Shura and Independence Party's vision of a parliamentary monarchic institution.

Because the monarchical institution considered that Moroccan people had risen against the protectorate and mobilized for freedom and independence owing to the deportation of King Mohammed V, it concluded that independence had came as a result of the efforts of several forces, and thus did not give the parties the right to govern.[5] Instead, the monarchy argued that the situation had to be restored to the preprotectorate status quo, a situation in which the king exercised power directly and effectively. In contrast, the demands of the national parties ranged from calls to participate effectively in public affairs next to the king as exemplified by the position of the Independence Party, to the desire to form a constituent council, as was the position of the Shura and Independence Party and the National Union of Popular Forces (NUPF).[6]

The monarchy was successful in managing the postindependence turmoil, exploiting both inter- and intraparty conflicts. The state followed a well-defined agenda with clear priorities. It dismantled the liberation army, which had organic links with some leaders of the Independence Party and dissolved it into the official army and other state organs. It attracted a number of prominent figures in the resistance movement and granted them some concessions. It also benefited from the experienced security and administrative organs inherited from the colonial era and from the conflict over leadership between the syndicate and the political wings of the party. Finally, the monarchy's resources were further augmented by a number of international alliances with the powers that had wanted Morocco to distance itself from the calls of socialism and Nasserism.

The best way of achieving independence was hotly debated among the various political parties of the time. The Independence Party insisted that the king should return first from his exile in Madagascar to Morocco before any negotiations began regarding independence. The Shura and Independence Party, on the other hand, believed that the demands of the Moroccan people should focus on independence first, and that securing independence would automatically allow the return of the exiled king. As for the liberation army, a number of commanders believed that the independence of Morocco would not be realized until its desert extension was freed from Spanish control and the remainder of the Arab Maghreb was liberated. The Shura and Independence Party, the resistance command, and the liberation army had lost trust in one another in the aftermath of Morocco's independence. Some of the political leaders considered the acts of violence committed by the resistance forces acts of sabotage. They sought to convince the French administration to speed up the process of declaring independence because they feared that they could lose control over resistance operations. On the other hand, part of the liberation army commanders believed that a treaty would only grant Morocco a superficial and formal independence.

The series of conflicts outlined above led to the depletion and fragmentation of the national movement and to a shift in its demands from the call to form a constituent assembly or participate in rule with the king to acceptance of the idea of working under the auspices and supervision of the monarchy. The ousting of the government of Abdullah Ibrahim and the declaration of the first constitution in 1962 were important turning points that consolidated the political defeat of those seeking political power in their own right. The groups that had founded the Independence Party adopted contradictory positions toward the constitution, a move that terminated the conflict over legitimacy in favor of the monarchy. In the aftermath, El Mahdi Benbarka drafted an important political document titled "The Revolutionary Option," which included self-criticism of the party, reviewing all the errors committed by the Moroccan opposition, which he called the three fatal mistakes.[7]

One can consider the emergency that was declared in the aftermath of the bloody vents in Casablanca in March 1965 as an extension of the political crisis that erupted as a result of the dissolution of Abdullah Ibrahim's government and the cruel verdicts issued against the party leaders who were accused of contriving a conspiracy against the crown prince. The palace, now relatively strong as a result of the parties' weakness, sought to liquidate the contentious wing within the NUPF. Some movement leaders also used the international conflict and Moroccan-Algerian historical sensitivities that stemmed from the Morocco-Algerian border conflict of 1962 to stage a number of armed operations against some of the remote military bases, giving the Moroccan political regime the pretext to use all available means to put an end to the struggle.

New Opportunities for Political Participation: 1975–1992

The year 1975 represents the second turning point for the early development of the contemporary Moroccan regime. After two failed coup attempts in 1971 and 1972 and the establishment of emergency rule, it was clear to the king that the security approach alone was insufficient to secure the stability of the regime. He recognized the need for sufficient political liberalization to placate some disaffected members of Moroccan society, a need that had become particularly apparent after the National Bloc refused to participate in the referendum on the constitution in 1970, which they saw as a decline of the values stipulated in the constitution of 1962.[8]

King Hassan thus began a series of long negotiations with party leaders in order to convince them to return to work within the official political institutions through a package of concessions that included a new constitution and new municipal elections. The Third Extraordinary Congress of the NUPF in 1975 was one of the strong indicators of the progress achieved in the negotiations. The party raised the slogan "Strategy of Democratic Struggle" as an alternative to the "Movement of Popular Liberation," strongly signifying that the party was pursuing a new trend under a new name: the Socialist Union for Popular Forces (SUPF). This change came not only as a result of their call for the unity of Moroccan territories, which required the unity of the internal front, but also as a result of the information leaked about the prior knowledge and coordination between leaders of the NUPF and the persons responsible for the second coup attempt of 1972.

The monarchy considered itself the patron of the Moroccan nation and, accordingly, rejected the notion that the parties could act as mediators between the palace and the people. The king's relation with his people, according to Hassan II's interpretation, is a direct relation in which the pledge of allegiance (*al bai'a*) takes precedence over all other contracts. According to this system, the pledge of allegiance acquires an individual character (an individual commitment by each person) that is both absolute and eternal. The fact that power was conceived by the monarchy and by a majority of the Moroccan people as the divine prerogative of the monarch made it impossible to spread the idea of democracy during this period. Instead, issuing a call to liberate the Sahara and engage in efforts toward the unity of Moroccan soil was regarded by the opposition as an honorable way to reintegrate the political system and move toward a national reconciliation. This took place within the context of a purely monarchic initiative that made King Hassan II the unifier of contemporary Morocco.

However, in 1975 a critical benchmark in Moroccan political life was reached: For the first time the leadership of the NUPF was confined to leaders residing inside Morocco, and the message of Mohamed Al Basry, a traditionally influential national leader who was exiled in France, was not read out at the party's extraordinary congress.[9] Moreover, the suspicious assassination of the trade union leader Omar Benjelloun led to weakening the rigid wing of the trade unions inside

Morocco, thereby opening the door for reconciliation between the monarchy and the internal leaders of the Socialist Union Party.

In the end this extraordinary party congress had three main outcomes: (1) the final divorce between the NUPF and the dissident wing, the SUPF, (2) the shift in power within the SUPF from the exiled leaders to those that resided on Moroccan soil, and (3) the readiness of the party to engage in a new political game based on recognizing the legitimacy of the monarchy and working within the framework of the Moroccan constitution.[10]

Unfortunately, these changes simply paved the way to new elections marked by flagrant violations by the regime and complete loss of political credibility. The extensive fraud in the outcomes of the 1977 elections was proof that the Moroccan political regime did not seek to establish partnership or reconciliation with the Moroccan parties. Rather, it wanted to transform them into political tools to enhance its own legitimacy, which had been severely compromised after two failed military coups. The parties were drained of all their energy as a result of the continued repression. They also lost strength and credibility because of internal cleavages and divisions and had no alternative but to take one of two paths: stay on the margin of political life in Morocco and wait for a slow death or engage in the political process despite all its shortcomings. That they chose the latter path was evident in the collusion between the regime and the parties in the preparation for transfer of power to Mohamed VI, Hassan II's son, on July 23, 1999, after Hassan had fallen terminally ill at the end of the 1990s. The succession preparations took two approaches: an external approach with Morocco's strategic partners and an internal approach that sought to evade any social turmoil or security problems. These measures could not have been adopted without cooperation with the opposition and their involvement in shouldering the responsibility of rule so they would become part of the solution and not part of the problem.

The Reinstatement of Constitutional Institutions: 1975–1992

Nevertheless, during the period now in question, there were some improvements as the king, aware that the security organs were incapable alone of protecting the regime, opened a new dialogue with the opposition and produced a measure of reconciliation during the 1977 elections. The monarchy had, however, by no means decided to give up any of its traditional authority. Instead, it sought to present a new arrangement for the public sphere that would attract parties to participate in political institutions while also seeking to discredit their political programs and undermine their social appeal.

Among the manifestations of this weakening process was the suppression of political activity, putting on trial politicians whose positions were not sufficiently flexible. In addition, the regime set up its own "administrative parties," used elections purely as ceremonial cover for cooptation of national level party elites, and contained party elites at the local level by selective prosecution of illegal or irregular activities by local party leaders and party representatives in local government posts.

Administrative Parties

The aim behind the formation of the National Coalition of Liberals, which was initiated by the late king's brother-in-law Ahmed Osman, was to bring together a new set of businesspeople who had benefited from state concessions and use them to weaken and disarrange the opposition. The party was primarily composed of a number of figures who were independent of parliament, had the support of the regime, and considered themselves spokespeople of the silent majority. Through the resources placed at its disposal by the state and its large number of deputies in parliament, the party was able to play the role designated to it for several years before it divided as a result of internal conflict between urban businesspeople and rural landowners over positions of leadership. In the aftermath of the 1984 elections, a new administrative party came to life, the Constitutional Union, which was formed by Almoati Bouebeid, one of the men who broke off from the NUPF, consolidated previous party practices, and operated the Constitutional Union as a state-sponsored party in the government and parliament.

The Ceremonial Character of Elections

During this period one of the main goals of parliament was to contain efficacious figures by giving them many privileges and thereby benefit from their influence and popularity in order to manipulate various social strata and achieve the goals of the regime. The election process was a sheer formality because the monarchy was not able to accept any "improbable" results. The state was keen on orchestrating activities within parliament by securing the loyalty of political leaders, party and syndicate members, syndicate leaders, and urban and traditional landowners. Through these elites and due to the immunity and concessions provided to them by parliament, the state was able to control the rules of the political game. Parliament was becoming similar to a "house of property owners," despite the presence of election mechanisms. When Abdelrahim Bouebeid tried, for example to break this tradition in the 1977 elections, and run for elections in Agadir instead of Salla, the constituency to which he had been assigned, he was punished by his defeat in elections.[11]

Containing Party Elites at the Local Level

Local leadership in parties and government was another level at which party elites could be contained and transformed into mere extensions of the state. The majority of the historical parties consisted of teachers and low level employees who lacked moral support from their party and faced huge responsibilities in managing large constituencies without any prior legal or financial training. As a result of incompetence, a large number of financial and legal violations were committed by these low-level party elites, leading former Minister of Interior Driss Basri to threaten to put them on trial.

Similarly, the local rural and municipal councils formed the focal points of endless incidents of political corruption, starting from the election campaigns, use of bribery, abuse of the mass media, direct fraud if necessary, and ending with the random use of resources by candidates in local government departments. This voluntary and organized dissipation enabled the regime to place the individuals it desired on top of the municipal councils and control their political views through concessions and blackmail if necessary.

Constitutional Engineering of Alternation in Morocco: 1992–2007

By the beginning of the 1990s, Morocco's rulers were ready to take another step forward into the "reconciliatory alternation" stage. By now, three groups of parties could be identified:[12]

1. The technocratic parties, which were formed by recommendations of Moroccan authorities during elections in order to fill a political vacuum and control the legislative authority. This group included the National Coalition of Liberals, which was formed on the eve of the 1976 elections and relied on a large number of independent MPs, the Constitutional Union, whose formation coincided with the 1984 elections, as well as the Popular Movement and other subsidiary organizations.
2. The newly born Islamist parties in Morocco, which were introduced to political life in Morocco after a long period of hibernation within the Popular Constitutional Democratic Movement. The nucleus of this movement stemmed from a number of elements that were active within the Islamic Youth headed by Abdel Karim Moti' in 1969, later dissolved in the aftermath of the assassination of Omar Benjelloun. A number of leaders of the Islamic Youth organization condemned the previous acts of violence, announcing that they had broken their relations with the past and were now ready to engage in legitimate political action.
3. The National Democratic Bloc, which consisted of the Independence Party, the SUPF, the Progress and Socialism (ex-communist) Party, and the Organization of Democratic Popular Work, in addition to the NUPF, which had announced earlier its withdrawal from the coalition.

The king's announcement that he was ready to begin a new stage heralded a new political dynamic as the parties of the National Democratic Bloc submitted their first memorandum for constitutional reforms on October 9, 1991. This memorandum was successfully followed by the declaration of the 1992 constitution. The new constitution laid the necessary legal base for a more balanced system of government by committing the government to present its election program before the House of Deputies, urging the ministers to respond to the queries of deputies within 20 days, granting parliament the right to form a fact-finding committee, as well as the nondissolution of parliament in case of the declaration of a state of emergency.[13] Despite the lofty ambitions of the second reform memorandum presented by the National Bloc on April 25, 1995, the most significant amendment introduced in the constitution was the establishment of two legislative chambers.[14]

The king was frank about his views on power rotation. He distinguished between the terms alternation and exchange. The system desired by the king would be based on a broad reconciliation between a wide range of political organizations with different political ideologies and referential frameworks. He wished to involve institutions in the management of public affairs without necessarily associating this role with critical electoral dividends. Conversely, alternation was based on the king's prerogative as he appointed and dismissed the prime minister and other ministers, not on voting outcomes. In addition, political forces took turns managing affairs in accordance with the instructions of the king and not on the basis of their party programs. This clearly meant that the king did not give over any of his jurisdictions to the prime minister and that the government was always there to manage current affairs.

The 1992 constitution reorganized the political sphere in Morocco on three main levels: reinforcing the role of parliament, enhancing local governance to a constitutional institution, and regulating the parties.

Reinforcing the Role of Parliament

Partisan politics in Morocco before 1992 were to a large extent superficial, for no matter how strong any party's presence was, it did not ensure effectiveness on the executive level. Parties were confined to the marginal exercise of politics through expressions of content or dissatisfaction. Their programs could not find their way to implementation because there was no logical link between the political discourse of party programs and actual political practice, or between winning a political majority and forming government. Moreover, these parties could not exercise effective opposition because the government was accountable only to the king. Thus, the parties were nothing but superficial mechanisms used to contain internal discontent. The threat by members of the Socialist Union to withdraw from parliament in 1981 and present a petition in 1990 were two significant signs that the framework endorsed by the 1972 Constitution was incapable of responding to the needs of Moroccan society.[15] It was clear that the structure of political life had to be altered in order to retain the political regime's efficacy.[16]

The Moroccan parliament had been subject to a strict government mentality as a result of this situation. Since the king appointed and dismissed the prime minister and the cabinet, the successive governments in Morocco were primarily formed of technocratic parties or administrative figures. To a large extent, the ministers regarded the parliament with disdain and did not feel any genuine commitment to its deputies, instead preferring to answer only to the king. The guiding role of the king's speech at the parliament's inaugural session, which the constitution stipulated was beyond discussion and was binding for all government policies, further undermined the power of the legislative body. This gave the parliamentary majority a merely theatrical role in the legislative process.

The 1992 Constitution did not stipulate that the prime minister must be a member of the majority party in parliament, nor did it adopt the principle that an absolute majority was necessary and that a government should have a unified and harmonious political program. It only pointed out that it was necessary for parliament to vote on the program of the government formed by the king, which was sufficient to restore some respect to the legislative authority and strengthen the parliamentary character of the Moroccan political system. However, this transformation did not result in a direct revival of Moroccan political life because of the multiplicity and fragmentation of parties. Cabinet portfolios became an end in themselves. Despite all the positive elements introduced by the constitution, the king still had a monopoly over the main powers of government, given the guiding nature of the inaugural speech, his power to appoint and dismiss ministers, his presidency over the cabinet, which endorses laws, and his power to appoint senior civil and military officials who supervise the management of major economic and administrative utilities, particularly the *walis* (local administrators) and the governors, who enjoy great power.[17]

Establishing Local Government

Establishing an effective local government had been the long-standing dream of King Hassan II. Local government and the development of the rural areas, or the empowerment of local populations to manage their own affairs, were repeatedly emphasized in the king's speeches, both under the title of decentralization. The call for local government acquired legitimacy from the semiofficial discourse, which states that the cultural and ethnic diversity in Morocco precludes the concentration of power in the hands of any particular group due to the potential disorder that might ensue as a result. Only the monarchy enjoys this privilege of unchecked power, theoretically because of its honorable descent, which goes back to the ideology of the prophet and command of the faithful.

Although the unity of the Moroccan nation and its multiculturalism are often a part of the rhetoric of the official discourse, these statements lose credibility when one considers the powers assigned to the municipal councils as well as their financial and legal constraints. As a result, there is a clear caution against enhancing the powers of local government too much or giving independence to any specific institution. This fear is manifested in the large powers enjoyed by the appointed *walis* and governors in contrast to the elected heads of municipalities. The hesitation that preceded the announcement of self-rule of the Moroccan Sahara also showed a reluctance to decentralize power.

There has also been a greater effort to reduce corruption at the local level. Until 1996, the general trend was the selected manipulation of corruption cases. However, a new constitution adopted in 1996 stipulated the appointment of local tribunals to examine financial books of local governors, and this has expanded the circle of judicial control to encompass the space that used to be occupied by blackmail and political maneuvers. If this new development is capitalized on correctly, it could transform local governments from tools used to manipulate social dynamics and bribe political elites to vehicles for local democracy and development. The Moroccan state gave a strong signal by contesting, for the first time ever in its political history, the results of the September 8 elections, which were marred by a number of political corruption accusations. The public prosecutors opened a judicial investigation with 17 candidates for the Council of Consultants (the second chamber) who belonged to a wide range of political trends in Morocco. These individuals were accused of making phone calls and engaging in transactions to buy the votes of senior voters.

While granting local governments additional protection was among the main goals of the 1992 constitution, the impact of these reforms remains limited due to partisan fragmentation and the fact that the elected head of the municipal council remains under the direct control of the *walis*. The distribution of administrative power in effect today is a mechanism ensuring a reciprocal relationship based on mutual needs of the elected and the appointed institutions. Such a situation has forced the two sides to reach a series of reconciliations, taking into account that the elected local governor is subject to a series of constraints on his decision making, while there are no restrictions on the head of the executive body except that he must follow the instructions he receives from the central administration. The head of the local government council, on the other hand, is bound by political agendas that are often contradictory, as well as a number of partisan interests representing a mosaic of corporate and ordinary individuals whose votes determine his activities. He is equally subject to the restrictions of the budget and the different forms of tribal controls, which cannot be overruled for fear of legal retribution. Moreover, he is bound by the signature of the *wali* or the governor on the budget.

The promotion of local government as a constitutional institution is an expression of a strategic choice by the Moroccan state. However, implementing this strategy is a very complicated matter. No final decision has been reached about the state's geographic or administrative borders or the exact identity of the different territories. It remains to be seen whether the territories will be divided up on the basis of culture and descent or on a socioeconomic basis in accordance to a developmental approach built on the integration between the resources and the potentials of different areas.

The state's political practice still suffers from indecisiveness in this domain. On the eve of independence in 1957, some rural landowners adopted a populist and sectarian discourse in order to break the monopoly of the Independence Party over popular representation and to avoid the pitfalls of a single-party state. However, encouraging identity discourse cannot be in line with the modernizing aspirations of the political institutions. Moreover, opening the way for populist political discourses might be one of the obstacles hindering building a democratic nation-state, along with hindering the endorsement of citizenship as the basis of relations amongst civic actors. Populist political discourse also runs the risk of stifling the trend toward an integrative rational federal system. In other words, the logical response to Islamism, if it indeed constitutes a danger to democracy, can only be allowing for more democracy.

POLITICAL PARTY REGULATION

A series of changes have been introduced to strengthen the institutionalization—but also the control—of the political parties. Most notably, a new party law has been passed and rights of partisan participation have been extended to women and youth.

The New Party Law and Its Repercussions on Partisan Life

The new party law, issued in 2006, has been a source of great concern for a number of the traditional political parties, which used to benefit from the legal vacuum, apparent in their suspicious handling of financial matters and the delay in holding congresses, in addition to various other flagrant violations in various aspects. For these reasons, the new party law encountered obstacles and delays in parliament. This new party legislation simultaneously provides necessary space in which political parties may operate and sets up controls to push parties to open up, change their leadership, and modernize their programs. Thus, while political parties have long criticized the state's traditional and conservative character, calling on it to modernize, the situation has been reversed, as the state is now pushing parties to reform under the new law.

To fully understand the impact of the changes now being put in place, it is important to remember that the political parties stemming from the national movement in Morocco operated as a movement of protest that criticized the large powers of the palace and its applied social policies, but did not have a real social program. The slogans of the Socialist Union and the Independence Party were merely attempts at mobilizing the people by highlighting points of disagreement with the enforced policies rather than providing their own unique vision for Morocco's future. In addition, the movement was confined to a limited geographic and social stratum. As for some of the administrative parties established later by the state, they also lacked the minimum requirements of a political party, in particular regarding the autonomy of their decisions, the existence of a viable political program, and possession of the appropriate institutions.

Overall, the parties and even individuals engaged in various aspects of organizational continuity have not necessarily agreed on any common theory or ideology. Oftentimes their offices have been open only around election times and closed again until it was time for the next campaign. These democratic deficiencies have characterized the Popular Movement, the Constitutional Union, the National Democratic Party, the Democratic Socialist Party, the Democratic Social Movement, the National Coalition for Liberals, and the National Popular Movement (combined in the political bloc called the Reconciliation). All these parties are composed of traditional rural leaders, with the exception of the National Coalition for Liberals, which consists primarily of urban elites.

In contrast, the Democratic Bloc parties have had the minimum requirements of a political organization given their long history and organizational links, but despite many of their positive aspects, their leaders tend to keep their positions for life, and their political life largely corresponds to their biological life. They have offered no opportunities to shift party positions or to rotate power.[18] They have rarely organized their congresses according to the scheduled dates, and, even when they do, the congresses rarely result in the renewal of leadership.[19] This situation has led to the disintegration of these parties' grassroots base because of the scarce opportunities for promotion within the party or for delegation of responsibilities.

What the New Law Requires

The new party law seeks to correct these deficiencies. It stipulates the need to respect principles of democracy so that all members would be able to participate effectively in party activities. This, of course, means selecting party candidates democratically. It also urges parties to hold their annual congresses within a specified period of time and declares that parties that do not comply within a period of five years will no longer receive funding. This mechanism, if respected and applied, will accelerate the maturity of the Moroccan political culture and provide opportunities to renew party leadership. The law also seeks to limit the movement of deputies in parliament from one party to the other and to dissuade parliamentarians who obtained their seats with the endorsement of a specific political party from subscribing to another party until the end of the electoral term.

As for the parties' financial resources, legal guidelines regarding transparency and funding criteria, in accordance with parliamentary representation, have been given for the first time. Parties are now obligated to disclose their sources of funding and keep records of their financial transactions for 10 years. In addition to their annual auditing, their accounts became subject to the supervision of the Higher Accounts Council. These stipulations are important in that they limit the process of transferring funds allocated to political parties or placing these funds under the personal disposal of their leaders. It also limits the illegal transfer of resources of local government in the interest of the political parties that run them.

The new law also promotes the role of women and young people in the parties. Political parties in the Arab world are primarily male parties dominated by men over age 60. Morocco is no exception, and this partially explains the prevailing spirit of political abstinence among young men and women, even though they were the backbone of leftist and radical movements in the 1970s and Islamic groups at the end of the 1980s. The new political parties law stipulates the need to allocate a quota for young men and women. In addition, the elections law provided national regulations favoring women as a type of positive discrimination to ensure a minimum representation of women in parliament.

The new law also reiterates the stipulation in the constitution that under no circumstances may a party encroach upon the Islamic religion, the monarchy, or the integrity of Moroccan territories. At the same time, no party shall be formed along ethnic, religious, or territorial lines. Membership of any party shall span half the regions of the kingdom. Not only does the law provide red lines, but it also judges a party according to the intentions of members. Thus, a political party is not dismissed based on its official position, but rather it is dismissed based on its predicated actions. However, there is a great deal of flexibility in practice. For example, the Communist Party was prohibited from operation after independence on the grounds of apostasy until it changed its name and regained its respectability and legal status. Moreover, religiously and ethnically oriented groups are very active in civil society organizations and parties. Indeed, the regime has always preferred to tame some trends that it did not legally recognize by condoning the related activities of civic and political actors, conferring upon them a semilegal status and allowing the actors to promote these trends in public. This secured their activities and allowed these actors to maintain dialogue with the regime within the possible limits.

The parties' code stipulates that the 300 founding members of a political party must hail from half the regions of Morocco and specifies a minimum of 5% representation in the parliament in order to benefit from public funding. On the other hand, the electoral code stipulates that a party must obtain 6% of the votes in order to have the right to participate in the parliament. The code devotes a large space to the procedures of merging and the creation of coalitions that comprise a group of parties.

THE POLITICAL MAP AFTER THE 2007 ELECTIONS

Party Dynamics Today

Dispersion is the main feature of the political map inherited by Morocco in the aftermath of the alternation experience. Currently, there are more than 35 parties, 22 of which are in the incumbent parliament. What is new in this situation is that the fragmentation of partisan life, which was an international demand until the alternation stage, is reversing today. A number of indicators and dynamics point out that the main political parties have sought to reassemble party life by encouraging the recruitment of new leaders and platforms to the right, left, and center. On the one hand, the SUPF, being the major leftist force in the government, seeks to create the grand socialist party, which is supposed to include all leftist organizations. It sought to achieve this goal through merging with the Socialist Democratic Party. It is noteworthy that, despite this trend toward unification, some leftist parties still witness cleavages. For example, the schisms within the National Congress Unionist Party, a wing that split off from the SUPF, led to the formation of a new party under the Socialist Party led by Abdelmeguid Bouzouboua, the former secretary general of the Unionist National Congress.

A number of political parties present themselves as liberal parties, but there are no authentic right-wing parties. Several historical and political arguments presented by the Independence Party in Morocco are closer to the values of the conservative right, although this party adopts a parallel social democratic discourse. One of the unique features of the Moroccan political scene is that the Independence Party has found itself forced to ally most of the time with its long-time rival, the Socialist Union, despite differences in their referential frameworks. The alliance between the two has often been circumstantial and related to the organization of elections or the formation of governments and has often failed due to competition over parliamentary nominations and ministerial portfolios.

The new element in the postreconciliatory alternation stage is the conviction of the political decision makers in Morocco that political life must be rebuilt on new a foundation. The state's need for political parties with a genuine popular base as well as political programs with an ability to take initiatives is part and parcel of the process of modernization launched by King Mohamed VI. They also mirror the same need to create a political base capable of facing the rising Islamist tide, which opinion polls show is enjoying large popular appeal and is qualified to win more popular support.[20]

Moroccan Islamism

The release of some members of the Islamic Youth from prison reopened the debate on the assassination of trade union leader Omar Benjelloun and the extent of involvement of Abdelkarim Moti in the incident.[21] The resulting negotiations ended in the group's decision to engage in the political community through joining the Popular Democratic Constitutional Movement led by Abdelkarim El Khatib. Despite its political realism, the decision was not unanimously endorsed by Moroccan Islamists, sparking the appearance of other Islamist parties such as the Cultural Alternative and the Movement for the Nation, both of which have been highly critical of the Islamic movement and have adopted liberal platforms. The Cultural Alternative succeeded in winning political recognition as a political party with a liberal program and an Islamic referential framework.

The Islamist organization Justice and Charity was an unknown entity in the Moroccan political equation until recently, due to its unique status. This group does not have a legal base, yet is one of the largest and strongest organizations, as indicated by its significant solidarity demonstrations with the Palestinian and Iraqi peoples, as well as the marches of the first of May and protests organized in the past. This group also has almost full control over the student organizations in the university and is active in the area of social services. It has started to organize summer camps on beaches since 1998 in order to expand its popular base. The camps were a great success and have had large popular appeal because of the services and security they provide. However, the authorities finally realized the goals behind these activities and sought to put an end to them in what came to be knows as the "war of the beaches." They stopped hosting "open days," which the organization had formerly arranged in order to introduce its activities in a number of Moroccan cities.

The result of the new political climate has been the engagement of Moroccan political parties in two contrasting dynamics: a dynamic of fragmentation and contraction and a dynamic of integration and expansion. The two dynamics have run parallel to each other and coincided at some points of time. However, the fragmentation and contradiction dynamic seems to be receding in favor of the more contemporary integration model.

Dynamics of Disintegration

A number of political parties have suffered several divisions after the alternation experiment, the most important division being that of the Socialist Union, which split into three parties. The political leaders (the majority of the political bureau members) kept the historic name of the party, while the syndicate wing formed the National Unionist Congress in 2001. The majority of members of the youth organization, which had been part of the party, formed their own political framework called Loyalty to Democracy, in addition to the already existing divisions. The National Unionist Congress was once again divided within itself between a purely trade unionist wing and a political wing that relied on the support of the trade unions since the time of the Socialist Union. At the same time, the Democratic Popular Work Organization was torn between one wing that was faithful to the history of the organization, abstaining from voting on the constitution and participation in the cabinet of Al Youssoufi, and another wing that sought to find common grounds of reconciliation with the government, forming the Socialist Democratic Party in October 1996.

Within the Islamic circle, Justice and Charity also suffered a severe division within its leading command center.[22] The debate focussed on the second man in the organization, Mohamed Al Bashiry, and resulted in his resignation in 1997.[23] Despite his high position, Al Bashiry's resignation had only a limited impact because of the charisma of the spiritual leader of the community and group founder Sheikh Abdelsalam Yassin. Within the Justice and Development Party, the old guards and companions of Abdelkrim El Khatib of the Popular Democratic Constitutional Movement found themselves in a state of gradual marginalization, which resulted in their split from the party and the formation of a new party under the name of Awakening and Renaissance under Mohamed Al Khalidy in 2006.

These divisions do not at all mirror the general trend of partisan politics in Morocco. They are, in fact, symptoms of the political stagnation from the previous time period in which conflicts were played out privately within parties, rather than becoming public affairs. These divisions also resulted in complicated and entangled relations with state organs. Official support was no longer offered to some figures who thus became incapable of playing the role of traditional mediators with the state and consequently found themselves weak and isolated from their parties.

These divisions also reflect the difficult choices that the parties have had to make as they attempt to balance their political and ideological character with the negative consequences of reconciliation. The SUPF found itself compelled to form a coalition government with administrative parties and to forgo the demand to take over the sovereign portfolios, leaving them instead for palace-appointed individuals. As a result, the government lost its partisan effectiveness. The pressures exerted on the grass roots to endorse the constitution, the decision to join the cabinet, and Al Youssoufi 's refusal to disclose the list of potential ministers he wished to propose to the party's central committee—all these elements weakened the party and made it open to more divisions.

Dynamics of Integration

The Islamist movement was a pioneer in the process of unification following the 1996 merger of its political components, the Reform and Renewal Movement and the League for the Islamic Future, as well as the formation of the Reform and Unification Movement. This latter movement combined elements of Moroccan Islamism and acted as an ideological, theoretical, intellectual, and educational force. It also acted as a fallback organization in case the experiment with the party of Dr. El Khatib failed. A number of factors contributed to the success of the integration process, including the controls established by Dr. El Khatib for the party in the transitional stage during which he acted as the party's secretary general. Also, the high level of flexibility demonstrated by the leaders in their relationship with the state facilitated the integration process. This flexibility manifested itself in a number of events, particularly the 2002 party elections, when the party presented its nomination in half the election constituencies only in order to avoid the state of terror that could result from a sweeping Islamist victory. It also prevented Parliamentary Deputy Mustafa Al Ramid from heading the parliamentary team of the Justice and Development Party, despite his victory in the party elections.[24] The party refrained from any act that could be interpreted as opposition or reservation against the king's religious role as the "commander of the faithful." Observers were surprised by offensive statements made by El Khatib against Ahmed Al Rayssouni, head of the Reform and Unification organization, but those remarks were in response to some of the views that Al Rayssouni expressed about the religious tasks of the king as the commander of the faithful. Al Rayssouni was forced to resign from the organization so as to protect the group's relation with the palace.

Integration was also abetted by the Moroccan state's need for an effective and credible Islamist organization to create a balance with the Justice and Charity organization and limit its expansion and increasing influence. This situation is similar to the complex relationship between the state and the Justice and Development Party. The rising and, to some, frightening popularity of the Justice and Development Party was the price that had to be paid to confront the more critical Islamist tide represented by the Justice and Charity Party.

Political unification and integration was not only a trend of the leftists and Islamists but also extended to the administrative parties. The federation of popular movements organized a preliminary congress on March 24–25, 2006, in preparation for a larger meeting scheduled for March 2007, with the participation of the historic Popular Movement, the National Popular Movement, and the Democratic Union, in order to prepare for elections and to unify the parliamentary blocs.

THE 2007 PARLIAMENTARY ELECTIONS: DEMOCRATIC MYTH AND REALITY

As Morocco approached its next parliamentary elections, held in 2007, it was concluding more than a decade of reforms. It had witnessed the endorsement and enforcement of a number of vital charters and reform packages. Furthermore, these reforms ran concomitantly with more liberalization in the private sector, trade, and economy, signing partnership and free exchange agreements with the European Union, the United States, Turkey, and a number of Arab countries like Egypt, Tunisia, Jordan, and the United Arab Emirates.

Nevertheless, the monarchy remained in charge of all the most significant projects, modernizing legal codes and expanding infrastructural projects and social work. There were few signs that it was capable of working harmoniously with the other institutions of government, the parties, or civil society. The parties in particular remained busy with their small battles over leadership, election constituencies, or cabinet portfolios. The monarchy's control over the social and political space in all sectors and activities left little for the government, the parties, or civil society to do.

The importance of the 2007 elections and their aftermath lies in the fact that they tested the true intentions of the regime, since the king had more than once expressed his determination to lay the foundation for a state governed by laws and declared his readiness to embody and uphold the values of modernity and democracy. These were the first elections that were monitored by external observers, and they did in fact meet basic international criteria for free and fair contested elections. However, the results of the elections, and the consequences for the values that the regime intended to establish, were nonetheless disappointing.

The political culture that had taken root during the long years of autocratic rule, the authoritarian structure of political parties, and in particular the widely accepted pattern of ad hoc voting that fragmented political life, rather than organize it, have not disappeared. Morocco has not yet rid itself of its old political ways and the corruption of political life cannot now be blamed solely on the Moroccan state. Voter turnout was only 37%, and 19% of the ballots cast were invalid, indicating that in fact the largest party is that of the boycotters and rejectionists. Otherwise the most salient feature of the elections was the political fragmentation they produced, a fragmentation that tends to give political life a frivolous aspect. The leader of the winning party in an election is supposed to become prime minister, but the Independence Party (Istiqlal) won less than a sixth of the total seats, while nine other parties failed to gain a single seat.

This dismal picture is attributable in large measure to several interlocking factors, the most important of which is that the electoral process itself and parliamentary effectiveness, under the slate system and proportional representation, have lost all credibility among the general public. The weakness and fragility of political parties and the paucity of their resources led them—in exchange for payment—to nominate rich candidates who in fact never had any previous relation with the party. Party programs seem empty of any real content, and the same elites have been returned to power. In addition, the current electoral system fails to produce a truly representative parliament. In most districts the difference in votes won by the front runner far exceeds those of his runner up, yet both win seats in parliament.

As for the parliament itself, past experience has shown that as a legislative body it has little influence on major policy decisions, all of which remain largely in the hands of the king and his close advisers.

Currently, the ruling regime and conditions in Morocco do not yet encourage the formation of strong political parties and a robust and democratic political life. Perhaps a new constitution and a new electoral law will help produce a more vigorous and dynamic political arena in Morocco in the future.

SUPPLEMENTAL BIBLIOGRAPHY

Albrecht, Holger and Schlumberger, Oliver. "'Waiting for Godot': Regime Change without Democratization in the Middle East." *International Political Science Review / Revue internationale de science politique* Vol. 25, No. 4 (Oct.,

2004), pp. 371–392. Sage Publications, Ltd. Stable URL: http://www.jstor.org/stable/1601605

al Etri, Abdelrahim. *Manufacturing Elites in Morocco*. Wijhat Nadar, 2006.

al Fassi, Allal. *Movements of Independence in the Arab Maghreb*. Allal Al Fassi Foundation, 1993.

Ayash, Albert. *Union Movement in Morocco*. Dar Al Khatabi, 1988.

Beck, Colin J. "State Building as a Source of Islamic Political Organization." *Sociological Forum*, Vol. 24, No. 2 (June 2009), pp. 337–356. Springer Press. Available at: http://www.jstor.org/stable/40210404

Bendourou, Omar. "Power and Opposition in Morocco." *Journal of Democracy*, Volume 7, Number 3 (July 1996), pp. 108–122. Johns Hopkins University Press.

Bouaziz, Mostapha. *The Left in Morocco, the Genesis Process: 1965–1979*, Tinmel, 1993.

Cavatorta, Francesco. "Civil Society, Islamism and Democratisation: The Case of Morocco." *The Journal of Modern African Studies*, Vol. 44, No. 2 (June 2006), pp. 203–222. Cambridge University Press. Available at: http://www.jstor.org/stable/3876155

Daadoui, Mohamed. "Democratization in Morocco: The Political Elite and Struggles for Power in the Post-Independence State." *International Journal of Middle East Studies*, Volume 41, Number 4 (November 2009), pp. 693–695.

El Chaoui, Abdelkader. *Istiklal Party: 1944–1982*. Al Najah, 1990.

Hamzawy, Amr and Ottaway, Marina. "Fighting on Two Fronts: Secular Parties in the Arab World." Carnegie Endowment for International Peace. Middle East Program. *Carnegie Papers*, Number 85 (May 2007).

Hochman, Dafna. "Divergent Democratization: The Paths of Tunisia, Morocco, and Mauritania."*Middle East Policy* 14.4 (2007): 67–83. International Module, ProQuest.

Howe, Marvine. "Morocco's Democratic Experience." *World Policy Journal*, Vol. 17, No. 1 (Spring 2000), pp. 65–70. The MIT Press and the World Policy Institute. Available at: http://www.jstor.org/stable/40209678

Laroui, Abdallah. *Morocco and Hassan II*, Presses Inter Universitaires, 2005.

Saaf, Abdallah. *Political Transition Challenges' in Morocco*. Dafatir Siyassia, 2004.

Sarah, Fayez. *Party Political Forces in Morocco*, Riad Rayess Books, 1990.

Sater, James N. *Civil Society and Political Change in Morocco*. Abingdon, Oxon, UK and New York: Routledge, 2007.

Sweet, Catherine. "Democratization without Democracy: Political Openings and Closures in Modern Morocco."*Middle East Report*, No. 218 (Spring 2001), pp. 22–25. Middle East Research and Information Project. Available at: http://www.jstor.org/stable/1559306/

Waterbury, John. *The Commander of the Faithful: The Moroccan Political Elite—A Study of Segmented Politics*. Arabic Translation: Abou Al Azm, Abdulghani, Ahad el Sabti, and Abdel El Falk, Abdellatif. Al Ghani Foundation, 2004.

Yassine, Abdessalam. *Debate with the Virtues Democrats*. Al Oufok, 1994.

CHAPTER 5

Tunisian Political Parties, Democratization, and the Dilemma of the Political Regime

Salaheddine Jourchi

INTRODUCTION

The Tunisian political arena witnessed the rise of political parties before independence and the establishment of the nation-state. Although civil society predates political parties, the latter have contributed, upon their birth and over the course of their development, to the consolidation, modernization, and expansion of civil society in order to achieve the objectives laid out by the national movement during its call for independence. However, after independence, political pluralism was conflated into a single party with full control over public life and the fate of Tunisian society. This reductive process started in the early 1960s and reached its peak by the mid-1970s, when pluralism began to find its way back into Tunisian society through the establishment of independent and opposition political parties.

With the advent of the 1980s, attempts were made from within, as well as from without, to pressure the regime into accepting a multiparty political system. Reluctantly, President Habib Bourguiba acquiesced to a political opening, which was fettered with many restrictions. Moreover, he refused to legislate this political pluralism into law and took measures to ensure that no political parties other than the ruling party could control any popular representative institutions. However, when Zine El Abidine Ben Ali replaced Bourguiba as head of state on November 7, 1987, the new regime adopted a different approach toward political parties. It opened a dialogue with them and then gradually began to sort out their organizations. This process ended up allowing some of the opposition parties to retain a modest presence in parliament. It is, however, unanimously recognized that these parties were weak and incompetent. Tunisia currently entertains a formal kind of pluralism, ensuring in practice the perpetuation of the single-party rule, notwithstanding the legal recognition of eight opposition political parties.

This chapter will examine the objectives of Tunisian political parties and the reasons that prevented their transformation into effective tools that would integrate Tunisia into the third international democratic wave.

Tunisia is a presidential system governed by a single state party, which dominates society and the entire public space. The Tunisian government is formed primarily of members of the ruling Neo Destour Party, which is currently led by President Ben Ali and enjoys an overwhelming majority in Parliament, the Council of Counselors, and the Economic and Social Council. It also controls all the municipalities and the majority of the municipal councils.

THE ROOTS OF AUTOCRACY

The features of the unitary nation-state began to take shape within the womb of Neo Destour, which led the national independence movement that began in the 1930s.[1] This monopolization of power was consolidated after independence under President Bourguiba's autocratic rule, in which he dominated both the party and the state.

All civil society institutions were subservient to the rule of the single party and its cadres, on grounds that this would best serve the public interest, strengthen national unity, and be the most effective strategy in the struggle against backwardness. In this context, all mass organizations and associations, including trade unions (the Tunisian General Labor Federation), were appended to the ruling party.

This absolute control of public life continued until the early 1970s when a political crisis developed within the ruling party as a result of the failure of the regime's socialist experiment. A number of high-level party officials and key groups withdrew, demanding the right to form opposition parties. In the 1980s, the situation gradually changed, particularly following a confrontation with the Tunisian General Labor Federation on January 26, 1978, and the resort by some nationalist Nasserites to armed conflict (the famous Gafsa incident of January 27, 1980).[2]

In the aftermath of these critical events caused by the lack of political openness, the opposition raised its voice and made its presence gradually felt. President Bourguiba was forced to lift the ban on the Communist Party and recognize the Democratic Socialist Movement, whose founders had split away from the ruling party in the mid-1970s.

Toward the end of the Bourguiba era, the country witnessed unprecedented political and social mobility, which political parties fed and also benefited from. However, they did not succeed in controlling or using this increased mobility to achieve democratic transformation. Change had to come from within the ruling power when former Prime Minister Zine El Abidine Ben Ali succeeded in overthrowing an aging and increasingly incapable President Bourguiba on November 7, 1987, in a bloodless palace coup. Thanks to this putsch, the regime regained its vitality and succeeded in manipulating the various elements of the situation to serve its purpose. As the regime took the initiative away from the opposition parties, the latter found themselves revolving in the orbit of the ruling power, surviving on its handouts and accepting the roles that it assigned to them.

THE CURRENT POLITICAL SCENE—FROM ABSOLUTISM TO FORMAL PLURALISM

Distinguishing itself from the Bourguiba era, the new regime adopted a political discourse that was largely in harmony with the demands and slogans of the opposition parties, such as the call for the rule of law and institutions, as well as democracy and the enhancement of civil society. The regime also practiced what it preached, particularly in the first two years of its rule, by adopting a set of legislative measures that were enthusiastically supported by all political forces.

This structural transformation in the official discourse caused the opposition parties to lose their distinctive discourse. This at first caused confusion, and those parties that enjoyed legal recognition gradually gave up their traditional functions and moved from the position of opposition to a critical, and later absolute, support of the regime.

Moreover, the positive political climate inspired the various ideological political groupings to establish party organizations and by the end of 1988, no fewer than 15 groups had declared themselves political parties, causing some concern about the possible fragmentation of the entire political system.[3] However, political developments and the process undertaken by the regime ultimately resulted in the demise of many of these groups, some because of their own lack of viability and others as a consequence of conflicts between them and the ruling elite, in which the latter eventually succeeded in banning their political activities entirely.

The regime recognized five other parties in addition to the Socialist Democratic Movement, the Tunisian Communist Party (which later became known as the Renewal Movement after it relinquished Marxism and dissolved the Communist Party), and the Popular Unity Party, all of which existed during the Bourguiba era. The process of oppositional party recognition took place over two distinct periods of time. During the first year after President Ben Ali took over, three more parties were recognized. The first was the Progressive Socialist Party (September 12, 1988), which sought to encompass different political trends (later dropping its socialist aspect and changing its name to the Progressive Democratic Party) and is currently the major opposition party, with a large expansion in its membership. The second party recognized at this point was the Liberation Social Party, a very small organization that was born weak and experienced several internal crises. The third party, the Unionist Democratic Union (November 30, 1988), led by its founder Abderrahmane Tlili, succeeded in convincing the Nasserite and Baathist nationalists and the Arab socialists to unify their ranks under one Arab party. Later Tlili—once very close to President Ben Ali—was implicated in a case of mismanagement of public funds and was given an 11-year prison sentence.

The next 16 years witnessed the stagnation of political and party life until the state recognized two additional new parties in 2006. One was the Democratic Bloc for Freedom, which was led by Mustafa Ben Gaafar and included among its members a number of well-known figures in the political and public arenas. It was an independent opposition party with democratic orientations and was still under formation. At the same time, a group of democrats requested license to form an independent Green Party in defense of the environment. However, instead of licensing it, the regime encouraged some of its own allies to establish a similar party. By so doing, the regime took the winds out of the first group's sails, causing a wide-scale critical reaction. In addition to the aforementioned licensed parties, other unlicensed ones nevertheless continued to operate without harassment by the regime. Among these were the Tunisian Communist Workers Party, an active leftist organization that adopts Leninist Marxism; the Islamic Renaissance Movement; and the Conference Party for the Republic, a lesser known "nonrecognized" party.

A WEAK CIVIL SOCIETY: A LIBERAL PRIVATE SECTOR WITHOUT LIBERALISM

Following the revival of civil society in the 1980s and up until the early 1990s, political party development suffered a relapse because of the harsh political climate that developed as a result of the all-out open confrontation between the regime and its Islamist adversaries. In this context, a number of major civil society organizations weakened and others disintegrated. This included traditionally active organizations such as trade unions, as well as normally politically active sectors of society such as university students. Weakness and disintegration characterized relations among civil society organizations and sectors during that time period. A brief look at some examples will help us gain insight into the present weaknesses of political parties and civil society in general.

Civil society and the democratic movement in Tunisia lack the experience of an enlightened business class that supports political reform. In the minds of the majority of Tunisian businesspeople, democracy is not related to the priorities of economic development and the enhancement of civil society. Businesspeople active in Tunisian politics are mostly representatives of a class that is keen on separating money from politics, although clearly the two are inseparable. Private capital seeks policies that would protect and help develop it, and it seemed to the Tunisian business sector that the shortest path to that end was to join the ranks of the ruling party and maintain close ties with the centers of power and influence.

Nor has the trade unions movement played a strong role in fostering democratic parties. The Tunisian General Federation of Work has historically been considered the main engine that drives the other vehicles of civil society. Historically, it had been the Constitutional Party's partner in leading the national movement and obtaining the country's independence. It had also been President Bourguiba's main ally in spearheading the project to establish the nation-state. For this reason, in addition to the federation's historical role and size, Bourguiba sought to undermine its autonomy and integrate it within his vision of centralized authority. When the syndicate movement regained independence in the mid-1970s, it had several run-ins with the Bourguiba regime that weakened it greatly and exposed it to divisions and random destruction. As soon as Ben Ali took over power, he released leaders of trade unions that had been imprisoned by his predecessor and to a large measure achieved reconciliation between the regime and the Tunisian General Federation of Work. In return, the federation decided to support the regime, particularly in its struggle against the (Islamic) Renaissance Party. Furthermore, the federation halted its previous persistent advocacy and activism in defense of democracy and civil society. Thus from once being the locus of aspirations of a new generation of democrats it now became a tame ally of the regime and its previous strong links with civil society associations were left to wither away. However, in recent years trade unions have exhibited renewed interest in contributing to any prospective democratic reforms.

The student movement has also disappointed those who might have hoped it to be a strong partner in the development of a democratic party system. In the beginning, the regime was convinced of the need to handle students constructively. It opened dialogue with the two main political trends that swept the student scene, the first of which included leftist political and ideological groups. This bloc adhered to the General Federation of Tunisian Students and believed it was the only legitimate structure that could encompass all students. On the other hand, the Islamists, with more affinity to the Renaissance Movement, stood as opposition and called for an organizational and political boycott and for severing relations with the federation. Later on, the Islamic trend in the university called for the establishment of a new student organization, and its supporters succeeded in amassing no fewer than 15,000 student signatures. They held a plenary conference in the university on April 18–20, 1985, which they called the General Conclusive Conference. At that time, however, the regime refused to recognize it, and subsequently, due to the conflict between the regime and the Renaissance Movement, dissolved it. Its structures were eliminated, its leadership put on trial, and its cadres and supporters placed under surveillance. They have remained so up to the present time. Only the General Federation of Tunisian Students remained and observers predicted that it would be able to fill the vacuum and convince students to support it. However, this did not happen. The ideological and partisan conflicts within the leftist movement reflected negatively on the federation's internal front. It lost credibility by entirely isolating itself from the student body.

The fragmentation and demise of the student movement impacted all independent democratic parties as they found themselves generally isolated from the young people and university students in particular. For over 15 years, young men and women separated themselves from politics and civil society organizations and as a result their political culture was severely impoverished. Political abstinence became an obstacle facing all attempts to establish new social movements or enlarge the base of existing political parties. The ruling elite did not realize the critical nature of the events until the Salafi religious movement swept through the universities and academic institutions to the isolation of all other parties, including the Renaissance Movement itself.

HUMAN RIGHTS UNDER SIEGE

The human rights movement in Tunisia was the fruit of political developments in the late 1970s and the reconciliation between a number of opposition parties that realized at this stage that democracy is closely linked to the spread of the culture of human rights and respect for all parties including ruling regimes. Within this context, the Tunisian Association for the Defense of Human Rights (TADHR) was established.

This kind of détente and concomitance between what is political and what is rights-based has continued through the 1980s and 1990s until the present time, despite the recurring crises experienced by the association. However, following the decision to eliminate the Renaissance Movement, the regime had a violent run-in with the TADHR, which condemned the regime's extensive resort to violence and the violations of the defendants' rights during the trials of the movement's leaders and cadres. Thereafter, the TADHR association had several heated battles with the regime, demanding the protection of the independence of its decisions and defying the new associations law. Skirmishes between the regime and the rights movement affected negatively almost all civil society organizations, including political parties, for whom they proved a difficult test. None of the parties took a firm position vis-à-vis human rights activists. Moreover, many of the partisan organizations were keen to see the regime rid the political scene of the Renaissance Movement, their recalcitrant adversary.

A CAREFULLY PROGRAMMED ROLE FOR THE OPPOSITION

When he endorsed the multiparty system in the early 1980s, Bourguiba was not convinced of its necessity. He believed that pluralism constituted a danger to the "strong unity," which represented one of the pillars of his political project. However, in light of the crisis faced by his regime in the early 1980s, he found no other alternative but to lift the ban on the Communist Party and to declare in his famous speech that "there is no reason to prevent the formation of political parties."

The situation changed, however, with the new political leadership. President Ben Ali did not show any opposition to the formation of parties and organizations; indeed, he was keen from the beginning to open the door to these organizations and he offered them different kinds of assistance. All he required in this new stage was that political parties' participation in public life and parliamentary institutions be gradual, describing it as a "drop by drop" process. This meant that the timing, the form, and the volume of opposition would be controlled, and that it would be subject to the political will of the president. In other words, the president felt that the parties' participation should take place without the expression of any dissident viewpoints, without any form of protest or pressure on political authorities, and without threatening the continuity of the regime or violating the existing balance of power in society.

Thus, the regime sought to control any kind of independent sociopolitical initiatives or transformations. This is what Sadok Chaabane, former minister and law professor, described in his book *Ben Ali and the Road to Pluralism in Tunisia*, where he spoke about the transitional stage that requires, according to him, preparing the pluralist alternative by building a controlled democratic opposition to prevent democracy from being "devoured" by extremists.[4] This policy was adopted by the regime but has had serious repercussions on the future of democratic reform. It is a pluralism that is not allowed to go beyond a predetermined ceiling and that is restricted to a game whose rules it has no ability to amend or change.

In this context, the regime discovered that it committed a grave mistake when it intervened to prevent the opposition from joining the House of Representatives in the first elections that took place under President Ben Ali. The 1989 politically uniform parliament allowed public contestation of the very discourse on which the new regime was based. Thus, in the beginning, the regime tried to absorb the state of dissipation that hit the political elite by adopting mitigating measures. After its victory over the Renaissance Movement and its full control over the political map, the regime decided to support the parties that were willing to operate within the controls and orientations it laid for the new political stage. Not only did the regime thus allow a form of political pluralism, but it also considered itself primarily responsible for establishing "democratic opposition."

Based on the above orientation, the regime lent financial support to the parties in order to help them issue their papers and cover their financial obligations and participation in electoral campaigns. It also helped them secure the full-time commitment of some of their leaders and members. In addition, it offered concessions to their secretary generals, such as protocol privileges and the appointment of some of them in consulting institutions such as the Economic and Social Council and the newly formed Council of Counselors. Moreover, some of the party figures were appointed heads of major public sector economic companies and institutions, which was earlier under the monopoly of the ruling party members. For the first time in Tunisia's political history, ambassadors were appointed who had different political affiliations from the ruling party. However, the most important achievement of the political regime in this respect was its decision to amend the elections law and thereby allow a number of party representatives to join parliament in the March 10, 1994, elections.

CHANGING THE RULES: A NEW ELECTIONS LAW

Although the 1994 elections changed the parliamentary scene in Tunisia by introducing a dose of pluralism, this was not the outcome of popular or democratic electoral labor, nor did it result in an actual authentication of pluralism in society.[5] Political parties had been yearning for membership in the House of Representatives in order to overcome their structural crisis and make up for their isolation from the public. Having failed to achieve these goals through democratic competition and free and fair election procedures, they decided to accept a compromise reconciliation with the government, one that allowed the regime to maintain full control over political affairs and practical control over the growth of parties and that eventually restricted their movement, curbed their growth, and undermined their political future.

The new electoral law introduced at the end of 1993 brought a calculated dose of proportional representation to the 1994 elections. Earlier the number of members in the House of Representatives was equal to the number of parliamentary seats allocated for actual constituencies (one deputy representing 60,000 persons, for a total of 144 members). Legislative elections used to take place in one round, with victory going to the candidate winning the most votes. Electors also had the right to eliminate names of candidates and replace them with names from other lists. Article 72 of the new elections law amended the electoral law of 1969 to provide one seat for every 52,500 persons, which meant a discrepancy between the total number of seats and the total number of seats allocated to constituencies. In the new electoral law, the government used a system of amended proportional representation, which combined the system of majority and proportional representation. It ensured the presence of members from the opposition regardless of the number of votes they obtained: lists that obtain the majority of votes in constituencies automatically gain seats, but now defeated lists are allocated the votes they received on the national level, and the remaining seats are distributed among them according to their size and order. Opposition lists have the privilege of amassing the votes they obtained in all constituencies, unlike the independent lists. The new amendment also eliminated the right to combine two lists, which means that an independent candidate who wishes to have a chance of joining parliament must look for a party with which to become affiliated. Some jurists considered this a violation of Article 19 of the constitution, which stipulates that "electors elect their representatives directly and on an individual basis." In this case, however, they are appointed by their parties.

Although the results of the 1999 and 2004 parliamentary elections seem to enhance the pluralist experience, they have deepened the crisis of the participating political parties (Table 5.1). The fixed quota system, which guaranteed seats to opposition parties that were defeated in local constituencies (see above), helped them secure higher numerical representation in parliament, but they came out exhausted from the test on several fronts. They suffered mainly from undermined credibility, which opened the way for the question: Can the fixed quota system, used when needed to maintain the representation of minorities and marginalized groups and grant them the opportunity to acquire experience and maturity by opening the doors of parliament, contribute to the growth and development of partisan politics, or does it perpetuate their weakness and change the nature of competition to a rivalry among themselves to obtain the required quota rather than one between them and the ruling party?

Table 5.1 Results of Legislative Elections of 1994, 1999, and 2004

	Seats (% of vote)		
Party	*1994*	*1999*	*2004*
Constitutional Democratic Party	144 (97.7)	148 (81.3)	152 (87.7)
Movement of Socialist Democrats	10 (1.1)	13 (7.1)	14 (4.6)
Renewal Movement	4 (0.4)	5 (2.7)	3 (1.0)
Unionist Democratic Union	3 (0.3)	7 (3.8)	7 (2.2)
Party of People's Unity	2 (0.3)	7 (3.8)	11 (3.6)
Social Liberal Party	NA	2 (1.1)	2 (0.6)

Note: NA, not available.
Sources: 1994 data: http://www.uam.es/otroscentros/medina/tunisia/tunpolpol.htm; 1999 data: http://195.65.105.150/parline-e/reports/arc/2321_99.htm; 2004 data: http://en.wikipedia.org/wiki/Elections_in_Tunisia

The political parties that have submitted to this formula of political participation have found themselves hostages of the state, which now controls their mobility and political future. This takes place through a number of mechanisms including controlling funds and determining the size of participation in parliament and municipalities. The imbalance that characterizes the relationship has also transformed membership in parliament to a kind of "concession" offered by the ruling party in return for "flexibility," which parties have to exercise vis-à-vis crucial issues such as basic rights and freedoms.

INTERNAL AND EXTERNAL FACTORS CONTRIBUTING TO PARTY WEAKNESS

Scholars agree that political parties in Tunisia are weak and lack competence. They are incapable of changing the balance of power in their interests and in the interest of democratic change. This weakness has forced them to accept compromises and at the same time seek to improve their performance and secure their sustained presence through their involvement in a political game imposed and entirely controlled by the regime. The weakness of political parties can be explained in large part by a number of internal and external factors that impinge directly on what they are able to accomplish.

Internal Factors

Partisan politics in Tunisia is an old phenomenon and yet parties have continued to suffer from a number of endemic internal obstacles. For the purpose of this chapter, I examine three of the major ones. First, with the exception of the Renaissance Movement before it experienced public repression, political parties suffer from meager membership and support. Their growth is slow compared to the increase in population and the large base of young people, particularly educated youth. The exact number of members is difficult to discern, but estimates vary from 100 to 700 members for each party, which amounts to their being elitist parties, unconnected to grassroots support. They tend to exist in the capital or large cities and their presence is limited in the governorships. They do not enjoy any kind of genuine or formal presence in poor neighborhoods and rural areas, nor do they have access to universities and youth groupings. They have no strong links to workers or leftists. The majority of party members hail from the middle class and work mainly in the education and business sectors. One can therefore say that partisan politics in Tunisia is totally separate from social mobility. Parties' organizational and political conditions have not qualified them to incorporate potential social movements. In addition, members tend to drop out of parties and move from one party to another, particularly in times of crises or close to the periods of parliamentary or municipal elections.

A second internal weakness of the parties is their lack of internal democracy. This has placed political parties in the trap of the contradiction between discourse and practice. The irony is that, while political parties are critical of the principle of "presidency for life," the tenure of their own leaders in office is very extended, on average for over 20 years. The self-criticism they exercise is weak, and criticism of their own leaders usually leads to fragmentation. Genuine and pluralist elections that engage different trends and programs within the same party are rarely held. In addition, the "number one" man in the party is expected to decide all matters involving the party's moral, political, and legal responsibilities. This explains why the regime seeks to foster special relations with the parties' secretary generals, which in turn enhances the status of the latter and gives them a monopoly of contact with the highest figures in the regime. Thus they tend to also monopolize information and influence within their parties.

This special status of the secretaries general has been useful to the parties in many respects, in particular in helping them achieve continuity. But on the other hand, it also gave rise to internal conflicts, which have had a detrimental impact on the organizational unity of the parties, which has often led to the loss of their best cadres. The personality of the secretary general usually takes center stage, drowning out the voices of the parties' individual members. Some even believe that the crisis of political parties emanate from the domineering character of their secretaries. While this might be partially true, it is important to point out that the matter is extremely complex and differs from one party to another. There are, indeed, instances of secretary generals sharing power, such as the decision made by the former secretary general of the Progressive Democratic Party, Néjib Chabbi, to voluntarily give up the position of secretary general, allowing Maya Jribi to be the first female leader of a political party in Tunisia.

The third internal factor weakening the parties is their lack of competence and alternative programs. Although partisan politics has existed for a long time in Tunisia, it has always been characterized by arbitrary struggles and identity politics, since most of the party cadres lack any established deep traditions and many of them do not possess any kind of solid political culture that would make them open to the experiences of other modern political parties. Political discourse within democratic circles maintains an attitude of protest and opposition. It focuses on pinpointing the mistakes of the regime, casting doubt on its legitimacy, and holding it responsible for all that is wrong in the country. On the other hand, the discourse does not have the power to generate alternative programs that would enable the parties to play a legitimate role in parliament, offering them a genuine opportunity to embarrass the regime by appearing more competent in economic and social issues. In many cases, it is hard to distinguish between the programs of political parties, which seem to use identical language and carry the same slogans and whose proclaimed policies, particularly on the economy, differ very little from the policies of the ruling party.

External Factors

Tunisian political parties, particularly those that refuse to accept the rules of the game dictated by the regime, operate under difficult circumstances. In particular, they must struggle to obtain legal recognition, they are constrained in their efforts to obtain adequate funding, they are often unfairly treated in the media, and they must constantly contend with the bias of the administration, leading to unfair and unequal treatment by the state. Here each is considered in turn.

None of the parties can function in a normal manner without first engaging in the battle to obtain legal recognition. Tunisian law grants the minister of the interior wide jurisdiction to control the present and future of political parties. For example, the Renaissance Movement, despite its weight and large number of supporters, has operated illegally since 1981. Thousands of its cadres have been charged and tried for maintaining an affiliation to an unlicensed association. Other parties and organizations, such as the Communist Tunisian Labor Party, have met similar fates.

A second external problem is posed by the laws governing political funding. Democratic parties cannot survive and grow, or function effectively, unless they succeed in resolving the problem of funding. In Tunisia, the law prevents political parties from obtaining any sort of financial support from foreign agencies. Although the regime has endorsed formulae for lending financial support to parties, these were accompanied by stipulations that allow only parties with parliamentary representation to receive this assistance. Such assistance includes financing the opposition press. Since parliamentary membership is related to accepting the electoral formulae mentioned above, parties and organizations that lack representation in parliament are deprived of any governmental financing, even if they are licensed to operate and have legal recognition. This, of course, is a mechanism that distinguishes between parties and does not grant them all the same rights and opportunities.

Next, there is a strong link between the growth of parties and their efficacy, on one hand, and the freedom of press and expression, on the other. The problem in Tunisia is that the regime dominates the media sector both directly and indirectly. Tunisian parties would not have experienced their revival in the 1970s and 1980s if it had not been for the modicum of press freedom that existed then. Independent opposition newspapers and even commercial newspapers contributed effectively in covering the activities of the parties. The press engaged in running dialogues and debates with parties, drawing public attention to their presence, their ideas, and their alternative prescriptions for the country's problems.

Since the end of the Gulf War, however, freedom of the press retreated in a manner unprecedented since the 1960s, causing parties to place freedom of the press at the top of their list of demands. It is now unanimously agreed that freedom of expression in Tunisia has deteriorated to an extent that has severely undermined journalism as a profession and inhibited all other aspects of freedom in general. Blame for this status is now directed at both the official and the independent press.

The government's assault on the freedom of the press has had a negative impact on political parties, particularly those that the regime dislikes. These parties are seldom mentioned in the audiovisual mass media—which is totally owned and tightly controlled by the state—and there is a long list of opposition figures and leaders who have not appeared on television since the early 1990s, with the exception of a few minutes during election campaigns. This has deepened the gap between parties and other citizens who know very little about the programs and demands of the opposition. Highly critical parties are seldom referred to in newspapers and magazines, which fear the government's reaction. Although some parties are licensed, they seem to function in a secretive manner. However, due to several local and international factors, some of the opposition newspapers have recently succeeded, to a limited extent, in breaking these barriers of fearful silence, becoming platforms for free expression and criticism of current conditions, and a venue for the dissemination of news on freedom-related issues. For example, *Al Mawkef* is one newspaper that has succeeded in raising the ceiling of criticism to a remarkable degree. However, due to a shortage of funds and lack of experience, opposition newspapers are still incapable of reaching out to the masses. Thus, *Al Mawkef*, despite its achievements in critical and independent expression, still does not distribute more than 5,000 copies.

Finally, the bias of the administration in favor of the ruling party is a continuing factor limiting the role of the opposition parties. Opposition parties do not compete with the ruling party but find themselves in confrontation with the entire state and its various apparatuses. The political conflict is imbalanced from the start, and any peaceful change based on public opinion and the ballot box is almost impossible to achieve by the standard recognized methods. This is particularly true during elections when the administration's bias and the organic link between the ruling party and the state become particularly manifest.

In addition to the above factors directly impinging on the parties, their weakness is also due to certain aspects of the overall culture in which they must function.

Prevailing Political Culture

Tunisian political parties also face a dominating political culture that does not give the same priority to freedoms and pluralism that it does to raising the standard of living and the increase of wages. This political culture shows a clear preference for the stability that is associated with the presence of a single statesman who has full control over the institutions of power. Pluralism, as understood since the time of President Bourguiba, does not seem to be a prerequisite for stability. Moreover, freedom of the press and media are of secondary importance within this prevailing culture, since citizens do not seek to obtain information from other than the official sources, nor are they inclined to exert any effort to learn about different points of view. This helps explain the low readership of the opposition newspapers. This does not necessarily mean rejection of the opposition or indicate strong mass support of the political regime, but rather the large degree of political apathy among citizens who have lost trust in politics and politicians. Many now believe that their opinions will have no impact on the course of events or on policy-making decisions. Moreover, it is a commonly held belief that interest in politics, particularly opposition politics, will only bring trouble, exposing citizens' interests to harm and loss and negatively affecting people's lives. Thus, politics is perceived by many as either hypocrisy or pandering to the powers that be or a dangerous activity that invites risk to the individual and his or her family. Thus, prevailing political culture constitutes a major obstacle to the growth, power, and influence of Tunisian political parties.

THE IMPOSSIBLE ALLIANCES

Given the multitude of obstacles impeding their movement toward a fair and democratic party system, Tunisian parties have made several attempts to work together, seeming to form large coalitions that will make them appear as vital forces vis-à-vis the ruling party. This, however, has represented a major challenge for the political parties in Tunisia. All attempts made to establish a permanent mechanism for coordination or alliances between two or more parties failed remarkably due to several interrelated reasons, most importantly, the weak culture of coexistence and the tendency toward personified leadership in a situation of waning political activity. The experience of the Tunisian left had indicated that it was possible to create a mass organization that would give political contestation the ideological and social dimension that it sorely needed. However, despite the continuous appeals and attempts to establish a party for the working class or a forum comprising several platforms for a democratic left, the left has remained fragmented and composed of conflicting factions. Not only has it failed to unify its ranks within one party, but its different wings have also failed to coexist.

More important, the left has not been able to manage the conflict between its different sections. Its state of incessant divisions and schisms has substantively affected in the most negative way the tasks and roles it attempted to perform or was expected to perform. This has compromised its political future and prevented the democratic movement from developing a competent dynamic cadre capable of attracting a large constituency among the masses by presenting a consistent ideological identity and a specific social orientation. This political and cultural malaise also afflicts all ideological schools: the nationalists, the liberals, and the Islamists.

This difficulty of forming alliances cannot be attributed to structural social diversity, for Tunisian society is highly homogeneous. Tribes no longer form a social force capable of attracting members, and there are no cleavages on the sectarian level. Sunni Islam prevails and Tunisians generally follow the Maliki school of Islamic jurisprudence. Thus, such primordial factors play no part in the current internal fragmentation of political parties and their inability to go beyond their narrow organizational interests to build sustainable alliances and fronts.

CURRENT POSITIONS OF THE PARTIES VIS-À-VIS THE REGIME

In addition to matters related to ideologies and stances on the question of national identity, the current position of political parties shows disagreement on two main issues: the first relates to their position toward the regime, and the second concerns their position toward Islamists.

At first, the political parties welcomed the initial liberalization by the regime of Ben Ali toward political parties and the various intellectual and political trends. However, following the developments reviewed in previous sections, positions changed, and the relationship with the regime became a subject of disagreements and schisms among opposition parties. The disagreements may be said to fall into two broad positions.

Proponents of the first position believe that the regime has a reform project and that it is genuinely committed to establishing democracy, albeit in a gradual and piecemeal fashion. They have reservations concerning the slow pace of political reform but recognize the noticeable progress already made and trust in the regime's political will to achieve the promises made by President Ben Ali when he took power in 1987. Like the ruling party, this group points to some concrete data and other indicators that support their view. To back their position, they refer to the pluralist parliament, the financial support to parties, opening the door for heads of parties to run for presidential elections, and the appointment of two ambassadors affiliated with opposition parties. But they also point to several negative aspects that characterize the regime, such as the domination of the ruling party over the mass media. However, they do not cast doubts on the legitimacy of the political power of the regime and the authenticity of its reform project.

They believe that political interest in enhancing democracy requires avoidance of the provocative discourse expressed by opposition parties, which, in their opinion, would only lead to the intransigence of the regime and delay further progress. They accuse their political adversaries of turning to external powers to exert pressure on the regime and believe that such a measure undermines state sovereignty and opens the door to foreign powers to interfere in local affairs. Thus, they do not hesitate to respond to what they consider uncalled-for campaigns occasionally organized by international human rights organizations or Western governments that seek to pressure the Tunisian government to carry out political reform.

In general, these parties emphasize the need to develop internal dialogue with the regime and consider dialogue the only road for expanding political participation. They also highlight the need to avoid crossing the red line represented by cooperation or alliances with the Islamists. In this respect they generally agree—with some variation among them—with the regime and respect its instructions. The parties that form this cluster are of varying sizes and importance and have an open relationship with the regime. While they intersect on the need for positive interaction with the regime's concessions and services, there is much that separates them, and each of them relates to the regime in a different manner.

Despite the symbolic role played by these parties in imparting a pluralist character to the Tunisian political regime, they have nonetheless been repeatedly criticized by President Ben Ali and by the mass media. Their performance, despite all the assistance they have received, is still weak. Furthermore, they have failed to attract citizens and young people and seem unable to fight religious extremism effectively. Four of these parties have decided to abandon efforts to put in place mechanisms permitting coordination with one another and activating a joint role in Tunisian politics. The Socialist Democratic Movement refused to join the four-party coalition that became known as the Democratic Reconciliation. Although it has been considered the most vital political force with potential to inherit the role of the constitutional party after Bourguiba and has the largest number of seats in parliament, it refused to be listed along with other small parties with no political past.

In contrast to the parties that believe in the current pluralism of the system, despite its failings, the other opposition parties adopt a totally different outlook. They believe that the current pluralism is nothing but a facade, an empty shell. They condemn the entire regime as an autocracy and contest the legitimacy of political parties that have agreed to play by the rules set by the regime, disdainfully calling them "cardboard" or "administrative" parties, created by the authorities to undermine and marginalize the democratic movement.

This cluster of parties calls for genuine democratic reforms, including free elections, separating the ruling party from the state, reducing the powers of the president, exercising genuine separation between powers, establishing genuine independence of the judiciary, and issuing a general legislative pardon whereby all political prisoners would be released and dissidents outside Tunisia encouraged to return.

These parties are not homogenous and do not agree on the proper approach for change, nor do they adopt a unified position on the terms that should govern their relation with the regime. However, they do agree on the necessity to go beyond the current piecemeal attempts at reform to seek a radical restructuring of the entire political regime. Among this group, the Renewal Movement (formerly the Communist Party) deserves special attention. In the past it was among the parties that accepted the regime's strategy of gradual reform and defended it vehemently. But later it reconsidered its position and became increasingly critical of the regime, calling for more profound political reforms at a faster pace. Thereafter, it was punished by the regime, which granted it only two parliamentary seats in the most recent elections. Having failed to attune itself to the regime, the movement gradually regained its position through the role it played in the 2004 elections. Many independents believed that the only legal way to nominate a political figure capable of standing against a candidate of the ruling party would be to nominate a candidate from the Renewal Movement. Cooperating with the Renewal Movement, independents succeeded in mobilizing politically during the 2004 election campaign. This experiment motivated the movement to negotiate with the democratic independents to convince them to engage with the movement and work together to create a "democratic front" that would be capable of competing effectively with the ruling party, while simultaneously also preempting the Islamists. However, many factors still hinder the achievement of this goal.

The other parties, such as the legally recognized Progressive Democratic Party, the Democratic Alliance for Work and Freedoms, and the Conference Party for the Republic, operate outside the circle of the regime authority and struggle against it—a fact that has prevented them from entering the parliament and the municipal councils. These parties have gone one step farther than others in criticism of the regime, accusing it of violating the constitutional order by introducing amendments that now permit the president to run for an unlimited number of terms in office. However, with the exception of the Conference Party for the Republic, the rest of the parties still adhere to the principle of piecemeal struggle and are ready to respond positively to any effective reforms undertaken by the regime. But Moncef Al Marzouki, head of the Conference Party for the Republic, has decided to sever relations completely with the current regime and embark on the creation of a new peaceful movement that seeks to overthrow it through civil mutiny. Despite his efforts to incite the public, his call remains unanswered and has not produced any noticeable response—perhaps in part due to the strict security surveillance he has been subjected to upon his return to Tunisia.

Despite the multiple attempts of political parties to introduce change, and despite the campaigns launched by international civil society organizations and the "calculated pressure" exercised by some Western governments that have friendships and strategic interests with the Tunisian government, the political outcomes on the domestic front have been limited. They have not had any marked impact on the regime itself or on the way it manages public affairs. This collective inability to push forward reform made the approach to change one of the main issues of concern to democrats. It is being debated in all circles, including political parties that have chosen to boycott the regime.

In the latest conference organized by the Progressive Democratic Party—one of the more active and vital political organizations in the area of democratic protests—the participants disagreed on the question of the kind of relations that should be maintained by the opposition with the regime. Two leading figures in the party, Mohamed Goumani and Fethi Touzri, presented a concept paper for discussion, an unprecedented measure in a party general meeting. The paper contained criticisms of the party experience in managing conflicts with the regime.

The document indicated that the main feature of the current regime is its monopoly over power, and that the regime has consistently turned its back on the nation's demands for reform and insisted on distinguishing between the opposition of reconciliation and loyalty, on the one hand, and independent opposition, on the other. The document maintained that a major problem within the party was that it remained torn between whether it should operate as a reform party or as a group calling for boycotting, confrontation, and resistance. The document criticized the boycott option that has proved in the past incapable of effecting any change of the political equation. There was thus no alternative to accepting participation in a system where progress was often infinitesimal and attempting to achieve democratic progress gradually by maintaining political pressure.[6]

The problem facing this kind of option lies in the lack of the necessary conditions conducive to openness. The debate within the Progressive Democratic Party highlights the impasse facing the democratic movement in Tunisia, which, after a long history of struggle and protest against regime policies, finds itself stagnating, unable to move forward, having failed to achieve a cumulative qualitative development that would result in substantive changes in the political status quo. This condition has led some democrats to admit that the opposition parties are neither ready nor qualified to secure a peaceful change of government, and to recommend that instead they initiate coordination and alliances with reformist wings within the regime itself, since change is not expected to occur, save from within the regime, not from outside it. But once again the proponents of this school face the uncertainty of the democratic function within the regime, even if it seeks political reform and is prepared to cooperate with the democratic movement.

THE STRUGGLE BETWEEN THE REGIME AND THE ISLAMISTS: THE PROBLEM OF DUAL POLARIZATION

The Islamist movement has and continues to constitute a significant challenge to the state's authority as well as to the Tunisian elite. This challenge gained salience when the Islamists participated in the first parliamentary elections that took place under President Ben Ali in 1989. Their participation revealed that they enjoyed unprecedented public appeal, one that no other political force has ever enjoyed, with the exception of the Constitutional Party during the struggle for liberation. Regardless of the circumstances surrounding these elections, official results acknowledged that the Islamist Renaissance Movement won 17% of votes cast, while the other opposition parties combined won only a very small percentage. This strong showing by the Islamists set the scene for a political and security battle between the two poles.

Despite reservations expressed by some concerning the conditions of the battle between the regime and the Renaissance Movement in the early 1990s, large sectors of the elite were psychologically and politically ready to accept the idea of expunging the Islamists from the political map. This is why several parties stood by the regime and consciously chose to support it with a view to developing political life but also to reap some party gains. These parties believed that among all Arab and Islamic countries, Tunisia has been uniquely capable of preventing the Salafi religious movement from ascending to a position of prominence, and this has been an important basic factor in maintaining a national consensus.

In 1990 a bitter struggle that had begun in 1989 between the regime and the Islamists resulted in the exclusion of the Islamists from the political process. This was followed by the state's determined efforts throughout the 1990s to "uproot" them entirely from society and Tunisian culture. However, as much as the confrontation with the Islamists provided the regime with a new opportunity—on both the domestic and external fronts—to justify its imposition of absolute control over the country, this political battle came eventually to be used as the template on which the relationship between civil society and state, on the one hand, and between the former and the Islamists, on the other, was finally based.

Following years of arrests and trials contested by human rights organizations and entailing a steady rise in the number of victims, some political, social, and intellectual circles began to question the consequences of this severe conflict, among which, as became quite clear, was that the regime acquired absolute power over the political and social aspects of life, without establishing any foundation for an eventual inclusive democratic system. The battle against the Islamists has enabled the state to acquire exceptional powers and jurisdiction. Naturally, this has occurred at the expense of civil society and the democratic movement, which suffered from the expansive powers of the state and its massive intervention in the public arena. The following dilemma has thus come to the fore: How can democracy be defended—in this case against a presumed illiberal Islamist movement—without jeopardizing its philosophy and main components?

None of the political forces are now able to endorse publicly the regime's policy of repressing Islamists or keeping them in prisons. All Tunisian elites have gone beyond this position, which is in direct violation of human rights. Almost all parties outside the circle of rule now call for a general legislative pardon whereby all political prisoners would be released and dissidents residing abroad would return home. Dissidence, however, revolves around two issues: the first is the extent of the right of Islamists to organize politically, and the second is how to deal with Islamists, and, if possible, to coordinate and build alliances with them.

A number of political groups still fear the repercussions of recognizing the right of Islamists to political organization, reiterating the need to separate religion from politics. And so, whereas they recognize the need to release Islamists from prisons after 16 years of arrest under harsh conditions, they have reservations about granting them the freedom to move and form legal political parties. The question for which they have no answer is: If these groups insist on practicing what they consider an inherent right—to inject religion into their political platform—can they be imprisoned again, and can they be excluded from political life by force?

Another opinion recognizes the right of Islamists to form political parties, but with strict conditions that ensure that they do not monopolize religion. Safeguards need to be put in place and all alliances with them should be avoided in order not to enhance their power any further. In essence this strategy requires that the Islamists not be oppressed, but that they be isolated and confronted by a broad front combining secularists and anti-Islamists.

A third group has gone beyond this by demanding that the approach of demonizing Islamists be completely abandoned. They assert the need to begin a profound dialogue with them in order to understand their political project and to seek to develop with them a discourse based on common denominators and to lay safeguards against the possibility of overturning democracy in a future stage. Aziz Krishan, a leftist intellectual, has made a noteworthy attempt in this direction, arguing that failure to establish an alliance with the Islamists will help keep the regime in power and make democratic transformation more difficult to achieve. The following section will examine this approach in greater depth.

THE OCTOBER 18 MOVEMENT AND POLITICAL ALLIANCES

The regime has considered dealing with the Islamists, particularly the Renaissance Movement, but has accused the party of being a terrorist movement seeking to establish theocratic rule. Consequently, the regime considers that any dialogue with the Renaissance Movement and any attempt to help it revitalize its political project is counter to nationalist aspirations.

This official policy had an important impact during the 1990s during which it succeeded in virtually isolating the Renaissance Movement, as most other parties avoided any contact with it. However, response to this moral pressure gradually receded as the political regime expanded its circle of adversaries and enlarged the scope of violations that included among its victims supporters of the Renewal Movement and its cadres, who had never advocated the radical transformation of the regime.

The psychological barrier that the political authority helped build between the Renaissance Movement and the political elite began to crumble gradually by the end of the 1990s. After the convening of the Information Technology Summit in Tunis in November 2005, the psychological barrier collapsed entirely when a group of opposition political figures and members of civil society organizations decided to organize a collective hunger strike, which began on October 18, 2005, and lasted over a month. The aim behind the strike was to draw the attention of local and international public opinion to the shortage of human rights and the plight of political prisoners in Tunisia. This initiative caused a civil and political upsurge. What best characterized it was the participation of elements attuned to the Renaissance Movement, with its Islamist leanings, in addition to several leaders from leftist and secular parties including Hama al Hamami, leader of the Tunisian Workers' Communist Party on the far left, and Ahmed Nejib Chebbi, former secretary general of the Progressive Democratic Party, which served as a liaison between the democratic left and the Islamists. Also among the supporters of the strike was the leftist human rights activist Khamis al Shamary, who, upon return from exile in the 1980s, emphasized the need to find formulae that would include the Islamists within the democratic transformation project.

Following the end of the collective hunger strike, the participants in this joint action developed from merely engaging in activities that demanded press freedom and the release of political prisoners (most of whom were Islamists) into a political initiative that sought to establish a coordinating mechanism between five political parties: the Progressive Democratic Party, the Tunisian Communist Party, the Democratic Coalition for Work and Freedoms, the Renaissance Movement, and the Conference Party for the Republic, along with support from other political and intellectual players such as the Nasserites. The initiative was called the 18 October Movement.

This movement, while succeeding in dealing a mortal blow to the psychological barrier that had been established by the authorities between Islamists and other political organizations, nevertheless failed to achieve a broad consensus within the democratic movement on how to deal with the Islamists. The Renewal Movement and other groups on the far left, as well as a large number of secular liberal intellectuals and the women's movement, did not believe that coordination with the Renaissance Movement would assist in achieving a safe democratic transition.

Creating much confusion was the surprising position taken by the Tunisian Communist Party, a deep-rooted leftist group with commitment to the theoretical and political doctrines of Marxism that enjoys relative representation among the Tunisian student movement and syndicates. Whereas in the past the party leadership stood in opposition to the Renaissance Movement and considered it the flip side of the regime, now it believed it was a potential partner in the struggle to change the balance of power and so recognized its right to political action. Accordingly, the Workers' Party revised its doctrines, claiming now that political alliances need not be based on doctrinal or ideological compatibility, but should rather be guided by the compatibility of the political programs and the positions of the different parties vis-à-vis the regime and the nature of the dominant problems to be faced—what the party called the main contradictions that divide society at the present time.

An important faction within the Workers' Party went even further. Its leader, Hama al Hamami, made a distinction not only between the ideological and the political, but also between the strategic and the transitional. He stated that his party's position toward the Islamist movement is based on the latter's position toward issues of concern to the nation and international questions. When the movement adopts what the party considers to be a "positive" stance toward autocracy, imperialism, or Zionism, it seeks to support them and deal with them. The party finds no difficulty reconciling Islamic-Arab culture with its own Marxist Leninist ideas, inasmuch as the Tunisian people are mostly Muslim and the party defends the identity of Tunisians. It does, however, distinguish among three levels in its dealing with Islam. First is the level of the faith, which is a matter of personal freedom, then the level of the Sharia, viewed as a "historical product" produced by Islamic jurists, and finally the level of Islam as a civilization and a culture which exhibit a variety of diverse features, some reactionary and others progressive. Thus the political position of the Workers' Party toward the Islamists has gone beyond a mere political posture to crystallize a holistic position concerning Islam and how to deal with it in the political arena. Undoubtedly this, in itself, is a remarkable development in the vision of a Marxist group on the extreme left that traditionally harbors a deep enmity to Islamist movements.

Despite these and other efforts, however, the history of partisan activities in Tunisia has never witnessed any lasting coordination between two or more parties. Fragmentation and attempts to monopolize the decision-making process are characteristic features of the Tunisian political scene. Can it be that the October 18 initiative is the exception to the rule? Can it overcome the many obstacles in the way and succeed in establishing traditions of cooperative work and life together? While the left party participating in the initiative has given precedence to pragmatism over ideology, the leaders of the Renaissance Movement have also shown a great deal of flexibility and have pledged to make serious efforts to make a success of this collective enterprise.

The October 18 initiative did not limit itself to the political level by merely issuing a joint communiqué. It also created an intellectual forum to deepen dialogue with the Islamists on a number of issues related to society and the democratic system, such as the nature of the political system to which opposition forces should aspire and the question of religious freedom. It was not a coincidence that women's issues occupied a central position in this dialogue, given the remarkable gains accorded to Tunisian women since 1956, beginning promptly after independence. There is no issue that so raises the fears and apprehensions of the democratic movement and civil society in Tunisia as the possibility that with growth of power the Islamists would eventually undermine the gains and rights acquired in the area of personal status. But these circles were surprised at the high degree of flexibility shown by the Renaissance Movement in dealing with this sensitive matter. Following an intensive internal discussion, members of the Renaissance Movement signed a collective statement on March 8, 2007, in which they declared their commitment to the personal status gains.

The collective statement indicated that the signing parties, including the Renaissance Movement, adhere to the gains stipulated in the Personal Status Code, including the ban on polygamy, that voluntary uncoerced agreement is the principle on which the marriage contract should be based, that women themselves are capable of marrying without the guardianship of others, and that women take part in running the affairs of the family. They considered these "the fruit" of the enlightened reform movement that respects and abides by the international conventions on women's rights. The signatories also demanded that the principle of equality between the two sexes be explicitly stated in the constitution and all Tunisian legislation, and that any elimination or revision of laws that leads to any form of discrimination against women or violates their full equality with men be eliminated. The Tunisian regime has, however, expressed reservations regarding such controversial issues as equality of inheritance between men and women and the clauses regarding women in some international conventions.

No doubt, this is one of the most important critical statements signed by the Renaissance Movement since its establishment. Never before has an Islamic movement along the lines of the Muslim Brothers adopted a position similar in spirit and letter. It was therefore natural that the main partners on the secular side that participated in the October 18 initiative consider this statement a confirmation of their belief that through dialogue much can be achieved that would never have been possible by repression and exclusion. Ahmed Nejib Chebbi pointed out that the statement, which was unanimously endorsed, was the first joint document issued in any Arab or Islamic country by secular and Islamic forces from all parts of the political spectrum.

Nonetheless, adversaries of the Renaissance Movement maintained their positions and cast doubt on the intentions of the party's leaders. They accused them of exercising "political deception" in order to be accepted and recognized as an integral part of the democratic opposition movement.

It is premature to pass judgments about the success or failure of this experiment. What is certain, however, is that the initiative has lasted over one and a half years without failure, despite the regime's scathing criticisms and harassment of its members, which added to the doubts cast by individuals who refuse to cooperate with the Islamists. Although this rapprochement between diverse opposition parties did not affect the system of rule, which has continued to ignore the demands of the opposition and the democratic elite, the initiative revealed the ability of the Tunisian political parties to go beyond their ideological differences and build alliances on the bases of joint interests and agree on a collective approach to both the present and the future.

This consensus, however, is still within the confines of the elite circles and needs to be translated into reality. It has not yet been taken to the streets and to the grassroots level, particularly in the absence of a pluralist and free mass media. Observers believe that the most important factor responsible for this gathering of Islamists, leftists, liberals and nationalists in a common front is the regime's intransigent policies. Having repressed all parties, these policies have encouraged former adversaries to unite and attempt to impose their own political will to counter that of the regime.

CONCLUSIONS

The pluralist experience in Tunisia still suffers from several shortcomings, and the nature of the Tunisian political regime of over half a century has not enabled it to develop a fully democratic party system, nor has the political regime offered Tunisian civil society the conditions conducive to growth, expansion, and influence. Yet it would be arbitrary to claim that parties have failed or been terminally disabled. While the regime is largely responsible for the conundrum in which the parties find themselves, the latter also take some responsibility for their impasse, for having failed to address seriously some of their internal problems. This in turn has prevented them from acquiring power and immunity and developing into grassroots parties whose legitimacy is recognized and defended by broad constituencies. Despite their democratic discourse and their calls for reform, it is still true that in the case of many of these parties, their organization structure and management system, their outreach mechanisms, and the management of party conflicts and relations with civil society all cast doubt on their sincerity in adopting a democratic project and their ability to change political life, especially since some of them continue to reproduce the very political system they oppose.

On the other hand, there is widespread concern among the elite about the political future of the country. The ruling regime is clearly in need of internal rejuvenation and profound reforms. However, the entire range of opposition seems weak and incapable of undertaking a politically transparent exchange of power. In the meantime, the Salafi religious discourse is spreading among youth, women, and the middle class, while the Renaissance Movement is witnessing a recession due to the severe repressive measures against it by the state and the slow pace of reforms within its own ranks. These issues raise disturbing questions, to which at present the political parties seem unable to provide clear, persuasive answers and a democratic vision capable of mobilizing Tunisians to move more effectively toward a fully democratic political system.

SUPPLEMENTAL BIBLIOGRAPHY

Ahmida, Ali Adbullatif (ed). *Beyond Colonialism and Nationalism in the Maghreb: History, Culture, and Politics*. New York, NY: Palgrave, 2000.

Alexander, Christopher. "Back from the Democratic Brink: Authoritarianism and Civil Society in Tunisia." *Middle East Report*, No. 205, Middle East Studies Networks: The Politics of a Field (Oct. Dec., 1997), pp. 34–38. Middle East Research and Information Project. Available at: http://www.jstor.org/stable/3013093.

Allani, Alaya. "The Islamists in Tunisia between confrontation and participation: 1980 2008." *The Journal of North African Studies*, Volume 14, Issue 2 (June 2009): 257–272.

As'Ad, Abukhalil. "Change and Democratisation in the Arab World: The Role of Political Parties." *Third World Quarterly*, Vol. 18, No. 1 (March 1997): 149, 163. Taylor & Francis, Ltd. Available at: http://www.jstor.org/stable/3992906.

Brand, Laurie A. *Women, the State, and Political Liberalization: Middle Eastern and North African Experiences*. New York, NY: Columbia University Press, 1998.

Entelis, John P. "The Democratic Imperative vs. the Authoritarian Impulse: The Maghrib State Between Transition and Terrorism." *The Middle East Journal* 59.4 (2005): 537–558.

Murphy, Emma C. *Economic and Political Change in Tunisia: From Bourguiba to Ben Ali*. Basingstoke, Hampshire: Macmillan, New York: St. Martin's Press, 1999.

Sadiki, Larbi. *Rethinking Arab Democratization: Elections without Democracy*. New York, NY: Oxford University Press, 2009.

Willis, Michael J. "Political Parties in the Maghrib: the Illusion of Significance?" *The Journal of North African Studies*, Volume 7, Issue 2 (Summer 2002): 1–22.

CHAPTER 6

Democratic Transformation in Algeria: The Role of the Parties

Abderrazak Makri

INTRODUCTION

The democratic experiment in Algeria presents serious challenges and potential opportunities as well as a history of radical transformation. Political parties have played an important and complex role in this experiment, one that cannot be understood without understanding the background and present characteristics and tactics of the ruling regime, which are covered in the first section of this chapter. A second section constitutes the main body of the chapter and focuses directly on the parties and electoral politics. The chapter concludes by offering a summary of the factors impeding democracy and those contributing to its further development.

This study is based on field work and participant observation of the development of political life in Algeria. There is very little in the literature on the recent political party transformations in Algeria and their impact on the future of democracy in the country. However, whenever possible, I refer to useful references.

THE RULING REGIME

The Algerian ruling regime is no different from other systems in the Arab world in terms of its authoritarian character, its desire to hold on to power indefinitely, and its fear of democracy and the interaction within a free society. Thus it shares the same poor democratic performance and the limited developmental achievement in all areas, despite the large resources available. However, the Algerian regime is different from its Arab counterparts in terms of its history, structures, and the different considerations in the balance of powers that govern its style of performance and its development.

Consolidation of Power

The Algerian political regime was shaped within the bosom of the national movement and the liberation revolution during the 1920s, a time when the political and the military were able to coexist without contradiction. The political national movement began in the late 1920s and by the 1940s had reached an advanced level of performance in its struggle for independence. At this point the intransigence of the French occupation forces was met by rising national consciousness among the Algerians, a combination that accelerated the revolution and changed the preferred means for its accomplishment. Armed activities became the main preoccupation of the new revolutionary structures, although other means were also used, including political and diplomatic efforts, the use of the media, artistic activities, and a civil struggle that contributed to building the leadership of the revolution.

As the revolutionary struggle continued, a major crisis developed between the political and military leaders of the revolution over whether the military or the political aspects of the struggle had primacy and which arenas should be given priority.[1] In the end, the conflict was resolved in favor of the military and the domestic over the civilian and the external. This result had long-term consequences: It determined that the future of power in Algeria would remain with the military rather than the civilian leadership. This conclusion came about via two junctures.

The first juncture was in the summer of 1962, when commanders of the national liberation army under Houari Boumédiène succeeded in allying with the prominent politician Ahmed Ben Bellah against the transitional Algerian government and took full control over affairs on the eve of independence.[2] The transitional government had been established on March 18, 1962, with the signing of the Evian Accords. On April 8, the vote for independence was 91% positive and another vote on July 1 of the same year reached 99.7% positive. Independence was declared on July 3, 1962.

The second juncture was on June 19, 1965, when Boumédiène overthrew his one-time ally Ben Bellah, who represented the political face of the Algerian government after independence and wanted to retain political power for himself by giving supremacy and ultimate power to the National Liberation Front (NLF) rather than to the military institution in the new Algerian regime.[3]

From that time on, the military became the core and essence of the ruling regime in Algeria, despite some changes from time to time in the form and the balance of power between the presidency and the army, without undermining the supremacy of the latter.[4]

The Boumédiène years from June 1965 to December 1978 were characterized by close ties between the presidency and the military under the absolute rule of the president. For this reason political parties were impossible to develop, despite efforts by eminent revolutionary figures such as Ayet Ahmed and Mohamed Boudiaf. Even the single existing party, the NLF, became nothing more than an administrative organ that performed no political functions except public mobilization for the president's programs.

After the death of President Boumédiène on December 27, 1978, the military returned to its former salience and unilaterally decided the future of rule in Algeria. In deciding the conflict of succession between Abdelaziz Boutaflika, who was close to Boumédiène and was his foreign minister, and Mohamed Saleh Al Yehiawy, the party coordinator, the military bypassed both and chose General Chadli Bendjedid, a man little known to the public, to be president.[5] With time, Bendjedid was able to liberate himself from the control of those who brought him to power. He promoted elements that were loyal to him in the higher echelons of the military and thus he also became an absolute ruler, albeit with a style less rigid and more open than his predecessor.

Bendjedid addressed the major problems that prevailed in the second half of the 1980s by laying the foundation for a pluralist system of government. However, these endeavors led to a severely polarized conflict that heralded the end of his rule. In June 1990, the Islamic Salvation Front won 55% of the seats in the municipal councils in the first multiparty elections and more than 70% of the state popular councils.[6] Then on December 26, 1991, the NLF once again confirmed its supremacy in the first round of the parliamentary election, winning 188 seats of a total of 220.

But the military was not prepared to accept an Islamist victory. Fearing the Salvation Front's extremist positions, a number of senior army officers forced Bendjedid to resign, annulled the elections, and dissolved the Salvation Front under the pretext that it had been planning to reach power democratically but then eliminate democracy, undermine the constitution, and destroy the country politically and economically.[7]

Thus Algeria threw the doors wide open to sedition. Force became the prevalent language, and the military and security organs became the sole decision makers. The military recognized the need for a facade that could give it credibility as it took over after the cancellation of elections, dissolved the victorious party, and imprisoned thousands. It chose Mohamed Boudiaf, a senior leader of the liberation struggle and head of the group of 22 that staged the revolution, to become president in January 1992 and provide that facade, presiding over a newly created State Council.

However, the choice was not a good one. Boudiaf did not have the temperament to accept a condition of dependence on a group of military men and associated civilians. He always believed he was above those and had for years opposed the regime that brought them to power. He therefore tried to assert himself by insisting on the constitutionally established presidential powers. He called for the dissolution of the NLF, which he considered a museum entity, and took measures to form a new party. An open political conflict arose that ended with the assassination of Boudiaf on June 29, 1992.

After the assassination of Boudiaf, Ali Kafi, the commander of the third army during the revolution of independence, was chosen as head of the State Council. Minister of Defense Ahmed Zerwal was asked to become a temporary president and then was elected president in the first multiparty elections held in 1995, meaning that the presidency once more was harmoniously incorporated within the military.[8] But this harmony did not last for long. A serious conflict took place within the ruling institution itself between retired and still serving military officers over positions, money, and ideologies. The conflict accelerated Zerwal's resignation after the fall of his counselor Mohamed Batshin, former head of the military security apparatus.

Feeling embarrassed, particularly on the international scene, the military once more felt the need for a strong political figure to maintain the stability of government and convinced Abdelaziz Boutaflika to run for president. Boutaflika entered the elections with confidence, knowing that his victory was certain after the withdrawal of the six other candidates and the elimination of the obstinate rival Sheikh Mahfouz Nehnah from the race.[9] He ranked second in the elections, obtaining 26% of the votes, sufficient to bring him to power.

From the beginning Boutaflika expressed his desire to enjoy full powers. He entered into several confrontations with the military, accusing it of having used violence to abrogate the 1991 elections. He accused some unnamed officers of corruption. This led to a hidden conflict, which ended with the resignation of Chief of Staff Mohamed Al Amary. However, close observers of the scene believe that a balance was finally struck between the military and President Boutaflika. Both finally realized that an attempt by either party to eliminate the other would be very costly. Consequently, a modus vivendi was reached, albeit within the context of an unstable balance that was vulnerable to emergency situations.

How was the military able to continue to exert influence despite the ousting of the chief of staff? The answer to this question is that the weight of the military in Algeria did not lie in the position of chief of staff but rather in the military security forces, which were more stable and had been the real decision maker since the resignation of Bendjedid. Therefore, one can say that the only center of decision making in the Algerian ruling regime is at the apex of the pyramid of power—the security institution—which is affiliated to the military. However, if the presidency is occupied by a strong man, the balance is disturbed and one of the following scenarios becomes possible:

- The president is in full control over the military institution and the latter becomes a tool in the hands of the president, as was the case with Boumédiène.
- The president is in full control but he cannot fully impose his will, as was the case with Bendjedid.
- A confrontation takes place and things end dramatically as the military takes control, as was the case with Mohamed Boudiaf.
- An unstable balance is struck that is temporarily in favor of the president, as was the case with Boutaflika.

Decision-Making Circles

The role played by others in making key decisions has also varied according to the balance of power between president and military. Under Boumédiène, the president was the sole decision maker. Under Bendjedid, the ruling institutions exchanged power and opinions but intense discussions often took place, particularly on issues related to identity and major economic choices. In the end, however, the decision was always the president's. After Bendjedid, and given the severe security crisis, decisive and critical issues were deliberated among senior officers. Under Boutaflika, important decisions were shared by the presidency and the military security apparatus, leaving a large margin of freedom of decision for the president. Once decisions are shaped, they are passed over to other institutions and the media for implementation. They, however, do not have the right to review or reconsider them. Implementing institutions include the military and security forces, the executive government and parliament, the political parties that respect the rules of the game, major civil society organizations, and administrative institutions at the central and local levels, including governors (*walis*) and heads of municipalities.

Bases of Power

A strong patriarchal tradition, a conservative ideology, regionally located tribal blocs, and contemporary interest groups underlie the power of Algeria's rulers. The patriarchal tradition reemerged as revolutionary stamina diminished and the idea of a "natural interest" that only revered leaders could discern and implement was revived. This tradition carries with it a tendency to distrust the integrity of the system and the ability of others to shoulder responsibility. Ideologically, Algeria's leaders have shared a fear of the rise of the Islamic tide and are moderately secular, depending on the support of conservative Arab Islamists as well as a pro-Western francophone camp. Regionally located tribal blocs have included the Algerian east, influential until the resignation of Zerwal, the Algerian west, whose influence significantly increased under Boutaflika, and the tribal bloc, with stable influence in all state institutions. Finally, contemporary interest groups with their own constituencies, centers, and factions also provide support and have some influence; indeed this may be the only dimension likely to gain greater influence and change the situation in the future.

The Art of Political Maneuver

Despite these bases of support, the regime must depend as well on its own capacity for political maneuver. Since it presents itself, both domestically and internationally, as a democracy governed by the outcome of contested elections, the decision makers have found themselves forced to resort to covert and sometimes overt interventions to maintain the existing balance of power between the different players, particularly in the aftermath of the victory of the Islamic Salvation Front, which overturned all the previously established assumptions. Eight such interventions have been particularly noteworthy:

- the cancellation of the 1991 elections;
- the use of electoral fraud to ensure the victory of Zerwal in the presidential elections of 1995;[10]
- the reinstatement of the NLF as an official party after the "scientific coup" against its secretary general Abdelhamid Mehry when he tried to join the opposition;[11]
- the establishment of a new party, the National Democratic Gathering, in 1996, followed by the use of electoral fraud to ensure a majority in both the legislative and municipal elections;
- taming and weakening the Islamist movement through the game of alternatives by (1) abolishing the Salvation Front, (2) undermining the emerging Peaceful Society Movement (formerly the Islamic Society Movement) by electoral fraud and by the co-optation of some of its leaders into ministerial positions (thereby undermining its public influence), (3) allowing Abdullah Gaballah, an influential figure on the Islamic scene, to establish a new party, the National Reform Movement, to ensure that the Peaceful Society Movement would not monopolize Islamist votes, but then excluding Gaballah from participation in the legislative elections of May 2007;
- assisting in the creation of a large number of small parties that appear only in political functions managed by the authorities, such as national dialogues and election events. Some of these parties have disappeared while others have achieved a controversial representation in the legislative elections of 2007;

- careful oversight, planning, and control of all election events and political processes related to the presidency; and
- assuming close control of the audiovisual media space. The mass media is tightly controlled by the regime, now under the terms of amendments to the penal code in 2002. Journalists have been arrested and even assassinated (with the blame placed on terrorist organizations) and newspapers have been suspended.

Control over Civil Society

Despite a large number of associations, Algeria's civil society lacks vitality and effectiveness. Political considerations govern which NGO's are permitted, and associations and organizations have been used by authorities as tools to manipulate society, by serving as alternatives to political parties to approve bills and support pro-regime candidates. In return, they receive financial support and their officials are brought closer to the regime. Those that refuse to be involved in such schemes are punished by loss of financial assistance, neglect, and the creation of internal crises and other forms of harassment. This situation has led to the rise of what came to be known in Algeria as the "beneficiary civil society."[12] Because of the critical nature of the roles played by these community organizations, they became an arena of conflict between the authorities and political parties, on the one hand, and among political parties, on the other, particularly the parties of the ruling bloc.

One can see parallels between some of the political maneuvers and games played by the Algerian political regime and those played in international conflicts, particularly in its efforts to maintain a balance of power between regime wings and between historic and regional factions. Other tactics are more distinctly domestic, such as:

- the game of blurring important issues by flooding political institutions, such as the parliament, councils, parties, and associations, with a torrent of unrealistic projects and ideas;
- the game of "political shocks," when the regime cancels the rights of the cadres of strong competing parties and ensures their defeat by electoral fraud, in the hope of driving them either to give up all political activity or resort to violence as a means of changing the status quo;
- the game of false opposition, when the regime assigns certain individuals from within its own supporters to play the part of an opposition, thus defusing popular anger without violating public order;
- the game of intimidation, played by maintaining open files that potential leaders know can be used against them at the right time;
- the game of political neglect;
- the game of creating political scandals;

- the game of undermining political parties and organizations from within;
- the game of the carrot and stick;
- the game of tactical political bargaining;
- the game of closed projects;
- the game of legal adaptation;
- the game of media misinformation; and
- the game of committees.

While some parties choose to play as well as they can within the rules of these confusing and threatening games, it is not surprising that others simply withdraw altogether.

Possible Regime Goals

Will these maneuvers continue forever? Is the possibility of Algerian democracy entirely blocked by the regime's intransigence? Not necessarily. The present situation is disturbing for decision makers themselves because it is costly and unprofitable, violates legitimacy and credibility, and threatens undesirable surprises. The strategy of the regime in Algeria is to reach a secure democracy in which rule is exchanged between the NLF and the National Democratic Gathering without fraud or administrative intervention. In order to reach that, the regime seeks to change the trends of the electorate by fostering despair among those in favor of the Islamic project and excluding them from the political game through oppression, fraud, and distortion. These endeavors seek, on the one hand, to stabilize an electorate that traditionally supports the regime's parties, particularly the Liberation Front, and, on the other hand, to encourage new generations of young people who have little to do with the Islamist trend to participate politically. To do that, religious elements are excluded from the formation of new election blocs that might vote for the Islamist parties; strong control is exercised over the educational system, the media apparatus, families, and religious institutions, including mosques; and legislation is passed with the intent of embarrassing the moderate Islamic parties into changing their discourse and their internal and international relations. The ultimate goal is to relegate these parties to the margin of political life, where they will exist only for the sake of maintaining a pluralist facade and to coopt the remaining Islamic youth into the acceptable political formations.

POLITICAL PARTIES IN ALGERIA AND THE DEMOCRATIC TRANSFORMATION

With an understanding of the history, tactics, and goals of the ruling regime, we are now ready to examine Algerian political parties and the role they have played in fostering or hindering democratization. We begin with a brief look at their history before independence and move forward to the present time.

Political Parties before Independence

Partisan politics are an old tradition in Algeria, having begun in the 1920s during the colonial era. At the end of 70 years of popular resistance in the countryside, marked by the destruction of traditional social institutions in the rural areas at the hands of the occupation army, the national struggle shifted from the rural to the urban areas and added national political resistance to armed struggle.[13] This transition was made possible by five factors: (1) the presence of an educated Algerian bourgeois class providing the personnel for the French administrative and educational institutions; (2) religious reform in the Islamic world and among the Algerian clergy; (3) the instruction in methods of political struggle Algerian migrants to France gained in the French leftist trade union movement; (4) the impact of World War I on the political consciousness of Algerians who fought within the ranks of the French army and came into contact with and were influenced by various political and intellectual trends; and (5) the rise of the leftist popular front in France to power after World War II, and the relative free space it provided.

All the above factors led to the formation of national, popular political trends of all shades: Islamic reformist, assimilationist liberal, and international communist trends that included a large number of independent figures, parties, associations, clubs, and mass media, eventually crystallizing into four main institutions: (1) the Association of Algerian Muslim Ulemas (1931), (2) the Star of North Africa political party (established in France in 1926 and arriving in Algeria in 1936, later becoming the Algerian People's Party), (3) the movement of the Victory of Democratic Freedoms, the Elite Confederation (1927), which later became the Democratic Union for Lovers of Algeria Communique (1946), and (4) the Algerian Communist Party (1936), initially a branch of the French Communist Party. All these parties were able to perform important political roles and made large contributions toward maintaining the social, cultural, and political aspects of the national struggle. However, colonial barbarism and its campaigns of distortion and repression eventually eliminated over time those intermediary political roles, and the Algerian struggle thereafter shifted toward a radicalism first adopted by the young men in the Victory Movement, which rejected partisan work, advocated a revolution, and demanded that all political parties dissolve themselves and join the NLF. The partisan dimension then virtually disappeared during the liberation revolution when, as already noted, the military won over the political in the final confrontation that took place between the advocates of each strategy within the leadership of the revolution.

Political Parties after Independence and before Multipartyism

After independence when the army general staff allied with Ben Bellah, it rejected the concept of a pluralist system and imposed a single party that dominated all political, cultural, and economic spheres. However, even that single party, the NLF, had little if any genuine political role.[14] The Boumédiène years stunted its role and transformed it into a mere bureaucratic apparatus that did not have the support of the rapidly increasing young population in urban centers as a result of its urban development efforts. The NLF became a vehicle for social and professional mobility for some professionals, such as employees and teachers (whose numbers increased as their social and symbolic status decreased), public sector officials, dwellers of rural areas, local landlords, and small and medium landowners. This single-party experience distorted partisan politics in the eyes of many Algerians and discouraged them from any engagement in public life, which became synonymous with opportunism and hypocritical allegiance to the ruler.[15]

However, some revolutionary political leaders attempted to establish clandestine opposition parties immediately after independence.[16] Ayet Ahmed formed the Front of Socialist Forces (FSF) in 1963, a party that still operates today as one of the relatively strong parties outside parliament. During approximately the same time, Mohamed Boudiaf formed the Socialist Revolution Party (SRP), which had a shorter lifespan because of its leader's decision to dissolve it in the early 1980s. The communists formed a party in 1966 under the name of the Socialist Vanguard. Some of the leading figures of the Islamic trend also organized themselves in associations to plan mosque-based, cultural, religious, and political activities, despite the ban on the activities of the Muslim Ulemas Association after independence. All the above political movements were subject to frequent harassment that sometimes reached the level of liquidation and torture of leaders who were often hounded even after they had fled abroad.

The Amazighi (an indigenous movement named after the Amazigh language, native to Algeria and now a national language) and Islamist trends were able to grow along the margin of the official party, while leftists, particularly under Boumédiène, chose to penetrate regime organs. Things remained unchanged until October 5, 1988, when a major schism occurred within the regime owing to deep ideological differences, the economic collapse resulting from the decline in oil prices, and severe social strains created by the large social changes initiated and dominated by the Islamist groups.

Political Parties under Multiparty Pluralism

The February 1989 constitution that endorsed pluralism was a result of the pressures and transformations noted above. In less than two years, the new 1989 law had allowed the establishment of 60 new parties. But only three political fronts managed to win seats in parliament in the legislative elections of December 1991: the Islamic Salvation Front (ISF), the NLF, and the FSF. Analyzing the election results party by party sheds further light on the political scene at the time.

The ISF was the largest winner in the elections. The irony that many observers tend to overlook is that the ISF alone reaped the rewards of all the Islamist advocacy groups, which had led the Islamic revivalist movement in Algeria during all the previous years. The long-lasting hesitation of these Islamic groups to form political parties allowed Abassi Medani and Ali Behlaj, who had not been members of any Islamic group, to form an Islamic party that was able to attract the overwhelming majority of social groups influenced by the Islamic discourse. However, the severely conservative discourse endorsed by the ISF expanded its appeal particularly among the marginalized categories that were heavily concentrated in cities and who were negatively affected by the economic changes and the political hegemony of the ruling circles.[17]

As for the FSF, it asserted its full control over the tribal area—with heavy Amazigh concentrations—where the ISF enjoyed little support. The FSF success in that region is attributable to several factors: its long-standing political presence in the area, the impact of the ethnic and cultural dimension on politics in the region, the historical and charismatic personality of its leader Ayet Ahmed, the strength of the FSF discourse, the deteriorating socioeconomic and political circumstances, and the long-standing grievance of the Amazighi that the regime since independence had discriminated against them and refused to acknowledge their independent identity.[18]

The NLF was the biggest loser in the elections, although the government contrived to support it by gerrymandering the election constituencies and promulgating a convenient law regulating elections. The NLF was barely able to evade a total collapse by virtue of its large constituency drawn from the revolutionary family (a large percentage of senior Mujahidin and children of martyrs) and the individuals and groups who benefited from the regime, particularly in the rural areas. However, as already noted, the elections were canceled before the second round could take place, and the victorious ISF party was dissolved. Legitimacy and the future of democracy in Algeria became the two central and most crucial problems facing the country.

Many parties attempted to revive dialogue between the conflicting parties. Numerous dialogue groups were formed that went under different labels, including the group of four, the group of six, the group of seven, and the group of seven plus one, but none succeeded in achieving the desired result. Finally, only two serious projects remained on the table. The first was an initiative sponsored by the Algerian authorities, which began with a series of dialogues involving the relevant parties and concluded with a national seminar in 1994. The second was an initiative of the opposition parties that carried the name of the National Contract or the Contract of Rome and that led to a meeting in Rome in 1995 in which the three fronts participated in addition to the Labor Party (Louisa Hanoun), the Renaissance Movement (Abdulla Gaballah), and Contemporary Muslim Algeria (Ahmed Ben Mohamed).

These activities ended with the organization of the first presidential elections in 1995, a crucial first step for the return to legitimate government. The elections were boycotted by the parties of the National Contract, while the Muslim Society Movement (currently the Peaceful Society Movement) participated with its candidate Sheikh Mahfouz Nehnah, the movement's leader who had participated in the first round of the Rome meetings but was convinced that the project of return to the election process suggested by the authorities was a better guarantee for the return to legitimacy. Participants in the elections also included the Gathering for Culture and Democracy under Saeed Saady and the Algerian Renewal Party under Boukrouh. Although the regime's candidate Lamin Zerwal won, the elections helped to highlight the strong presence of the Islamist movement in the Algerian streets as a result of the large public support for Mahfouz Nehnah and indicated that the Islamist trend was here to stay.

Algerian citizens participated heavily in the presidential elections, thereby endorsing the government's project for the return to legitimacy. This convinced all the parties to the National Contract to reconsider their boycott of the political process. Thus, new elected councils were formed and a new political map began to take shape and develop.

What are we to conclude from the outcome of the election process imposed by the authority in which the Algerian people took part and that was accepted by all the political parties? Does it promote democracy? Did the participation of the parties guarantee the democratic process? Or were the parties simply the chorus that had assigned roles to play? Were they convinced of the authenticity and usefulness of their roles? Or were they responding to the realities of the situation, over which they had little influence? Or is the truth somewhere in between? In order to answer these questions, we shall analyze three legislative elections that have taken place since 1995 (in 1997, 2002, and 2007). (There were also presidential elections in 1995, 1999, and 2004, as well as two local elections in 1997 and 2002.)

Political Parties after the 1997 Legislative Elections

The 1997 legislative elections came in the aftermath of several important political events. The NLF had been reorganized, changing its status from an opposition party to a party allied to the regime, the National Democratic Gathering had been created as a competitor of the NLF for positions inside state institutions, and the constitution had been amended and the parties and elections law modified to prevent the establishment of parties on religious or ethnic grounds. This final step was believed to be directed mainly against the (Islamic) Peaceful Society after the unexpectedly favorable results achieved by its leader in the presidential elections in which he garnered 26% of the vote. When the election was held, the rate of participation was an impressive 65.6%. The results are shown in Table 6.1.

Despite complaints of fraud by many opposition parties, this election produced a lively parliament with animated discussions shown live on television. It also reflected a remarkable diversity in views, visions, and stances, as well as a noticeable state of amicable coexistence between the deputies of the various parties. An energetic parliamentary movement was afoot, and members exhibited a great deal of vitality in establishing close relations with their constituencies. Additionally, the State Council established committees to investigate the allegations that massive fraud had marked the 1997 local elections.

Political Parties after the 2002 Legislative Elections

By the time of the 2002 legislative elections, other major developments in the political scene had taken place. There had been tangible improvements in the security situation. The president dominated the political scene, traveling constantly from one province to another, making

Table 6.1 Algerian 1997 Legislative Elections

Party	*Percentage*
National Democratic Gathering	32.12
Peaceful Society Movement	14.12
National Liberation Front	13.61
Renaissance Movement	8.32
Socialist Forces Front	4.80
Gathering for Culture and Democracy	4.03
Free Elected	4.17
Labor Party	1.77
Progressive Republican	0.06
Liberal Social	0.03
Union for Democracy and Freedom	0.04

Source: Algerian Ministry of the Interior.

frequent appearances on television and introducing political initiatives (civil harmony, codification of Amazighi language) and popular economic projects. Major changes also occurred with respect to political parties. The NLF was revitalized by the extensive support it received from the president who made Ali Benflis, the party's secretary general, his prime minister. Within the tribal area—which had witnessed constant conflicts between young people and the security organs since 200—a new political group, al Oroush, became the most significant party in the area, surpassing in popularity the already existing parties: the Socialist Forces Front and the Gathering for Culture and Democracy.[19]

Major divisions arose within the Renaissance Movement, and its leader left to form a new party called the National Reform Movement. In combination, these changes led to an election with a much lower turnout rate (46%) and the results shown in Table 6.2.

What characterized the parliament in its second term was the unexpectedly large number of seats won by the NLF, which ruled with an absolute majority (thanks to the regime's support and the bloc of some 1 million votes of military personnel). There was a clear choice on the part of the regime to lend support to the Front even more than to the National Gathering, which ranked second. The (Islamic) Peaceful Society Movement lost 31 seats, a result many observers attributed to its crisis in the presidential elections of 1999 and its long-standing links to the government. Overall, the Islamist movement witnessed a general decline. But the Labor Party rose as a new political force to contend with.

The new parliament in this second term lacked much of the credibility that it enjoyed in the first term. Its sessions were characterized by a large degree of monotony, and the council as a whole was much less active politically, with hardly any effort to exercise control over the government. This was due to the absolute majority of the NLF, supported by the National Gathering and the Peaceful Society Movement. The council was

Table 6.2 Algerian 2002 Legislative Elections

Party	*Percentage*
National Liberation Front	35.52
National Democratic Gathering	8.50
National Reform Movement	10.08
Peaceful Society Movement	7.74
Free Independents	10.65
Labor Party	3.16
Renaissance Party	3.58
Algerian Renewal Party	2.19
National Reconciliation Party	0.18

Source: Algerian Ministry of the Interior. These elections were boycotted by several Socialist and Islamic parties.

criticized by the press and the public, and even the president seemed to have little regard for it, refusing to deliver speeches there. Many believe that the image of the council truly reflected the democratic recession in Algeria at this stage.

Political Parties after the 2007 Legislative Elections

Once again there were significant political developments prior to the next legislative elections. Presidential elections had given another term to Boutaflika (more than 84% of the vote) who ran within a large alliance that included the NLF, the National Democratic Gathering, the Peaceful Society, and a number of national organizations and popular support committees. For the first time no one contested the results or the integrity of the elections, and a public referendum endorsed the national reconciliation initiative presented by Boutaflika. Moreover, the elections resulted in a major crisis within the Liberation Front. A conflict took place between its secretary general Benflis and President Boutaflika, despite their long friendship. A movement was formed from within the front, the Correction Movement, which supported the president and overthrew Benflis after he lost the presidential elections. Abdelaziz Belkhadem was invited to amend the Constitution and allow the president to run for a third term of office. The Peaceful Society Movement regained confidence after the death of its leader, and following multicandidate internal elections, resulted in the choice of a new leader, Abi Garra Sultani. Turnout dropped still further (35.65%) with nearly 1 million invalid votes. The results are shown in Table 6.3.

The limited voter turnout and the large number of annulled votes strongly indicated that citizens were not convinced of the viability of elections and their effectiveness to bring about change that would raise the living standard of the Algerian people. A cynical apathy seemed to have set in, and neither parliament nor parties and politicians were held in high regard. The people doubted that the regime had the will to introduce change or the intention to exchange power through elections. Indeed, the entire electoral process suffered from lack of legitimacy, which was not improved when the head of the national political committee, Saeed Bousheir, notified the president (who had appointed him) that fraud was taking place on a large scale in favor of the NLF. This report was endorsed by a large number of parties and highlighted by the mass media.

Within this context, the fates of the individual parties varied. The NLF did not achieve the same results as in 2002 but continued to occupy the top position as the main political force and together with the National Democratic Gathering was able to form a parliamentary majority. The advance of the Peaceful Society Movement was explained by observers as due to its ability to win the sympathy of the conservative electorate

Table 6.3 Algerian 2007 Legislative Elections

Party	*Percentage*
National Liberation Front	22.98
National Democratic Gathering	10.33
Peaceful Society Movement	9.64
Free Movement	9.83
Labor Party	5.09
Gathering for Culture and Democracy	3.36
Algerian National Front	4.18
National Movement for Nature and Development	2.00
Renaissance Party	3.39
Youth and Democracy Movement	2.31
National Republican Party	2.21
National Reconciliation Party	2.14
Algerian Renewal Party	1.80
National Reform Movement	2.53
Opening Movement	2.51
National Front for Liberals for Reconciliation	1.96
Pledge 54	2.26
National Party for Solidarity and Development	2.09
National Movement for Hope	1.73
National Republican Gathering	1.47
Algerian Gathering	1.75
National Democratic Front	1.38
Democratic Social Movement	0.89
Republican Progressive Party	1.42
Socialist Labor Party	0.75

Source: Algerian Ministry of Interior.

that approved of its approach to political participation, thus permitting it to penetrate electoral constituencies that traditionally voted for the regime's parties, while at the same time maintaining its strong ties to the traditional Islamic constituency. On the other hand, the (Islamic) National Reform Movement suffered a remarkable recession, obtaining only three seats, possibly as a result of the severe conflicts and schisms among its leaders. Overall, the Islamic trend witnessed a significant regression in the 2007 elections, which raises some questions regarding the future prospects of the Islamic movement as a whole.

In another interesting development, the tribal provinces were divided among a significant number of parties and free lists despite the presence of the Gathering for Culture and Democracy. The latter did not obtain any more votes than it had in 1997, despite the absence of its rival, the Front of Socialist Forces.

Finally, it is interesting to note the large number of small parties that now entered parliament via individuals who were not in fact party members, but in reality independent candidates who were allowed to run under the label of a party in return for a hefty donation to that party. This created a scandal that pointed to major failings within the political system.[20] Thus many big businesspeople and traders entered parliament through the small parties and the free election lists, although some others did secure seats via the larger parties. These small parties, moreover, engaged in fully exploiting their right to join the parliamentary political committees, organizations that are funded by the government to supervise central and local elections. To cash in on these government funds, the small parties would conclude agreements with individuals who were not politically related to them to represent them on these committees and split the remuneration paid by the government. Thus small parties made large profits in election events, but became a large burden that undermined the legitimacy of the state and the authenticity of the elections. Because of their large number and their dependency on the regime, the regime used them to support government bills and projects that came before the various committees.

Algerian Political Parties Today

The recent legislative elections have raised a wide-scale controversy on the future of partisan life in Algeria, particularly after the apathy expressed by the Algerian voters in the elections and their expressed rejection of the entire process via the enormous number of annulled ballots (about 17% of the total). Following the large deviation of small political parties, the official response was to purify the partisan scene by preventing parties from entering elections unless they obtained 4% of the electors' votes in any of the prior elections in 1997, 2002, or 2007. Parties that did not obtain this minimum threshold could not run in the elections unless they collected a large number of signatures; which was usually very difficult to amass.

With the implementation of this new rule, only nine parties have remained on the political scene: the National Liberation Front, the National Democratic Gathering, the Peaceful Society Movement, the Renaissance Movement, the Labor Party, the National Reform Movement, the Front of Socialist Forces, the Gathering for Culture and Democracy, and the Algerian National Front. Although some of these have been discussed in the preceding pages, others have not. What follows is a closer look at each of these members of the contemporary Algerian multiparty system.

The National Liberation Front

As we have seen, the NLF rose with the Algerian liberation war and took power in 1962 and remained the single party in Algeria until the adoption of a multiparty system in February 1989. The NLF was originally a socialist party but has moved to the center. Its core constituency is the members of the revolutionary family, war veterans, and the children of martyrs. By the early 1990s its initial popular appeal had waned considerably. It joined the ranks of the opposition and boycotted the 1995 elections. However, the change that took place later on in its leadership through the external intervention of the regime brought it back into power and it became the regime's favorite party. President Boutaflika became its honorary president and Prime Minister Belkhadem the head of its executive committee. However, the conflict that took place between its former secretary general Ali Benflis and President Boutaflika over the presidency in 2004 brought about a severe crisis that led to a the replacement of Benflis by Belkhadem and the effects of this crisis are still being felt. Nonetheless, the party remains an apparatus of the regime and represents one of its wings. At present some of its leaders now insist that the party must henceforward distance itself from the regime.

The National Democratic Gathering

The National Democratic Gathering (NDG) was established in February 1997 to support the elections program of the regime after the NLF boycotted the presidential elections and is known as the administration's party. It won the most parliamentary seats in the 1997 national elections, as well as an overall majority of the local councils in the municipal elections of the same year. It has been accused by all political parties and the mass media of having won its parliamentary majority by widespread electoral fraud. It has a liberal nationalist orientation. Originally it offered an extreme agenda dedicated to confrontation with the Islamists. Over time it has moderated its discourse, although it continues to focus on combating terrorism and supporting the self-defense groups formed by the security apparatus to combat armed factions. The NDG together with the NLF now represent the two wings of the regime's political party support. The founding members of the NDG include former veteran members of the NLF and several administrators and leaders of popular civil organizations controlled by the regime. The devotion to the regime of the party's leader, Ahmed Ouyahia, a man with no previous governing or political history, is absolute. He has openly declared that serving the regime has, for him, greater priority than serving the party.

Peaceful Society Movement (Hamas)

This movement was established on May 30, 1991, as the Movement of the Islamic Society, subsequently changing its name to meet the requirements of the constitutional amendments of 1997, which disallowed parties based on religious or ethnic grounds. Headed since 2002 by Sheikh Abu Garah Sultani, the party adopts a moderate Islamic orientation and seeks to establish peace and national reconciliation in Algeria without a priori conditions. It is keen to present an image of a peaceful democratic national Islamic movement, basing its principles to the original Muslim Brotherhood in Egypt.[21] It adopts the principle of political participation instead of supremacy and has contributed to disassociating religion from terrorism. It has made pioneering efforts in restoring the election process after its cancellation in 1991. It participated in more than six governments since 1994 and is the third member of the presidential alliance next to the NLF and the NDG. It experienced a severe drop in popularity in the 2002 elections but recovered somewhat in the 2007 elections. It is the site of wide-scale internal discussions about relations with the regime. Among the important issues that the party campaigns against are government corruption, the state of emergency, and the amended articles in the penal code that permit the imprisonment of journalists and imams. It advocates modernization of the political system and expanding freedoms, while upholding the moral principles of Islam as the basis for both the state and society.

Renaissance Movement

The Renaissance Movement was established in March 1989 and is now headed by Al Habib Adamy, secretary general after Fateh Rabi'y, leader of the party's general secretariat. It has moderate Islamist orientations that are quite similar to that of the Peaceful Society Movement. While it once boasted 34 seats in parliament, internal schism has greatly weakened the party, and it won only five seats in the 2007 elections, becoming thereby simply another one of the small parties in Algeria.

Labor Party

The Labor Party was established in 1990 as a leftist party with Trotskyite tenets and carried out its activities clandestinely prior to the establishment of the multiparty system. It expresses solidarity with the proletariat and the vulnerable social classes, resists any kind of privatization, and demands the protection of the public sector and state intervention to protect consumers. Its discourse has shifted from stringency to flexibility, and it has now established friendly relations with President Boutaflika who commends the party leader Louisa Hannoun in the mass media. This relation acquired strength when the president withdrew the combustibles law, which had granted large concessions to the foreign oil companies. The party's presence in parliament has grown steadily, rising from 4 seats in 1997 to 21 seats in 2002 and 27 in 2007. Among the main issues that the party staunchly advocates is abolishing the current family law, which is grounded in the Islamic Sharia, and codification of the Amazighi language (i.e., standardization of grammar for the different variations; adoption of a formal writing system).

Reform Party

The National Reform Movement, founded in 1999, has an Islamist orientation that is ideologically moderate but politically radical. Under its original leader, Abdullah Gaballah, it became a strong opposition party with 42 seats in the 2002 parliament, plus a significant presence in the municipal councils, but after Gaballah was ousted by internal divisions, its strength fell in 2007 to merely three seats. (Supporters of Gaballah joined small parties and also won only three seats.) Its current leaders are Mohamed Boulihia and its secretary general is Jahid Younessy.

The Front of Socialist Forces

The Front of Socialist Forces is the oldest opposition party in Algeria. It was established in 1963 following the disagreement that took place on the eve of independence between the main pillars of the liberation revolution. Confined now to a limited geographic tribal region, this party favors the reestablishment of a ruling system through a constituent assembly of moderate secular orientation that does not conflict with religion and that has strong links with the *marabouts* and the *zawayas* (the graves of particularly famous *marabouts* that are often the destinations of pilgrimages; such worship is contrary to the teachings of Islam, which does not recognize the holiness of these men). It totally boycotts all state projects and participates only in the local council elections of the tribal zones it controls. It participated in the first multiparty legislative elections of 1997 but boycotted all subsequent national elections. It has been headed since its establishment by Ayet Ahmed, one of the main figures of the liberation revolution who leads his party from his home in Switzerland.[22] The party is no longer prominent in the Algerian political scene because of its constant boycott of elections, limited participation, and absence of political initiatives. Internal cleavages have led to the resignation of several of its prominent cadres. Among its main demands are granting full cultural rights to the residents of the tribal region it seeks to represent and demilitarizing the ruling regime.

The Gathering for Culture and Democracy

The Gathering for Culture and Democracy was established in 1989, one week before establishment of the February 23 constitution endorsing pluralism. Its leading members include a number of dissenters from the Front of Socialist Forces (including its former leader Saeed Saady). The party, which has a secular radical intellectual orientation and supports the ethnic identity of the tribal region where it is confined, is closely allied to the regime. It won 9% of the vote in the presidential election of 1995 and joined the coalition government after the legislative elections of 1997 (in which it won 19 seats). It did not participate in the legislative elections of 2004 because of tensions in the tribal area at that time, but then participated again in the 2007 elections, winning 19 seats. Because of this participatory tendency and the influence of individuals close to the regime, its discourse and relations with the Islamists began to moderate. Among its main demands now are the liberalization of the economic system, eliminating the family law, codifying the Amazighi language, and secularizing the constitution.

The Algerian National Front

The Algerian National Front was established after the promulgation of the 1989 constitution and appears only on election occasions. In the 2002 elections it won 8 seats, and 13 seats in the 2007 elections. Its nationalist orientations are very close to the NLF and it is the only small party that made it across the 4% threshold.

Algerian Political Trends

Three political trends (fronts) are at present dominant in Algeria, and each of these is supported by three political parties. The nationalist trend includes the NLF, the NDG, and the Algerian National Front; the Islamist trend comprises the Peaceful Society Movement, the National Reform Movement, and the Renaissance Movement; and finally the secular trend comprises the Front of Socialist Forces, the Gathering for Culture and Democracy, and the Labor Party. The regime's favorite tactic, achieved via various plots and maneuvers but without resorting to outright fraud, is to ensure the exchange of power between its two major allies, the NLF and NDG. At the same time, the continuing conflict between these two outside the democratic framework ultimately leads to the failure of both, and the rise of the Islamic trend, seen as the only alternative capable of preventing a repeat of the events of October 1988, when the escalation of the conflict within the ruling regime led to the collapse of the whole regime and the rise of a radical Islamist party. But in order to achieve its goals the regime must continue to support its two major allies—the NLF and the NDG—and particularly the weaker NDG, which had been forcibly created and which some observers suggest may have benefited from regime interference in the 2007 legislative elections to achieve second rank among the parties.

In addition, to attain its ends legitimately the regime must closely monitor all the Islamic parties, with an eye on the specific weaknesses and strengths of each, forcefully resisting Islamic parties that adopt hard-line opposition postures and containing those that opt for participating, such as the Peaceful Society Movement, while adopting shifting policies toward these parties; alternately reinforcing some while weakening others so as to eventually weaken all, causing them to lose much of their popular appeal and to cease to represent any serious challenge to the regime.

As for the secular parties, they pose no direct threat to the regime itself but have the ability to destabilize the tribal area due to their weight there and benefit as well from the external pressures exerted by foreign circles concerned with civil society, particularly the Front of Socialist Forces, which is affiliated to the International Socialist Forum. Thus the dilemma facing the regime with respect to the secularists is to find a political party that can win enough popularity to inflict a defeat on the Socialist Front and at the same time present a convenient cover against foreign threats. Within this context, the Gathering for Culture and Democracy seems a viable option, especially given that it has not been reluctant to play this role since its establishment. At the same time, the Labor Party, with its traditional ideological opposition to Western liberalism, could be used to fill the ideological gaps within the secular trend, particularly since the party has exhibited a remarkable aptitude of late to assume that new role.

In all cases, the ninc parties are all cards that might be used in case the available scenarios fail, particularly since they all accepted the rules of the game and have realized that they could not survive and thus do not desire any existential confrontation with the regime.

This is the dream of the regime as indicated by long and accurate observations of its conduct, the information available, and its long historical record of expertise in the art of political maneuvering. However, these schemes of the regime are not an inevitable fate for Algerian parties and the development of Algerian democracy. The best laid plans have failed before. These maneuvers from above have been the main cause for the continuous political crises in Algeria. The future cannot be guaranteed without a democracy passed on the supremacy of law and the maturity of a public opinion nurtured by the guarantee of freedom to all. Only such a political system can prevent political parties from transgressing on democracy and prevent any political regime from imposing its hegemony over society.

CONCLUSIONS

We can now sum up the conditions that impede and those that facilitate democratic transformation in Algeria. Those that impede democracy are all related to the political will of the regime and whether it will continue to intervene in the political and social balance of powers while ignoring all legal and democratic frameworks, manipulating the administration and state institutions to support the parties it favors and restricting those it wishes to curtail, encouraging corruption and manipulating money and businesspeople, derailing civil society from its original paths, and weakening mass media, particularly the audiovisual media. Permitting and even sponsoring election fraud remains the biggest problem that undermines every possibility for empowering democracy in Algeria.

But the political parties share responsibility for the slow progress of democracy. Parties have passed up opportunities to foster democracy by using verbal and material violence and by presenting dogmatic and radical visions. Moreover, some political parties have become servants to the regime, seeking only to achieve gains for their parties and members. Political opportunism has also spread among large categories of party leadership, which have enjoyed the opportunities they had for social mobility and do not wish to change the status quo. To put an end to this conundrum, it is important that party leaders become aware of the poor prospects for all if political horizons remain so limited in the future in the developmental, social, and cultural domains. The situation will not be remedied unless ideas, programs, interests, and visions are exchanged in accordance with a social contract that will ensure a democratic transition and exchange of power.

Another major impediment is corruption and the remarkable resistance among mass media, political parties, and the judiciary waging a serious campaign against it, despite the extent to which it threatens political development and social stability in all corners of the polity.

There are, however, a number of factors conducive to democracy in Algeria today. The acute conflict within ruling institutions and political parties opens the door to restore the balance of political power in favor of the independence of political parties, mass media, and civil society. Public awareness is growing among new groups of elite and intelligentsia who have not grown too weary of the political opportunism rampant among different social groups. There have also been impressive signs of a new willingness and ability of the political class to develop and improve its performance, particularly on the Islamic front. Moderate Islamist political parties have risen and narrowed the gap between themselves and others, normalizing relations wherever possible, including those with the regime.

It is also the case that the present degree of freedom in the information and civil society sectors, while by no means perfect, is perhaps sufficient to help Algerian society achieve at least a minimum level of democracy. And finally and very important, we must not forget the importance of any and all international developments that reject oppression and defend human rights.

Finally, then, we must say that the gains achieved by democracy in Algeria are large and cannot be underestimated. Algerian democracy is approaching the point of no return. Coexistence between ideas and trends is appreciated by all parties. Joint work is under way, and the existential conflict between parties has disappeared. Elections, despite their shortcomings, are a positive undertaking. Qualified political human resources and advanced institutional frameworks as well as NGOs with the capability to learn and develop are abundant. Media freedoms are expandable. Unless a setback happens, we believe that this is the normal course of democratic development.

SUPPLEMENTAL BIBLIOGRAPHY

Almost nothing has been written previously concerning political parties in Algeria. Hence there was little material in the literature on which to base this chapter. The following is a bibliography, therefore, of a more general nature. The authors are noted historians and prominent figures that participated in the Algerian revolution.

Arabic:

Abu-Aziz, Yehya. *Al-Aydiologiyat al—Siyassyya lil-Haraka al-Watanyya min Khilal Watha'iq Gaza'iryya.* Al-Gaza'ir: Diwan al-Matbu'at al-Gaami'iya, 1990.

Abu-Aziz, Yehya. *Al-Tarikh al-Siyassy lil-Gaza'ir min al-Bidayya wa Lighayt 1962.* Beirut: Dar el-Gharb el Islami, 1997.

Bahimi, Abdelhamid. *Fi Asl al-Azma al- Gaza'irieh, 1954–1999.* Beirut: Narkaz Dirassat al-Wehda Al-Arabyya, 2001.

Gabi, Nasser. *Al-Gaza'ir min al-Haraka al-Ummallyya-al-Niqabyya ila al-Harakat al-Igtima'yya.* Al Gaza'ir: Dar el Ma'had el-Ali lil-Amal, 2001.

Gabi, Nasser. *Al-Intikhabat, al-Dawla, wal-Mugtama'.* Al-Gaza'ir: Al-Qassba lil-Nashr, 1999.

Muhammad, Ali b. *Gabhat al-Tahrir ba'd Boumedien.* Al Gaza'ir: Haqa'iq wa-Watha'iq Dar el-Umma, 1998.

Nu'man, Ahmad b. *Faranssa wal-Itruha al-Barbaryya, al-Khalfyyat, al-Ahdaf, al-Wassa'il, al-Bada'il.* Al-Gaza'ir: Dar el-Naba.

Nu'man, Ahmed b. *Al-Hawyya al-Watanyya, al-Haqa'iq wal Mughalatat* (Al-Gaza'ir: Dar el-Umma.

O'Sadiq, Fawzi. *Al-Haraka al-Islamyya fil Gaza'ir, 1962–1988.* Al-Gaza'ir: Dar el-Intifada, 1992.

Qiqa, Khaled Omar b. *Fessoul min Qissat al-Damm fi al-Gaza'ir.* Cairo: Beit al-Hekma, 1997.

Rahmatallah, Mahfouz Nehnah. *Al-Gaza'ir al-Manshouda, al-Mou'adalla al-Mafqouda: al-Islam, al-Watanyya, al-Dimouqratyya.* Al-Gaza'ir: Dar el-Naba, 1999.

Saadallah, Abu-el-Kassem. *El-Haraka El-Watanyya al-Gaza'iryya.* Beirut: Dar el-Gharb el-Islami, 2000.

French:

Abbas, Ferhat. *L'autopsie d une guerre.* Paris: Garnier, 1980.
Abbas, Ferhat. *L'independence confisquée.* Paris: Flammarion, 1984.
Ageron, Charles-Robert. *Les Algériens Musulmans et la France 1871/1919* 1. Paris: Ed Puf.
Ahmed, Hocine Aït. *Mémoire d'un Combattant, L'esprit D'indépendance 1942–1952.* Alger: Ed Barzakh, 2002.
Azzedine, Commandant. *On Nous Appelait Fellaghas.* Paris: Stock, 1977.
"Berbére." *Revue naqd* 19–20 (2004): 27–54.
Bouchama, Kamal. *Le FLN a-t-il Jamais eu le Pouvoir/1962/92.* Alger: Al Maarifa, 1995.
Boudiaf, Mohamed. *Oú va l'Algerie?* Librairie de l'Etoile, 1964.
Courrière, Yves. *L'heure des Colonels.* Paris: Fayard, 1967.
Courrière, Yves. *Les Feux du désespoirs.* Paris: Fayard, 1971.
Courrière, Yves. *Le Temps des Léopards.* Paris: Rombaldi, 1976.
Dahleb, Saad. *Pour l'indépendance de l'Algérie, mission accomplice.* Alger: Ed Dahleb, 1990.
Harbi, Mohamed. *Le FLN Mirage et Réalité, des Origenes á la Prise du Pouvoir ed.* Naqd/enal 1993.
Harbi, Mohamad. *Aux Origines du FLN, le Populisme, Révolutionnaire en Algérie.* Paris: Christian Bourgeois, 1975.
Harbi, Mohamad. *Les Archives de la Révolution Algérienne.* Paris: Jeune Afrique, 1981.
Kaddache, Mahfoud. *Histoire du Nationalisme Alggérien* 2. Alger: Ed Enal.
Layachi, Azzedine. "Ethnicité et Politique en Algérie, Entre L'inclusion et Particularisme Redjala, Ramdane." *L'Opposition en Algerie Depuis 1962.* Alger: Ed Rahma, 1988–.
Sari, Djilali. *Le Désatre Démographique.* Alger: Ed Sned, 1982.
Yefsah, Abdelkader. *La Question du Pouvoir en Algérie.* En. A.P. Edition, 1990.

PART II

Neighboring States

CHAPTER 7

Institutional Incentive and Attitudinal Deterrents: Parties and Democracy in Israel

Yael Yishai

INTRODUCTION

The year 2008 was a thorny one for Israeli democracy. President Moshe Katzav was forced to resign after being accused of sexual harassment; Finance Minister Avraham Hirchson was tried for financial fraud; and Prime Minister Ehud Olmert was subject to six corruption investigations. This incomplete list reveals the depth of leadership crisis in the country. Public opinion surveys show a growing discontent with the political process, as well as a substantial loss of faith in political leaders. Political parties, the vestiges of democratic politics in Israel since the prestate era, appear to be ineffective in rectifying the situation and restoring faith in democratic institutions. This chapter will address the role parties play in Israel's democracy.

That political parties are crucial for democracy is almost a truism. In a widely cited comment, E. E. Schattschneider noted that "political parties created democracy and modern democracy is unthinkable save in terms of political parties."[1] It has been generally agreed that parties are inevitable, and that democratic government cannot work without them. Cases of democratization, where parties were attributed privileged position within the democratic institutions, provide an unequivocal testimony of their importance.[2] In their capacity as the main tier of democratic politics, parties play a mediating role, providing linkage between society and state.[3] In doing so, they shape the political agenda, recruit leaders, and organize stable and effective governance. These functions, however, are not confined to democratic regimes. The People's

Action Party in Singapore, the Communist Party in North Korea, and even the Patriotic Front in Zimbabwe were all engaged in setting the political agenda, recruiting leaders, and forming a government. The test of democracy should be sought in the linkage of parties to society. Do parties provide adequate representation to minor and marginal groups? Do they encourage individuals to participate in the electoral process and educate them with regard to political choices?[4] Put differently, do parties perform their participatory linkage?[5] It is to these questions that this chapter addresses itself by observing parties and democracy in Israel.

Political parties act within a legal framework, inhibiting or encouraging the fulfillment of their democratic functions. The major argument of this chapter is that Israel has established an institutional-legal framework that provides a congenial environment for democratic partisanship. An extreme proportional electoral system allows organized groups easy access to elected institutions. State law gives wide leeway to parties, and state funding further enhances their capacity to mobilize support. These arrangements made parties representative, in the sense that they mirror the composition of the population. But they have not been effective in terms of socializing the public and securing legitimacy for the democratic process. In the absence of legitimacy, they are unlikely to settle crises such as the one in which Israel is currently engulfed.

The analysis of political parties' contribution to democracy in Israel will proceed as follows: First, the historical and contemporary characteristics of the party system will be reviewed. Then the institutional aspects of partisan activity will be discussed, with its resulting high representativeness. Next, public attitudes toward parties will be explored. These include trust in parties, electoral turnout, and support of antiparty parties. Finally, a brief answer will be provided to the question why things went wrong in an attempt to understand what has happened to party development in a nation which formerly served as a vivid example of a "party state."

THE PARTY SYSTEM IN ISRAEL: HISTORY AND DEVELOPMENT

The story of political parties in Israel is that of continuity and change. Institutional structures have remained practically intact since independence (1948), but functions have been altered and power configurations have undergone changes. Two prominent factors mold the structure and functions of political parties in Israel: ethnic cleavages and the security imperative. These two factors were sustained by a legal framework that evolved during the state's history.

From its inception Israel has been an immigrants' society, with Jews arriving literally from all corners of the world. The raison d'être for establishing a Jewish state was to provide a safe haven for all Jews who chose to immigrate. In addition to those who arrived in the early days of Zionism, mainly from Eastern Europe, there were Holocaust refugees, people from Arab-speaking countries who found it difficult to remain in their country of origin after the escalation of the Arab-Israeli conflict, Jews from the former Soviet Union, who took advantage of the opening gate and emigrated to Israel, and Jews from Ethiopia. This incomplete list demonstrates only one aspect of the demographic variety in the country. People of Israel are also divided along national and religious lines, with an Arab minority comprising about one-fifth of the population and orthodox Jews distinct from the secular majority. All these divisions have structured the party map and served as a basis for political mobilization. Political parties were formed when the Zionist settlement in prestate Israel was still in its infancy. Whereas in the United States, for example, parties were regarded as an unpleasant reality, a hardy weed that sprouts up in what would otherwise be the well-tended garden of democratic institutions, in Israel they constituted the essence of the democratic haven. The debate over the role of political parties in the process of nation building had already been settled in those early days. Fulfilling an important absorptive function, political parties played a vital role in the provision of services, particularly, but not exclusively, to new immigrants, from the cradle to the grave. In fact, Israel constituted a good example of a "party state,"[6] in which parties fulfill social, economic, and cultural roles as well as political ones. Political parties were all-encompassing organizations, on whose allocation of benefits the population depended.

In the years following independence, the ruling party Mapai, a moderate socialist party, was the epitome of a dominant party. It was the largest vote getter, the key ingredient of any government coalition, the standard bearer of the society's goals, and the articulator of its aspirations.[7] Mapai also had the political advantages of a united and integrated leadership; a broad-based, well-functioning, and flexible political organization; and most important, it had no serious opposition. The party had control over the major economic and human resources flowing into the country from the United States and Germany, as compensation to Holocaust survivors.

However, ineffective party organization and internal disputes over political leadership led to Mapai's decline. In 1977, an upheaval occurred when Likud (former Herut) replaced Labour and took control of the government. The demise of Mapai (by then termed Labour) was attributed to several factors, including the bureaucratization of the state, which made parties redundant in the absorption process. The party, furthermore, was blamed for the plight of the immigrants from Asia and Africa (the Sephardim) who, despite absorption efforts, remained far behind their European counterparts. Their defection to Likud was another major reason for the political upheaval.

Likud was initially an antiestablishment party, serving as a blatant (though weak) opposition to the ruling Mapai, which attracted the votes of the veteran, mostly well-to-do Israelis. In 1977, it started to establish itself as the "party of the people," catering to the needs of marginalized groups. It successfully replaced Labour not only in the control of government, but also in providing an epoch, a doctrine, and an influence on public life. It also gave a clear voice to up to then marginal groups in society, particularly to the Sephardim, many of whom were recruited to party leadership positions.[8] Political parties played an integrative social role by enabling members of deprived groups to join mainstream politics, but at the same time they contributed to social segregation. Increasingly, parties were identified with socioeconomic indicators where the haves voted for Labour and the have-nots tended to support Likud.

The advent of Likud to power had a profound impact on the partisan map. At present, Israel is no longer a one-party state. Since 1977, the two major parties, in various forms, alignments, and coalitions, have alternated in control of the government. Yet despite shifts in leadership, in constituency, and in electoral style, Labour and Likud are firmly rooted in their historical origins. As noted by Arian, "their ideas, vocabulary, organization, and imagery come from the first half of this [20th] century and not the second. Their political world is one with a strong and leading socialist party and a beleaguered but persistent right."[9]

The number of parties has also remained stable. In the election to the first Knesset (1949), with an electorate of some half a million, the number of parties represented in parliament was 12. In 2006 (17th Knesset), with some 5 million eligible voters, the number of parties represented in the Knesset was still precisely 12. As in the past, partisan makeup reflects with great accuracy the map of social cleavages. Parties represent the two peoples living in the country (Jews and Arabs), the religious and the secular, the well-to-do and the blue-collar workers, the new immigrants, the advocates of territorial concessions, and the proponents of hard-line policies toward the Palestinians. Many parties cater to narrow social or ideological interests. At present, besides the two "establishment" parties—Likud and Labour—there are three Arab parties, two "Russian" lists, three parties representing the religious constituency, and one pensioners' party. The advocates of extreme militant solutions to the Israel-Palestine conflict are represented by three small parties, one party is adamantly pro-peace, and there are other small parties not mentioned here. Social cleavages continue to cultivate distinct lists, shaping both the structure and the agenda of political parties in Israel.

Security constraints have been the second factor affecting the party system. The Arab-Jewish conflict started with the first wave of Jewish immigration to then Palestine. The Independence War reflected its intensity and scope. Since its establishment, Israel has expended a sizable portion of its national income on defense, with repercussions on alternative budgetary items. A mandatory conscription to the army for both women and men makes it "a nation in arms." The fact that bloody wars erupt every few years accentuates the security imperative.

The prominence of the defense issue on the national agenda had two ramifications regarding party politics: First, in line with consociational theory, parties formed an unstable alignment, contributing to a shaky coexistence between various strands of opinion. At the same time, however, the unresolved conflict animated the radicalization of the political map and intensified. Political parties were formed on both ends of the political spectrum. Some advocate the replacement of Israel by a secular-democratic state, implying the eradication of Israel as a Jewish state. Adversely, right-wing parties support the exclusion of Arabs from the democratic process. The fact that the security issue is so central in Israeli politics also framed the parties' agenda. Identifying with a party entailed the adoption of a certain stance on the Arab-Israeli conflict. This was the case not only with regard to the margins of the political spectrum, but also to the "catch all" parties, often in control of government. Voting for Likud, by and large, implies orientation toward a militant solution to the conflict; supporting Labour denotes willingness to retreat from the occupied territories.

To sum up, while Israel is no longer a party state in terms of the functions parties perform in encapsulating citizens, it has maintained many of its past characteristics. To a large extent parties still cater to social cleavages, be they ethnic, national, or religious. They also reflect clear stances on the perpetual Arab-Israeli conflict.

THE INSTITUTIONAL CONTEXT

Parties in Israel operate within a congenial institutional context that enables them to perform a constructive role in sustaining democracy. Four legal (or semilegal) arrangements provide institutional incentives to party democracy: the electoral system, parties' legal regulation, party finance, and leadership recruitment.

Electoral System

Israel has an extreme proportional electoral system based on nationwide proportional representation. Any party participating in an election is entitled to representation if it passes the qualifying threshold, which is currently set at 2% of the eligible vote. Until the 13th Knesset (1992), the threshold was only 1% and remained at 1.5% until the 16th Knesset (2003), which raised it to 2%.

The origins of the rigid proportional system are rooted in the prestate era in which various political organizations struggled to preserve their independence. It was the deliberate intention of the political leadership to grant representation even to minor, and perhaps trivial, groups. The justification given for the large number of parties that resulted from the system was that in a period in which far-reaching and rapid changes were taking place in the population make up as a result of immigration, it was important to enable maximum representation for various groups and opinions. It was also important to obtain the maximum possible consent of various groups to the dramatic steps that were about to be taken, particularly the declaration of independence. During the 60 years of sovereignty, pressures have been exerted to change the electoral system, but all have proved abortive. Minor parties refused to give up their rights to be represented in the national decision-making body.

Legal Regulation of Parties

In 1992, the Knesset enacted a Parties' Law, which mandates newly formed lists to register as a political party with the party registrar, a statutory official. The main provision of the law, subject to much debate and litigation, is that the parties' goals should not violate Israel's status as a Jewish and democratic state. This clause appears to demonstrate strong state involvement in parties' goals. However, on only a handful of occasions has the state implemented the option of obstructing the establishment of new parties. Only in cases of clear racist overtones against Israeli Arabs were parties denied the right to run for Knesset elections. Although parties are required to operate in good faith and reasonableness and in accordance with the principles of equality, the state gave them wide leeway.

The law does not involve itself in the internal governance of parties or in the way they manage themselves. It is sufficient that the party possesses a charter that establishes its basic structural arrangements, including the manner in which Knesset candidates are selected. Parties in Israel are given a considerable degree of autonomy and freedom to handle their own affairs.[10] Israeli law strengthens the status of political parties by granting them legal status, by protecting their legal rights, and by allowing them freedom of action.

Party Finance

The Parties' Finance Law (1993) adds further vigor to political parties. The introduction of public subsidies to political parties has often been described as one of the important developments of modern democracy. Israel was one of the first countries to introduce fixed party financing. The number of members of the Knesset (MKs) a party has serves as the basis for funding, but financial aid is also given to aspiring lists, to provide them with seed money that will enable them to propagate their message. Between 1973 and 1998, a steady increase in party funding was evident. Relative to the number of voters nationwide, the public grants allocated to political parties in Israel were noted to be the highest in the world.[11] The parties that initiated public funding hold the purse strings by ensuring themselves absolute discretion in the use of money. State funds have no conditions attached, and the parties are not obliged to publish their accounts, only to report their expenditure to the state comptroller. In 1998, the authority to determine the "finance unit" upon which allocation to parties is based was transferred from the Knesset to a public committee chaired by a Chief Justice. But the manner in which the money is used remained solely at the discretion of parties themselves.

Candidate Selection

Candidate selection processes are not directly regulated by Israeli law although there are legal provisions that apply to their financing. Leadership recruitment is part of the institutional environment because it is grounded in partisan regulations and delineates the context in which parties operate. In the past, the way to get on a party's list was to be appointed by its top leadership. The list, made up by an appointment committee, was presented to a party institution for approval, which was automatically given. Israeli parties were undemocratic in the sense that a narrow oligarchy made up lists in smoked-filled rooms.

A major break in that pattern occurred in 1977 after a newly formed party (Democratic Movement for Change) introduced primary elections. It took several years and a gradual process until the two big parties, Labour and Likud, reformed their procedures for the selection of candidates in a manner that democratized the nominating process.

In 1992, the Labour Party adopted primaries enabling party members to decide the composition and rank of the candidate list on the basis of competition for positions allotted to the winners in a national contest and in several territorial and sectarian districts. Likud adopted party primaries, giving dues-paying party members the right to decide the composition and rank of the candidate list on 1993. In 1996, both Likud and Labour used primary elections to select their Knesset candidates. They both used a mixed national-district system. Members had multiple votes, but the party institutions had almost no role to play in them, other than approving the rules and supervising the election. Both parties held membership censuses that ended close to the day of primary elections.[12] The law partially regulates the financial aspect of the primaries, but parties are free to adopt a system in line with its members' or leaders' wishes. Religious parties do not have primaries, relying instead on rabbinical decision making. The freedom parties are given in this matter clearly reflects the autonomy they are granted by the state.

In conclusion, the structural aspects of party politics in Israel vividly reflect the factors underlying their evolution. The electoral system mirrors the heterogeneity of Israeli society and the wish of its founders to enable the inhabitants of the fledgling state to participate in political life. Legal regulation has been aimed at providing political parties, the touchstones of nation building, a sound and stable basis for activity. Party finance was adopted to manifest the salience of political parties in public life: The generous funding provided reminds Israelis of the role played by the parties in Israel's history. Leadership selection procedures, although not imposed by law, made the parties more susceptible to public input by expanding the size of the internal electorate. Judged by the institutional framework, political parties in Israel should be at the forefront of the democratic process. They have excellent chances of winning Knesset seats, their status is protected by law, they are funded, and they are free to adopt a leadership recruitment process suitable to their style and ideology.

Parties' contribution to democracy will be judged, as recalled, by reference to their representativeness, legitimacy, and role in inspiring participation.

REPRESENTATION: THE SECTORAL PARTIES

As noted above, Israel is divided along ethnic, national, and religious lines. According to the Ethnic Tension Index, Israel ranks very high, second only to Thailand.[13] The question under concern is whether these divisions find expression within the party system. The answer, briefly stated, is that Israel is currently moving toward more representation of minorities, and social groups are increasingly gaining weight both in internal party organization and on the national arena.

Ethnic Parties

Ethnicity here refers to the cleavage between Jews on the basis of country of origin and to the formation of Jewish parties reflecting those differences (not to national differences, as between Jewish parties and Arab parties). Although most Jews in Israel are second- (if not third-) generation native born, ethnic identity is still relevant for many voters. Three distinct groups are germane to party politics: Jews originating in Europe-America (the Ashkenazi), those from Asia-Africa, and those from the former states of the Soviet Union. The members of the first group do not constitute a numerical majority, but they also do not cultivate an ethnic identity. They are the "haves," controlling institutions of power. This is not the case with the Sephardim, whose parents (or grandparents) immigrated from Arab-speaking countries, nor with those who emigrated from the former Soviet Union.

Initially, Mapai, the dominant ruling party, fulfilled a major aggregative role, paying no heed to ethnic cleavages. Integration was all-encompassing. As noted by Medding, "The activities of the party branch embraced much of the member's social life and were his major source of information and guidance in political and social affairs. His employment, friendships, cultural interests and leisure hours were all deeply influenced by his party membership."[14] This applied to newcomers and veterans alike, to city and village dwellers, to young and old. The party was successful in performing its brokerage function not only because it captured a significant portion of the electorate, but also because it was able to manipulate the state to provide resources to its adherents. Minority groups had no access to the corridors of power or to the barrel of assets. They were mostly passive recipients of commodities and values, which, according to their view, were incompatible with their needs.

Attempts by Sephardic and other ethnic leaders to run ethnic lists with the support of new immigrants had only token success. In the first national elections (1949), a United Sephardic Party gained four mandates and a Yemenite list won one parliamentary seat. But in the next election (1951), the ethnic vote had already been absorbed by the veteran parties, particularly Mapai. Autonomous ethnic lists failed to pass the blocking percentage, and their appeal was not translated into particular ethnic demands. Ethnic identification was not a source of pride and dignity.

In 1984, a short-lived Sephardic party emerged (Tami) followed by Shas, which for the first time in Israeli history succeeded in mobilizing the Sephardim to vote on ethnic grounds. Part of its success may be attributed to the fact that it added religious symbols into its plank, thus expanding its constituency. In contrast to former ethnic parties, Shas institutionalized and became part and parcel of the party map. Shas is now a significant force in Israeli politics,[15] using traditional strategies to enlist support. It encapsulates its supporters with a wide network of community organizations, including schools, adult education programs, welfare services, and so forth. These institutions spur the members to value their ethnic identity and enable the party to maintain its power.

Ethnic parties became much more prominent in the 1990s, when the Russian immigrants sought representation via party channels. During the 1990s, Israel absorbed approximately a million immigrants from the former Soviet Union, constituting then about 20% of the population. Although the veteran parties attempted to capture the Russian vote, hoping to repeat the absorption of the new immigrants, their attempt proved to be futile. The success of the Russian immigrant party Yisrael Ba'Aliyah (Israel on the rise, or Israel in immigration) in the 1996 elections was unprecedented in the history of Israeli political parties. Never in the almost five decades of sovereignty had a group of relatively recent immigrants gained seven Knesset seats. Despite the socioeconomic and geographic variety, some 38% of the new immigrants supported the Russian immigrant party.[16] In sharp contrast to the past, when the overwhelming majority of the then immigrants gave their vote to the established veteran parties and shied away from immigrant parties, in 1996 ethnic solidarity flourished. Ethnic representation by political parties was in full swing.

The reasons for this turnabout are rooted both in institutional circumstances and in the immigrants' background. In 1996, direct election of the prime minister was introduced (to be annulled in 1999), enabling the voters to identify with mainstream politics and give vent to their own aspirations at the same time. The two ballots gave the voter a chance of splitting the vote, thereby expressing two different preferences.

Second, the newcomers of the 1990s were different from earlier waves of immigration. The Russian immigrants were far more educated than previous immigrants and most had worked in white-collar occupations in their country of origin. They developed a subculture, sticking to their own language and customs. Many of them had only a single Jewish grandparent and practiced Christianity rather than Judaism. They had their own school system, theaters, shops, and orchestras. They attempted to preserve their traditional way of life, regarding themselves superior to the native culture. Financial constraints also impelled political mobilization. The arrival of a mass of people in a short timespan strained the economy and overloaded its capacity to absorb and integrate. These circumstances facilitated a wide-scale mobilization process. The immigrants had real grievances regarding their economic plight. Having lived under a totalitarian regime, they were accustomed to political socialization and were readily available to charismatic leadership. Their breach with veteran Israelis was deep, and—from their point of view—would remain so. Party representation was perceived as an adequate pathway to promote seclusion, while at the same time practicing integration.

Seven years later (in the 2006 election), Russian communal politics was still evident. Admittedly the "Israelization" of the new immigrants had its momentum, and many of them were no longer in economic distress. In fact, many of them (42% to 45% of the total Russian vote) cast a ballot for mainstream parties, demonstrating their incorporation into Israeli society. But Yisrael Ba'Aliyah continued to be a community consensus party, attracting the vote of nearly half the Russians (48.4%).[17] The party of their choice was termed the "Russian party with an Israeli accent,"[18] revealing the desire of the Russian immigrants to integrate into the host society while simultaneously preserving the attributes of their own community.

Arab Parties

Arabs in Israel comprised in 2007 some 20% of the population. They are the most distinct group in the crisscross of Israeli society. The Arabs differ from the Jews on the basis of language, culture, geography, religion, political identity, and national aspirations. Political mobilization of Arabs was slow to emerge. During the formative years of the state (1948–1966), they were subject to military rule, which gave them minimal leeway to organize politically. Although there were some Arab lists during that period, they were for all practical purposes extensions of Mapai and did not represent the Arab constituency. Voting for a Jewish party was instrumental at that time, serving the collective and individual interests of the Arabs. Consequently, voter turnout was high (85% on the average) and four-fifths of the votes were cast for Jewish parties.

After the abolition of military rule (in 1966), an informal control system preserved this pattern for another decade,[19] although with growing erosion in its effectiveness. Both turnout and voting for Jewish parties dropped considerably. In the context of the debate over the occupied territories, and in view of the then electoral deadlock between the two major parties—Labour and Likud—two processes have emerged. First, Jewish parties, particularly the Labour Party, opened their gates to Arab representatives. The introduction of primaries accelerated this process with individual prospective candidates courting the Arab vote.[20] Simultaneously, Arabs have begun to shape their ethnonational identities via the partisan channel.

Admittedly, already in the 1950s there were buds of political self-actualization when the Arabs, organized mainly within the Communist Party, demanded the de-Zionizing of the Jewish state and aligning it with the Soviet bloc. But this party was aggregative in the sense it insisted on its Jewish-Arab composition. Although the party developed an Arab nationalist narrative, its purpose was not radical, but based on a demand for full equality for Arabs within Israel: the Jewish state. Across time the Communist Party, in its different forms and titles, gradually boosted its national attributes. By the mid-1970s, it became the single largest Arab party with a steady support of about one-third of the Arab electorate. Simultaneously, it has become a distinct Arab party, representing Arab demands. Although at present there is one Jew in its Knesset faction, the rate of support among the Jewish constituency is extremely low.

In the 1980s, and increasingly during the 1990s, Arab representation in the Knesset proliferated and simultaneously became more accentuated. The breakdown of the Soviet empire, the revival of the political Islamic movements, including one in Israel, the breakout of the first *intifada* (rebellion) in the occupied territories, and the active interest of the Palestine Liberation Organization (PLO) in the elections in Israel promulgated these shifts on the Arab electoral scene.[21] Since the 1990s, Arab voters have had a choice of various political parties. In 2006, for the first time a total of 10 mandates were gained by Arab parties (this number excludes Arabs elected to the Knesset on Jewish parties' lists). These represent three Arab lists. First is Hadash, previously the Communist Party under different titles, whose fortunes are somewhat declining. The second party is Balad (National Democratic Assembly), a nationalist party dedicated to fighting "Israelization" of Arabs. This party is the most radical of the three parties, demanding the replacement of Israel by a secular democratic state, which in practice implies the eradication of its Jewish attributes. The party also seeks to change the Jewish symbols of the state and to recognize Israeli Arabs as a national minority presided over by an elected assembly and executive. The United Arab List, allied with the Arab Movement for Change, is the third party. It presented a religious Islamic alternative to the more secular Hadash and Balad. It is at present the party with the most votes in the Arab sector. According to one commentator, its electoral success may be linked to the electoral gains of other Islamist parties in the region, most notably the Hamas in the Palestinian Authority.[22]

The Arab party map undergoes constant changes. Space limitations preclude the description of all mergers, alliances, and splits that took place during the past decade. Despite the schism among the Arab electorate, Arab parties are united on two issues: opposition to the discriminatory approach of the state and support of the Palestinian cause. These parties provide a clear and present channel of interest articulation for the Arab population. They offer a variety of ideological and social profiles, giving Arabs a genuine opportunity to raise their voice without expressing their loyalty.

Religious Parties

The proportion of the observant population among the Israeli Jews is estimated at around 30%. Despite the fact that a significant majority of the population observe some of the religious tenets (such as fasting on Yom Kippur), a clear, albeit not dichotomous, distinction can be made between religious and secular Jews. Religious representation in Israel is clearly on the rise. Between 1949 and 1973, the average representation of religious parties in the Knesset was 14.4 delegates. Between 1977 and 2006, it rose to an average of 24.7 MKs. Three reasons account for this growth: first, the integrative role of religious parties; second, the expansion of issues; and third, demographic processes.

Religious parties in Israel act as "camp parties,"[23] which do not settle for merely enlisting support during election campaigns, but are dynamic in a wide range of socioeconomic spheres such a employment, health and housing, as well as in sociocultural spheres like education. The linkage between religious parties and their constituency is thus two-edged. By virtue of the services they provide, the parties encapsulate their supporters and shield them from outside influence by forming an "enclave" that presents itself not only in the form of identity and cultural norms but also in terms of geographic context, a separate educational system, and a distinct way of life.[24] At the same time, however, they fulfill their representation function with a great measure of success. They raise the genuine, and often exclusive, voice of their adherents. Needless to say, an overwhelming majority of the relevant constituency votes for each party.

Religious parties have also expanded the issues they promote, a process leading to expansion of their electorates. In the past, the religious constituency was represented by two main parties: the National Religious Party (NRP), catering to the interests of the religious-Zionist voters, and Agudat Israel, representing the ultraorthodox non-Zionist constituency. Both parties enjoyed organizational and electoral stability. In the 1980s, with the entrance of Shas to the electoral scene, religious parties started to attract nonobservant voters. In the pre-1980 era, the definition of what constitutes a religious party was straightforward when leaders, electorate, and policy reflected religious mores and interests. This distinction is much less valid today with the expansion of the religious cause to both ethnic and nationalist directions. Shas is an ultraorthodox party so far as its leadership and parliamentary delegates are concerned. Its policies also cater to the interests of the religious constituency. However, the makeup of its electorate indicates that about half its voters are not religious.[25] They regard Shas as an ethnic party appealing to their identity as Sephardi Jews. Worth noting is that within a short period of time Shas became the largest religious party. Its continuing success "stands out because the Israeli political arena is renowned as a cemetery for new parties most of which fail to survive longer than two campaigns."[26]

In contrast, the NRP is religious in terms of its Knesset members, as well as in the composition of its constituency. Yet, the party is classified as right wing rather than religious, with Greater Israel at the center of its plank. The party has attracted a large measure of support among the secular right-wing voters. Only Agudat Israel is a full-fledged religious party in terms of leadership, voters, and ideology, catering to the interests of the ultraobservant community. This party, however, refuses to join any governing coalition and prefers to watch the political game from the outside, maintaining its pure ideological and social exclusiveness. What works best for this party is the demographic advantage.

In 2002, the ultrareligious population (aged 20 and upper) accounted for 6% of the Jewish total, yet its number of births was threefold—18%.[27] A recent social survey of the Central Bureau of Statistics shows that the ultraorthodox portion of the total Jewish population now stands at 8%. However, in the 20–29 age group, that proportion rises to 10.6%.[28] Furthermore, nearly 20% of the secondary school students are ultraorthodox and even more study in the moderate religious school system.[29] To recapitulate, the religious constituency in Israel has achieved clear and incontrovertible representation. Religious parties were extremely successful in mobilizing the orthodox vote. This success results from the "enclave" culture that ties voters to religious parties, from the expansion of issues, particularly the growing association between religiosity and ultranationalism and from the demographic advantage.

Discussion of the representative function of political parties in Israel cannot end without reference to a phenomenon that is perhaps not unique to Israel, but is very prominent on the national scene: "interest parties."[30] The term refers to what in effect is an interest group running candidates for legislative elections. Although it assumes the title and function of a party, the group remains focused on the quest for private benefits for a single issue. Such groups, reflecting a variety of interests, have often become parties, presenting lists to the Knesset elections. Among them have been groups as diverse as cab drivers, the disabled, potential drug abusers, divorced men, and Ethiopian immigrants, all seeking power through the partisan channel. Conspicuously absent from the list are women, who only rarely used the partisan channel as a means for promoting their interests.[31] The pensioners, however, have been particularly successful at aggregating their interests. There were several attempts in the past to mobilize the retirees' support for a Knesset list. In 2006, these attempts proved very successful as the Retirees Party gained seven mandates.[32] Despite the impressive electoral gains (forecast to be temporary), the pensioners constitute for all practical purposes an interest party.

To sum up, political parties in Israel did secure a considerable measure of representation. The three big sectors, identified on the bases of ethnicity, nationality, and religiosity, as well as members of other social groups, succeeded in articulating their interests by using the partisan channel. Does this process contribute to democracy? The answer is equivocal. Some critics regard sectorialism as a democratic deficiency because it inhibits intra- and interparty aggregative processes. They attribute all social and political malaise to internal divisions within society. Unity is often perceived as a panacea that provides peace and prosperity to all. Others, however, are content with the wide opportunity available for dissidents to influence "from within" and become legal, and legitimate, members of the political establishment. This is the voice that presumably averts exit.

LEGITIMACY: DISENCHANTMENT WITH POLITICAL PARTIES

The question of parties and democracy remains relevant, despite the gloomy mood of party scholars. As noted by Dalton and Weldon, "there is a long history of anti-party sentiment from Rousseau to Madison that criticizes the mischief of faction and the ways parties can impede the democratic process."[33] Contemporary scholars also question parties' general contribution to democracy's well-being.[34] Skepticism is corroborated by voluminous literature indicating a growing disenchantment with parties among western democracies. Parties are often seen as both the institution most susceptible to corruption[35] and the one least trusted by the public. Parties, in fact, have increasingly been defined as semistate agencies[36] rather than representatives of the people. A significant decline in both membership in, and identification with, political parties has been widely noticed. Has Israel escaped this fate? The answer is largely negative. As elsewhere, there is a considerable reduction in political parties' popularity, having three manifestations: public trust, party membership, and party identification. Data presented here are derived mainly from the annual Democracy Index based on surveys conducted by the Israel Democratic Institute.[37]

Public Trust

Political parties enjoy the least trust among political institutions. In 2004, 32% stated that they trust parties to a large degree or to some degree; in 2006, 22% did so and in 2008 a record low of 15% trusted parties. Some 40% of the respondents stated that they have no trust at all in political parties. Segmentation of distrust shows it is more prevalent among the ultraorthodox (although, as we have seen, they are adequately represented in the Knesset!) and among those with lower educational attainments. But disenchantment with political parties is not associated with political apathy. In the World Value Survey, 70% of the respondents in Israel reported they are interested in politics to a large or to some extent, the highest rate in western countries.[38] As noted by the authors of the report on democracy, "skeptical attitudes toward the parties are woven into the web of the public's high interest in politics."[39] It is precisely the parties that are the source of discontent.

Party Membership and Party Identification

As a result of the worsening image of parties, membership has declined from a height of 18% in 1969 to 16% in 1973, to 10% in 1981, to 8% in 1988, and to only 6% in 2006.[40]

Attachment to political parties was also examined by tabulating closeness to a particular political party. Data reveal an ongoing trend of decline in the number of people who see themselves as close to a particular party, suggesting a weakening of the party structure in general, not only for specific parties. In 1996, 64% of the respondents stated that they see themselves close to a particular party. The survey also gauged the extent of closeness. To a question asking respondents to indicate how close they feel to their particular party of choice, 37% answered "very close" in 1996. A decade later, the drop in attachment was clearly visible as less than a quarter reported high closeness.[41] Furthermore, in the 1980s, about 30% said that the most influential factor in their voting was identification with the party, whereas only 25% said that in 2006.[42]

All these data sum up to a gloomy picture of legitimacy. Parties are perhaps perceived as an essential evil, without which government cannot be formed, but they hardly attract sufficient legitimacy to enable them to play a key role in democratic life.

PARTICIPATION: LESS IN QUANTITY AND DIFFERENT IN QUALITY

The political malaise, with voters being critical of the polity in general and of political parties in particular, reveals the obstacles facing parties in fulfilling their democratic tasks. Disenchanted individuals can react in two ways: They can abstain from voting by keeping away from the ballot, or they can vote for "antiparty parties," channeling discontent in a democratic manner. These parties enable the disaffected to participate in the political process by alternative means of representation, instead of abandoning party politics altogether. As will be shown below, Israelis have resorted mainly to abstention to express their discontent. They have been more reluctant to vote for an antiparty.

Abstention: Ever Lower Voter Turnout

Political participation is the opportunity given to citizens to express their political preferences, as democracy is about ensuring popular sovereignty through regular and intensive participation of the great mass of people.[43] Although many strategies are available in democracies for citizens to communicate their views and influence decision-making processes, casting a ballot is one of the conspicuous ways to assess citizens' participation. Elections are critical junctures where individuals take stock of their various political attitudes and preferences and transform them into a single vote choice. One of the parties' primary tasks in a democracy is vote structuring, which is successfully achieved when they efficiently mobilize voters to cast their ballots. Low voter turnout might be indicative of a relatively low structuring capacity.[44] Abstaining from voting, common among Western democracies,[45] is one result of the declining role of political parties in democratic regimes. Comparative data reveal that turnout in elections has generally decreased across the advanced industrial democracies, especially over the past decade.[46] Citizens' refusal to vote was attributed to the weakening of social ties, the lack of public trust in the traditional party and parliamentary political system, and to a growing inclination to resort to alternative, extraparliamentary activity.

Data derived from the Inter-Parliamentary Union regarding voter turnout in 36 countries, within the period 1949–2006, show that Israel is no exception. In fact, it is placed in the lowest third of the scale, between Canada and Ireland,[47] in terms of voter turnout. Furthermore, a temporal analysis reveals a significant drop in voter turnout in Israel during the same period. In the first elections (1949), Israelis flocked to the polls, with 86.9% voting. Citizens were motivated to participate in the electoral process by enthusiasm for their recently acquired sovereignty and the wish to grant legitimacy to the new state. During the first 20 years of statehood, until the elections to the 7th Knesset (1969), the average voter turnout was over 80%. During the following two decades (until 1999), voter turnout declined somewhat to 78.8%. Since 2000, a substantial decrease in electoral participation is evident. In the 2003 (the 16th) Knesset elections, turnout was low: 67.8%, and three years later, in the elections to the 17th Knesset in March 2006, it reached a record low of 63%. These data represent a trend of increasing indifference to, and alienation from, elections and political parties.[48] Divided as abstention is across parties, they also represent a tendency of dissociation not from a specific political party, but from the entire party spectrum.

Electoral Choices: Antiparty Parties

Calling parties "antiparty parties" refers not to their position on the partisan map but to their ideologies. Antiparty parties are simply "anti: anti-establishment, anti-elite, anti-state, anti-politics, anti-anything outside their campaigns."[49] They are perceived as acting outside the party system, although they are themselves part of it. Some of them, particularly right-wing parties, describe themselves as victims of exclusion and use exceptionally aggressive tones in their messages. Others are content to present an antiestablishment novelty. They are the ones that will remedy the system and provide cures for its ailments. They too cater to the interests of those holding grievances against the partisan establishment yet are willing to play by the rules and cast a vote.

Antiestablishment parties were visible particularly (but not solely) on the right end of the political spectrum. The nonliberal context of the Israeli democracy and the divisive cut of its society create fertile ground for the growth of extreme parties. Furthermore, Israel's character as a Jewish and democratic state is also a source of constant antiestablishment agitation. The majority of religious parties would prefer Israel to be a Jewish state while forgoing its democratic principles, and most Arab parties would rather see Israel as a democratic state while relinquishing its Jewish attributes. The overwhelming majority of Israeli parties acted within a delicate balance, recognizing both the Jewish character of the state of Israel and its democratic commitments. Yet, there have been a few occurrences of antiestablishment parties, the most noticeable of which was Kach—an ultraright party in the 1980s.

Meir Kahane, leader of the militant Jewish Defense League in the United States, founded Kach. Kahane brought with him a new rhetoric and violent political style previously unknown to Israeli society or political life. The major goal of his party was to encourage (if necessary by force) Arab emigration in exchange for property remuneration. Kach alleged that the deportation of Arabs was the only feasible course toward a genuine resolution for the future of the Jewish nation, as the two people could not occupy the same land.[50] Kach ran for Knesset representation in 1981 but failed to pass the threshold (1% of the vote). Kahane was not successfully integrated within Israeli society, nor was he able to mobilize an adequate supporting public. In the next elections (1984), however, Kach successfully overcame judicial and political hurdles. The party was represented in the Knesset, albeit by one delegate—Kahane himself. Freedom of speech and expression overruled the revulsion he aroused among the Israeli public and law makers. Legal means were taken, however, to prevent future representation of racist parties. The Knesset introduced an amendment to the Basic Law stipulating that "a list of candidates will not take part in the elections to the Knesset if their goals or actions include, explicitly or implicitly, incitement to racism." On the basis of this amendment (1985), Kach was disqualified from competing. In line with the theory on antiparty parties, Kach disguised its racist ideology by hiding behind the democratic curtain.[51] As Kach continued to espouse the forcible expulsion of Israeli Arabs, it was banned from presenting an electoral list on the elections to the 10th Knesset (1988). But that was not the end of the militant antipolitical establishment parties.

The demise of Kach was followed by its splinter—Kahana Hai, which was a "flash party" not surviving the test of time, and by Moledet, which, in fact, was incorporated into the political establishment. Kahana Hai was disqualified by the Central Election Committee on account of its anti-Arab stance. In contrast, Moledet found its way to the heart of Israeli politics. It was founded by Major General (res.) Rechav'am Ze'evi, a revered war hero well integrated into Israel's social milieu. Fearing that the demographic scale would tip in favor of the Arabs, Moledet proposed to elicit voluntary transfer, spurred by generous financial compensation of both Israeli Arabs and Palestinians living in the occupied territories. Moledet distanced itself from Kach both socially and politically, claiming its policy positions are rooted in Zionist history. Appeals to disqualify the party have been abortive. Moledet survived a decade as an independent party and later integrated into the National Unity Party, thus ceasing to be an antiestablishment party. According to Pedahzur, the party's statements in the Knesset did not include straightforward racist messages or a genuine challenge to the democratic system.[52]

The second type of antiparty parties is described in the literature as "third parties."[53] As Israel is a multiparty system, "third" is not a viable option. Yet the dual dimension of the Israeli party system (left versus right, peace versus Greater Israel), enabled parties to identify with either of the sides, or alternatively, to distance themselves from the two poles and present either a neutral position on central issues or a third option. In this sense, third parties became a viable political option after the demise of Mapai as a dominant party (1977) as Israel has turned into a two-bloc system, a division based mainly on the parties' security attitudes. There have been numerous attempts to establish middle parties,[54] which were short lived. As noted by one commentator, "the history of middle parties in Israel is a combination of relative electoral failure and a definite failure to survive."[55] Only three parties—the Democratic Movement for Change (Dash), Shinui (Change), and Kadima (Advance)—attracted a significant number of votes and left their impact on the political scene.

The Democratic Movement for Change presented the first viable alternative to the political establishment. It was formed in 1976, just a few months before the upheaval that changed the structure of the party map in Israel. It was defined as a party "founded in order to bring a radical change in the practices of government, society, and the economy."[56] Dash was a middle-class party whose leaders were well-known figures in various walks of life, in the academy, the military, and the economy. The party was committed to liberalizing the economic system, cleaning up the polity and administration, and changing the electoral system. The voters were persuaded that change is imminent. Dash won 15 seats, for the first time in Israeli history creating a third option. The party was clearly distinguishable from the others. However, its success was short lived. Dash started to disintegrate before the end of the Knesset term, never to reappear on the electoral scene. Internal frictions, organizational decay, and public disenchantment were responsible for its demise.

Shinui was organized as an independent party prior to the 1999 elections. Basically a middle-class grouping, its agenda did not focus on foreign policy and security but on the secular–religious cleavage. The alternative to the political establishment was exhibited in the party's title: change. The party had no pretension of winning control of government. It shied away from the two blocs, giving low priority to Israel's major preoccupation with defense and focusing instead on the country's domestic problems. Shinui demanded a separation between state and religion, a political novelty in Israel never before offered to voters in such an explicit and militant manner. Shinui was not a party of compromise and moderation. It used expressions of delegitimization toward religious parties, emphasizing its struggle against religious coercion.[57] Shinui identified neither with the left nor with the right, giving vent to an antireligious sentiment prevalent in both political camps. The party's message fell on receptive ears and it gained 15 Knesset seats, becoming the third-largest party. During the 2006 elections, however, it failed to pass the threshold and disappeared from the political scene. Once again, internal conflicts that culminated in leadership rivalry removed a party from the political scene. Once again the option of a third party did not appear to be realistic on the Israeli political map.

Kadima made its first debut during the elections for the 17th Knesset (2006), taking the middle road. It can hardly be considered an antiestablishment party. Ariel Sharon founded it just before his stroke and collapse into unconsciousness in January 2006. Initially the party operated without an organizational infrastructure. Kadima, staffed mainly by defectors from establishment parties, attempted to capture both ends of the political spectrum. The platform presented a compromise between the aspirations of the right and the objectives of the left. It asserted that "the Jewish people have a national and historic right to the Land of Israel in its entirety." Simultaneously, the party supported the notion of "a clear Jewish majority within the state of Israel," implying retreat from most of the occupied territories. Kadima fared very well in the 2006 elections, winning a plurality of the vote and becoming the biggest party in the country. It is at present a serious contender for heading the government after the next elections. In contrast to the previous middle parties—Dash and Shinui—Kadima does not appear to be a flash party. But at the same time it cannot be counted as a protest against the existing party system. It is a mainstream party in terms of leadership (President Shimon Peres, Knesset Chair Dalia Itzik, and others), in terms of voters (divided across various sectors), and in terms of ideology.

In conclusion, although antiparty parties have occasionally emerged on the partisan scene, their success has so far been ephemeral and brief. Israelis tend to be disenchanted with political parties, but they do not express their discontent by turning to antiestablishment parties. In fact, they do not tend to protest at all. According to the World Value Survey (data from 2001), less than 25% participated in a street demonstration in the past and 44.4% do not have any intention of doing so in the future.[58]

WHAT WENT WRONG?

The major vulnerability of political parties in Israel is their inability to secure trust and legitimacy. Given the congenial environment provided by institutional structures, the question arises: What has gone wrong? Why can't parties be trusted as pillars of democracy? Why must they operate in a vacuum of confidence? The fact of the matter is that the law endowed parties with essential constitutional functions and corroborated their status by a firm legal structure. Yet, they have failed to fulfill expectations. Three explanations that may account for this failure are grounded in the polity, in society, and in the parties themselves.

Accounting for Failure: The Role of Government

Like many other industrial societies, Israel has privatized not only the economy but also other domains of public life. The electoral process is largely handled by public relations agencies, attempting to increase the rating of political parties and particularly of political leaders. Programs and ideologies remain vague. Commercialization of politics puts an emphasis on market strategy. Commentators have noticed the personalization of politics, whereby leaders have become marketable commodities.[59] Ideologies and worldviews matter very little.

Furthermore, globalization and the intricacies of policy making have shifted the onus of power from the elected representatives to the bureaucracy. The "Treasury Boys," consisting of senior officials in the Finance Ministry, are those responsible for Israel's policy output. They are the ones, together with the administrators in the Bank of Israel, who set up the budget and determine the allocation of resources. The answer to the question of "who gets what" was transferred from the Knesset, that is from the parties' elected representatives to the administration, remote from the public eye. Parties have failed to set up policy-making organs that would guide, or at least keep up with, the new rulers in the state's administration. They remained remote from the technological global revolution into which Israel has successfully integrated.

Accounting for Failure: The Role of Society

Israeli society has also undergone significant changes. The rise in national income is staggering. Although socioeconomic differentials are noticeable, the overall standard of living has risen considerably. The distribution of durable goods, density of living, and educational attainments are now a far cry from the conditions Israelis lived in only two decades ago. Occupational mobility is evident, with a substantial shift from blue-collar to professional and managerial careers. Economic changes were accompanied by value shifts. Money making, individual success, personal achievement, and social fame replaced the old values of austerity and communalism. Last, but certainly not least, Israel experienced a communication revolution when the government decided (in 1993) to revoke the monopoly of the national broadcasting services and to grant a license to cable television, allowing the majority of Israelis to watch a variety of channels broadcasting from every corner of the world. Israelis are now dedicated to the electronic media, with the number of Internet users (per capita) among the highest in the world.

Accounting for Failure: The Role of the Parties

Only political parties have remained nearly immune to these changes. Admittedly, as noted above, the selection of candidates is no longer monopolized (in some parties) by the elite, but in many other respects political parties have failed to adjust to the new era. Politicians consist of old-guard party activists. Outsiders, originating in the academy or in the professional world, are usually not welcome. The winds of new politics blowing on the social scene have not penetrated the iron walls of political parties. Furthermore, parties have failed to take advantage of the electronic network to mobilize, or reinforce, support. My attempt to learn more about parties or to establish contact with their headquarters through the Internet was highly disappointing. Political parties continue to fight with one another and within themselves as if the world stands still. They occasionally hold primaries to settle internal rivalries and attract public attention, but after the electoral storm the water is once again quiet.

Political parties lag behind changes, some of which are dramatic, taking place in all walks of life. They seem to have forgotten that Israelis have changed their lifestyles and are now much more educated and critical. They have also ignored the fact that the world is not standing still, and that Israelis are much more exposed to their outside environment than they used to be in the past.

SUMMARY AND CONCLUSIONS

Three questions were presented in the outset of this chapter: First, why should we expect political parties in Israel to be the backbone of democracy? Second, to what extent did they fulfill the expectations, in terms of their ability, to provide representation, enlist trust, and foster participation? And third, why did the parties fail democracy and what are the reasons for their vulnerability?

The answer to the first question relies on the institutional framework. Equipped as they are with a viable opportunity to gain representation, with laws providing them both recognition and resources and with freedom to act, political parties are expected to be the watchdogs of democracy.

The answer to the second question is equivocal. Political parties do fulfill their representative function. The public is not oblivious to this fact, as nearly 60% of the respondents in the Democracy Survey estimate that the Knesset represents the entire range of the population.[60] But the parties are not given credit for this accomplishment. In fact, data reveal a great sense of disillusionment and frustration manifested in distrust and distance, resulting in low turnout in national elections. Dislike of parties even seems to extend to voting for antiparty parties, using this channel to express their denial of, or distinction from, the mainstream system. Attempts to undercut antiparty sentiment as it affects electoral behavior have not been successful.

As for the third question, various explanations account for the visible decline in party attachment. Israel portrays many characteristics of the new politics, widely dealt with in the literature. But parties have largely remained deaf and blind. For them, old politics is still the name of the game. Scholars have been preoccupied with the possible freezing of the party system. In Israel, there have been significant changes on the partisan map, resulting from a volatile electorate, but the parties themselves have made small alterations with time. Their structure, mobilization, and linkage with affiliates have remained very much the same. If the world is moving quickly and the parties remain still, it is little wonder that people shy away from them. This split diminishes the parties' ability to perform democratic functions.

The picture presented above is gloomy both in regard to parties and to democracy. Parties are not dead, but they do need democratic resuscitation. For Israel, a shaky democracy, this is bad news. Democracy calls for strong and viable political parties enjoying wide public support. However, this chapter has focused on what is rather than on what should be. It has shown that Israeli parties have been partly successful in one aspect (representation) but have failed in others. They upheld the institutional infrastructure that served as a basis for Israel's democracy in its nascent stages but failed to adjust to changing mores and structures. Unfortunately, there is no blueprint for enhancing a party's contribution to democracy. But revealing vulnerability is perhaps the first and necessary, though certainly not sufficient, step.

CHAPTER 8

The Quest for Party Democracy in Turkey: Unequal to the Power of Historical Continuity?

Yunus Emre

It may be said that to write the history of a party means nothing less than to write the general history of a country from a monographic viewpoint, in order to highlight a particular aspect of it.

—Antonio Gramsci, "Selections from the Prison Notebooks"[1]

INTRODUCTION

Despite the long history of the Turkish experiment with political parties, one can hardly claim that there is a sufficient accumulation of analytical and critical knowledge about it. International scholars largely neglected Turkey's experiment with multiparty democracy, and local scholars have viewed it from constitutional and legal perspectives.[2] Some analyze political parties comparatively, having their European and U.S. counterparts in mind, with the aim of finding the missing dimensions in the Turkish case that hindered the development of the "modernity" and "maturity" of the society.[3] Only recently have political parties been analyzed on the basis of state–society cleavages and become a subject of interdisciplinary scrutiny.[4] Current scholarship on political parties in Turkey focuses on conceptualizing the Turkish experiment in comparison with the development of parties in similar cultural contexts. This was especially true after the rise to power of the Justice and Development Party (Adalet ve Kalkınma Partisi [JDP], the post-Islamist party in power as of this writing), when many scholars were curious about the political and social implications of this experience for other countries with ostensibly similar cultural and even "civilizational" backgrounds.[5]

Although I share these same methodological and analytical concerns and believe that the JDP experience presents an example that may be emulated by others in the Middle East and elsewhere, in this chapter I will emphasize the peculiarity of the Turkish experience within both the Western and Eastern contexts, making clear at the outset that the Turkish experiment in political parties and democracy has been shaped by rather unique historical conditions that may not necessarily be present in other countries. Party politics in Turkey has a relatively long history, secularism is deeply rooted, and state traditions are firmly embedded in the mindsets of the Turkish people.

This chapter is organized into three parts. The first examines the era from the late Ottoman period to the 1960 coup d'état, with the goal of explaining how political parties entered into Turkish political life and how they changed. The second part covers the period from the 1960s to the 2000s, discussing the impact of military interventions and the main political party traditions (the Republican People's Party and the Center Left, the Center Right, and the Nationalist and Islamist Right). The third part focuses on the JDP and the new political environment after this party's coming to power. Overall, this chapter questions state-society relations in Turkey and the place of political parties in that relationship by exploring the historical continuities and peculiarities of the Turkish case.

THE EMERGENCE AND DEVELOPMENT OF POLITICAL PARTIES: 1815–1960

Imperial Era, 1815–1920

Although political parties in the modern sense of the term appeared on the political stage in Western Europe and the United States in the mid-19th century, it took almost half a century to find them in the Ottoman Empire. Before then, organized groups, party-like structures in the then territories of the Ottoman Empire, were based on ethnic and religious preferences, mostly with a nationalist agenda and no legitimate role to play within the decision-making realm. The Balkan territories of the empire were particularly crowded with these nationalist, secessionist entities.

The first known such political grouping was Filiki Eteria (Friends Society), established by Greek nationalists in 1815.[6] In the first half of the 19th century, almost all of the Christian minorities of the empire had their own political organizations. Greek secession in 1830 encouraged other ethnic and religious groups, and Serbian, Bulgarian, Macedonian, Albanian, Armenian, Jewish, as well as Arab nationalist organizations reminiscent of their contemporaries in Western Europe were established.[7]

Country-wide political parties did not emerge until the first decade of the 20th century, despite the fact that constitutional developments and a semidemocratic experiment in Turkey had started much earlier. The 1839 Tanzimat reforms, with the goals of the modernization and provision of legal equality between the Muslims and non-Muslims of the empire, were the turning point in the constitutionalization of monarchy in the Ottoman Empire. The First Constitution of the Empire was issued in 1876. However, the two-chamber parliament that was established lasted only a year. In 1878, Sultan Abdülhamit suspended the constitution and closed the parliament on the pretext of the war with Russia.

After the suspension of the constitution in 1878, the autocratic administration of the sultan successfully defied any opposition, let alone the formation of parties. However, an underground opposition was organized in exile, particularly in Paris, against the absolutism of the monarch. The opposition to Abdülhamit II was crystallized through what was later called the Young Turks Movement. The Young Turks formed the Committee of Union and Progress (İttihat ve Terakki Cemiyeti [CUP]) in Paris in 1907.[8] As we shall see, this organization controlled the destiny of the empire in its final years.

In 1907, two organizations, the Ottoman Liberty Association (Osmanlı Hurriyet Cemiyeti) and CUP merged and began to recruit military officers and intellectuals in order to force the sultan to put the constitution into effect. To accomplish this goal, the still secret organization terrorized the political environment via violent activities. The insurgent officers of the Ottoman Third Army in Macedonia forced Abdülhamit to declare the constitutionality of his monarchy in July 1908.

After the proclamation of the constitutional monarchy, a new era primarily shaped by the leaders of the CUP began. During the 1908 Salonika Congress of the CUP, the Party of Union and Progress was established. In all the corners of the empire, the name of the new party was linked to constitutionalism and parliamentary monarchy. However, its opponents were not standing idle. In 1909, a popular riot against the CUP and the constitutional monarchy broke out in Istanbul. The CUP was able to take control, but only with the aid of the Ottoman Third Army in Macedonia that marched from Salonika to Istanbul after the riot. After the suppression of the rebellion, Sultan Abdülhamit II was overthrown by the CUP and his younger brother Mehmet Reşad was enthroned as the new sultan.

Despite two more elections (and one byelection) held after 1908, the CUP established its dictatorship, and a single-party regime was instituted. The members of the Central Committee of the CUP, and among them three strongmen, Pasha Enver, Pasha Cemal, and Pasha Talat,[9] replaced the mighty sultan and governed the country with an iron fist. The party administration led the country into World War I in November 1914 on the side of the Central Powers (Germany and Austria-Hungary). When the war ended in 1918, the leaders of the CUP fled the county. The end of the war brought the end of the party, too.

The CUP was just one front of the political alignments in the empire. The most important opposition party was the Entente Liberal (Hürriyet ve İtilaf), during the Second Constitutional period, which began in 1908. As the name suggests, this party was not a homogeneous political entity. It was a union of opponents of the CUP and was established after the dissolution of the Ottoman Liberals Party (Osmanlı Ahrar Fırkası), following the 1909 counterrevolution attempt. The Entente Liberal promoted free enterprise, liberalism, constitutionalism, and self-government.[10] The CUP government was brought to an end by a memorandum from the military and the Entente Liberal ruled the empire, briefly, between July 1912 and January 1913. When the city of Edirne was lost to Bulgaria in May 1913 during the Balkan Wars, a group of CUP officers led by Enver toppled the Entente Liberal government and took power again. The dissolved Entente Liberal was reestablished after the war and signed the Peace Treaty of Sevrés with the Allied powers, a treaty that met with outrage since it envisaged the liquidation of Ottoman sovereignty.

During the armistice period from 1918 to 1923, 55 political parties were established but none of them had any lasting impact on the fate of the country. In fact, during the semidemocratic parliamentary period of the decaying empire, only one left its mark on Turkish politics and that was the CUP, a party whose legacy, practice, and culture have survived even until today. The single party of the early republican period (1923–1946) and today's chief opposition party, the Republican People's Party (RPP), has been the successor of the CUP in terms of ideology and political practice.

The Kemalist Era (1923–1946) and Major Features of the Single-Party System

With the establishment of the new National Assembly in Ankara in 1920 and with the success of the new regime in defeating its foes and signing a revisionist peace treaty ending the war, a new era commenced in Turkish politics. A republic replaced the monarchy and the RPP replaced the CUP. A single-party parliamentary system similar in many ways to authoritarian systems elsewhere in Europe was instituted. Having been successful in navigating Turkey through the rough waters of the interwar period and carefully avoiding World War II with well-balanced diplomacy, the authoritarian single-party rule endured until 1946. In fact, had it not been for the need to ensure the security and the territorial integrity of the country, the system could easily have survived much longer. But democratization as such was an imperative in order to join the Western security community.

The leader throughout this period was Mustafa Kemal Atatürk, a general in the Ottoman Army and a former member of the CUP.[11]

After the occupation of the Ottoman Empire, he sought refuge in Anatolia and led a successful national resistance movement, Society for the Defense of Rights, against the Sevrés Treaty. Just before the signing of the new peace treaty (Lausanne Peace Treaty) in July 1923, the National Assembly was dissolved and elections were held. Atatürk and his followers carefully controlled the elections to be certain of securing ratification and won all of the seats in the assembly. When the assembly first met in August 1923, the Society for the Defense of Rights was transformed into the People's Party (Halk Fırkası).

The National Assembly had already abolished the sultanate in November 1922. The new political regime was proclaimed as the Republic of Turkey in October 1923, and Atatürk became the first president of the republic. In 1924, the Caliphate was abolished and the members of the imperial family were sent into exile. By the end of 1924, Atatürk's cadres were in complete control of the country.

But there was no consensus among the leadership on the future of the country. Most of the moderate and the liberal members resigned from the People's Party and established the Progressive Republican Party in 1924. The head of the party was General Kazım Karabekir, the former commander of the army in eastern Anatolia during the National War of Independence. Some public and intellectual celebrities such as Hüseyin Rauf, Refet Bele, and Adnan Adivar joined this party, and the Progressive Republican Party established its parliamentary group.[12] Thus, opposition to the RPP of Atatürk was constructed just a year after the end of the war.

However, the opposition did not last long. A Kurdish, but mostly religious, rebellion arising in southeastern Anatolia in February 1925 sounded the death knell for the opposition and for the cautiously guided multiparty experience. The parliament issued the Law on the Maintenance of Order (Takrir-ı Sükun Kanunu) forbidding civil organizations and publications.[13] The Progressive Republican Party was dissolved by the government and 1925 was the de jure beginning of the single-party system, which would last until 1946. The elections held in 1927, 1931, 1935, 1939, and 1943 served the purpose of rubber stamping the deputies nominated by the central administration of the party.[14]

Yet in between there was another guided trial of opposition in 1930, one that was not to last more than 90 days. In 1930, President Atatürk asked his seasoned friend Fehti Okyar, ambassador to France by that time, to form a new political party. Okyar set up the Free Republican Party (Serbest Cumhuriyet Fırkası) and entered the October 1930 municipal elections.[15] But the political environment became so tense that almost immediately after the elections, the party was dissolved by its founder. Even a guided opposition was not tolerable to the governing elite in the country.

Reminiscent of its contemporaries in Italy, in the Soviet Union and later in Germany, the RPP also unified itself with "the state." By 1936 the governors of the provinces were at the same time the local heads of the party and the secretary general of the party became the minister of internal affairs. The single party, single leader philosophy continued after Atatürk's death in November 1938. The new president, Ismet Inönü, a close comrade of Atatürk, was an ardent advocate of the strict control of an immature society and politics. In the First Extraordinary Party Congress of 1938, Inönü was proclaimed the unchangeable leader of the party and the "National Chief" (Milli Şef). Although his position was challenged in 1946 and four years later in relatively free elections he was relieved of his national duties, Inönü remained as the leader of the party until an advanced age and was not forced to retire by his secretary general Bület Ecevit until 1972.

Transition to a Multiparty System, 1946–1960

During World War II, Turkey was able to maintain its neutrality despite the treaty commitments to the Allied powers. At the end of the war, Turkey had a relatively sound economy, a robust political system, and an undefeated military. But it was isolated diplomatically and vulnerable to Soviet demands. It could only rely on U.S. support, which was conditional upon the country's having at least a semblance of democracy. This meant that elections, as the sine qua non of any minimal democracy, had to be held and political parties were required.[16]

The cautious transition to multiparty politics did not create a much more democratic Turkey by Western standards. The doubtfully democratic 1924 Constitution was the main barrier to any real democracy in the country, particularly the clauses that insisted on the impossibility of delimitation of the political power of the majority in the National Assembly. There were several other important restrictions that hindered the establishment and organization of new political parties. Any new party was expected to stick to the rules of the game set by the framers of the republic. They had to be secularist and nationalist, but not socialist. The first political organization to qualify was the National Development Party (Milli Kalkınma Partisi), founded by Istanbul businessman Nuri Demirağ in 1945.[17] However, it had no lasting impact on political life.

The party that would have a lasting impact on the politics of the country was the Democratic Party (DP). It was established by the opponent cadres of the RPP after two speeches by President Inönü emphasized the need for an opposition party.[18] An important cleavage opened within the RPP during a debate over the Land Distribution Act pending in the National Assembly. The future leaders of the DP, holders of large properties, opposed the draft bill and issued a memorandum declaring the necessity of democracy in Turkey. The party group of the RPP first dismissed the memorandum and later expelled its three drafters, Adnan Menderes, Refik Koraltan, and Fuat Köprülü, from the party. When Celal

Bayar, prime minister from 1937 to 1939, resigned from the RPP, the time was more or less ripe for the formation of a new state-sponsored opposition party. All that was missing was an official blessing. That blessing came from President Inönü on November 1, 1945, in his inaugural speech to parliament.[19] The new opposition party, in many ways reminiscent of its imperial forebear, was founded with the name of Democratic Party in January 1946 and lasted until the 1960 coup d'état. However, its legacy still remains in political life. Most center-right political parties have claimed the legacy of the DP. Its name also has survived to the present in different forms and platforms.

Despite rigging, unfavorable election laws, and unpleasant electoral surprises, culminating in the DP's inability to nominate more than 273 candidates for 465 seats in the parliament, the new party nonetheless obtained 61 seats in the 1946 elections. Even with relatively minor representation, they were able to voice the demands of their constituencies and be effective in leveling criticism of the lack of democratic and economic liberalization.[20]

During this time the emerging need was for Turkey to participate in such new international schemes as the Marshall Plan and the Organization for European Economic Cooperation. A year after the 1946 elections, the RPP had to charge its hardliner prime minister Recep Peker to cope with the new domestic and international realities. By the time of the 1950 elections, it had even produced a new liberal election law.

In 1950, the DP won the elections by a far higher vote margin. It received 53% of the total votes and, due to the intricacies of the election system, won 420 seats in the National Assembly. The RPP received 39% of the votes and only 63 of the seats. After the elections, the leader of the DP, Celal Bayar, became the new president of the republic and appointed Adnan Menderes as the new prime minister. During the DP's reign, two more elections were held, first in 1954 and later in 1957. The DP received, respectively, 57% and 47% of the total votes and 505 and 424 of the seats. The major opposition party, the RPP, received only 34.8% votes and 31 seats in the 1954 elections. In 1957, the RPP raised its representation almost sixfold by obtaining 41% of the votes cast and 178 seats.[21] If it had been given a chance by the military and the 1960 coup had not been launched, the RPP would have been able to topple the DP from power in the elections of 1961 as the masses and the intelligentsia were turning against the DP. But their term ended on May 27, 1960, with a military coup, less bloody during the initial phase than the one staged by the CUP in 1913, but more severe in terms of its human and political consequences. Just like the legacy of the party, the shadow of this coup remained over the country for decades. The coup is considered to have been legitimized by the masses and in fact the anniversary of the coup has been celebrated for almost two decades. Nevertheless, it ushered in yet another era in Turkish politics with a more liberal constitution, on the one hand, and a long lasting active military tutelage, on the other.

POLITICAL PARTIES FROM 1960 TO THE 2000s

The Impact of Military Interventions

After the May 27 coup d'état, the military junta dissolved the assembly and the cabinet.[22] Three of the DP leaders (Premier Adnan Menderes, Minister of Finance Hasan Polatkan, and Minister of Foreign Affairs Fatin Rüştü Zorlu) were executed after an intimidating and utterly questionable trial. Severe sentences were issued for the leading DP figures and their political power was curtailed. The DP was outlawed by a decision of a Court of First Instance. The RPP and other small parties, on the other hand, were largely left untouched. New parties claiming the legacy of the DP were established. One of them, the Justice Party (Adalet Partisi [JP]), ruled the country on and off during the following two decades, as will be more fully discussed in the next section.

The era from 1960 to 1980 was a period of social transformation. It was characterized by a rapid rise in population and urbanization, moderate industrialization, the emergence of a vibrant working class, and a burgeoning bourgeoisie that participated as independent political actors, as well as tense military-civilian relations. It was an era of two successful and at least two unsuccessful military intervention attempts. The first decade ended with a moderate military intervention on March 12, 1971, resulting in the toppling of the government, while the second ended in 1980 with a harsher one, reminiscent of the 1960 coup d'état.

On September 12, 1980, on the pretext of fighting terrorism, Turkish armed forces took power and retained it for three years. They designed a new political system with a new constitution allowing for the permanent presence of the military in the country's decision-making circles via the National Security Council. Fundamental rights were curtailed and violated. All parties were outlawed: This time even the RPP was unable to escape. When the new elections were held in November 1983, a 10% national threshold rule was in place and a totally new set of parties were allowed to run for the new unicameral parliament. Only the parties confirmed by the National Security Council, composed of the five leaders of the junta, were allowed to register on the tickets.

The Alignment of Political Parties in Turkey after 1960

The Center Right

As noted, after the 1960 coup d'état and the closure of the DP, that party's legacy was taken over by the JP, although its founder was a retired general, Ragıp Gümüşpala.[23] The party followed a moderate way, avoiding confrontation with the military, and received 35% of the votes cast in the 1961 elections. When Gümüşpala died in 1964, the JP had already established itself as the main opposition party in the country. Six months later, during the party's General Congress, Suleyman Demirel, the candidate of the liberal and moderate wing of the party, became the new (and almost permanent, as it proved) leader of the party. His victory was vindicated in the 1965 election when the party obtained 53% of the votes cast, and again in the 1969 elections, when it received 47% of the votes. However, the party was removed from power on March 12, 1971, when a memorandum from the military addressing President Cevdet Sunay openly threatened the government with another coup. The crisis could only be avoided with the resignation of Demirel from his prime ministerial post on the same day. Interim governments to rule the country until the 1973 elections were established and staffed mostly by bureaucrats.

This was the second in a series of serious military interventions in the republican period. Demirel's JP, after suffering a moderate defeat in the 1973 election, was only able to come to power in 1975 through a coalition of right-wing parties, as the name the Nationalist Front suggests. In the 1977 elections, the JP increased its votes to 37% and the Nationalist Front survived until 1978 when the resignation of 11 deputies from the JP caused the fall of the government, at which time Bülent Ecevit's RPP formed a new government. Two years later the JP was able to establish a single-party minority government, but another coup forced it to leave power on September 12, 1980. Soon after the military coup, like the other parties, the JP was closed down, and like other politicians, Demirel was banned from politics.

The JP, itself a substitute for the DP, was replaced in the first elections by the Motherland Party (Anavatan Partisi [MP], formed 1983).[24] Under the leadership of Turgut Özal, one of the protégées of Demirel and the main architect of the liberalization of the economy as a bureaucrat in the last Demirel government, MP received 45% of the votes in 1983 and established a single-party government. After long years of political instability and economic uncertainty, the MP remained in power until 1991. Özal served as premier from 1983 to 1989 and then was president until his sudden death in 1993. Throughout, he was proud to claim that his party was a coalition of the four main political currents (center-right, center-left, religious right, and nationalist right) in Turkish politics. However, to judge by its performance, its social base, and the views of most of its cadres, the MP was a center-right party.

When the MP left power after coming in second in the 1991 elections, it had completed eight years of mostly controversial and according to many corrupt practices. For the next four years it served in the opposition benches and then, in the period between 1995 and 1999, it took part in two coalition governments. Before its total political demise in 2002, the MP was a minor coalition partner for three years. The party was unable to pass the 10% national threshold in the 2002 elections and declined to enter the 2007 elections. As of mid-2009, the MP is a negligible political actor with no visible future.

The other center-right political party in Turkish politics in the post-1980 era was the True Path Party (Doğru Yol Partisi [TPP]).[25] This party was founded as the continuation of the JP when the leader of the JP, Demirel, was barred from political activities. In 1987, a referendum brought the restrictions on the pre-1980 politicians to an end, allowing Demirel to return to political life. In the 1991 elections, Demirel's TPP got the highest number of votes and established a coalition government with the Social Democratic Populist Party (Sosyal Demokrat Halkçı Parti [SDPP]). After the death of President Özal, Demirel was elected president in 1993. In the party congress, Tansu Çiller became the party leader and later the prime minister. This government of the TPP and the SDPP continued until 1995. The votes of the TPP gradually decreased after the 1991 elections. In the 1999 elections the party was barely able to pass the 10% national election threshold, and by the 2002 elections it could not.

Thus the two main parties of the Turkish center right were out of parliament after the 2002 election. Just before the 2007 elections, there was an effort to merge the TPP and the MP with the name of the Democratic Party, referring to the party of Celal Bayar and Adnan Menderes. However, the merger was not realized and again the MP was unable to pass the threshold in the 2007 elections, receiving only 5% of the total votes. In the multiparty period, the Turkish electorate generally voted for center-right political parties. However, today's center-right parties are far from passing the 10% national elections threshold. There are two main reasons behind the dissolution on the center right, one demographic and one political. The main social base of these parties was the peasantry in Turkey and once in office they granted high subsidies to the agricultural sector. However, with economic development, industrialization, and urbanization, the number of peasants in the whole population noticeably decreased, in turn decreasing the votes of the center-right parties. The second main reason was the transformation of political Islam. Through the 1980s and 1990s, the power of political Islam gradually increased in Turkey. However, in the first years of the 21st century, Turkish political Islam took a moderate path and tried to embrace all of society. So the former electorates of the center right transferred to these new conservative democrats. Thus the JDP today, although it does not come from center-right origins, covers the traditional social basis and legacy of the center right.

The Republican People's Party and the Center Left

The RPP continued to be one of the major parties of Turkish political life in the post-1960 period. It attempted to transform itself into a center-left political organization after 1965. However, the historical background, the peculiarities of Turkish politics, and the social bases of the party made it impossible for the party to change itself into a Western-type social democratic party.[26] Although it was closed down after the 1980 coup d'état, the heritage of the RPP was pursued by a number of parties, and in 1992 it was reopened. In this period, the party has been more powerful in urbanized areas, and modernism and nationalism have been the two main mottos of the party.

In the national elections that were held in October 1961, the RPP had 37% of the votes, became the major party in the parliament, and led three coalition governments in this period. Just before the 1965 elections, Inönü declared that his party was on the left of center in the political spectrum. This left of center discourse was different from the Western-type left of center politics in many respects. The main priorities were developmentalism and nationalism. This assumption of left politics did not bring electoral success for the RPP; on the contrary, it created a dramatic decrease in the voting rates of the party. Under those conditions, the RPP was able to obtain only 29% (the lowest rate for the RPP up to that date) of the total votes in the 1965 elections.

In the 1966 Congress of the RPP, Bülent Ecevit became the secretary general (the second man in the party organization after Inönü) and led the group that supported the left of center policy. Within one year the opponents of the policy resigned from the party. The RPP stood as the main opposition party in the 1965–1969 parliamentary period. Although in the 1969 elections the RPP's share of the vote dropped to 27%, the party continued its left of center discourse.

In March 1971, as mentioned above, the army issued a memorandum forcing Prime Minister Demirel to resign. After Demirel, a RPP deputy, Nihat Erim, became the prime minister with the support of Inönü. Ecevit, as the second man in the party, did not respect this decision and resigned from his post as secretary general. After one year of hidden struggle, Ecevit won against Inönü in the 1972 Party Congress.

Under the leadership of Ecevit, the RPP attempted to transform itself into a democratic left party. It changed its program and statutes in 1976, adopting the principles of western social democracy in these official documents. Moreover, in 1978 it became a member of the Socialist International. With its new leader, the RPP took 33% of the vote, the highest rate among the other parties in the 1973 elections. In 1974, Ecevit led a coalition government with the RPP and the National Salvation Party of Necmettin Erbakan, but that lasted only 10 months, and although the RPP received 42% of the votes in the 1977 elections, it was unable to get a majority and could not form a government. After the second Nationalist Front government, Ecevit's RPP accepted 11 deputies of the JP with the promise of ministerial positions. Ecevit formed the RPP government in January 1978. However, during this period Turkey entered a political and economic crisis, and the government was unable to cope with it. After an electoral defeat in the 1979 byelections, Ecevit had to resign, and the JP of Demirel founded a minority government, only to be overthrown, as noted, by the 1980 military coup. After the coup, the RPP was closed down as were the other parties and its leaders were banned from political activities.

By the time national elections were held again in 1983, the most dispersed political movement was the center left in Turkey. Before the elections two center-left political parties were established to take the social base and the heritage of the RPP. The first one was the Populist Party (Halkçı Parti [PP]), established in 1983. This party took 30% of the votes and became the main opposition party after the 1983 elections. However, the top cadres of the RPP joined the Social Democratic Party (Sosyal Demokrasi Partisi [SDP]). The PP merged with the SDP in 1985 and the Social Democratic Populist Party (Sosyal Demokrat Halkçı Parti [SDPP]), became the new name of the party.[27]

The leader of the SDP was Erdal Inönü, professor of physics and son of Ismet Inönü. Erdal Inönü's SDP was not allowed to enter the 1983 elections. Despite the merger between the PP and SDP, the votes of the new party, the SDPP, gradually decreased. It was able to become the minor coalition partner of the TPP in 1991, but after that government fell, the decline of public support for the party accelerated.

The SDPP was divided in 1992 with the reopening of the RPP. In 1995, those two parties, the RPP and the SDPP, merged. After a transition period, Deniz Baykal became the leader of the party. The party was not quite able to pass the 10% national threshold in the 1995 elections and dropped lower in the 1999 election. However, the chaotic environment of politics after 2000 made this party again one of the main political actors, and in the 2002 elections, the RPP became the only other party besides the JDP to pass the national threshold.

The former leader of the RPP, Bülent Ecevit, did not approve of the foundation of center-left political parties in the new environment because of the military tutelage they received. He disagreed with the direction former RPP officers were taking after the 1980 coup and did not enter or support any of those parties, preferring instead to found the Democratic Left Party (Demokratik Sol Parti [DLP]).[28] (The official founder of the DLP was the wife of Bülent Ecevit, Rahşan Ecevit, because Bülent had been barred from politics like other pre-1980 politicians for 10 years through the 1982 constitution. After the 1987 referendum that abolished this ban, Bülent became the official leader of the party.)

The DLP's views on the economy and religion were more liberal and moderate than those of the traditional RPP tendency, but it was unable to achieve electoral success until the middle of the 1990s. Then, after the failure of the SDPP in government, the electoral support of the DLP, as the alternative center-left political organization, increased. But during its government term from 1999 to 2002, Turkey went through one of the most severe economic crises and in the 2002 elections, the DLP, which had been the leading party in the 1999 elections, could obtain only 1% of the votes cast. To date, the party has not been able to recover from that blow, and despite its representation in the parliament with 13 seats, it remains marginalized.

Approximately 40 years have passed since the beginning of social democratic politics in Turkey. Yet one can hardly claim that a social democratic party representing the interests of labor has ever been present in Turkish politics. The left of center of Inönü in 1965 was a reproduction of Kemalist modernism and statism in the conditions of the Turkey of the 1960s, harmonious with the hegemonic views of that era and a strong focus on nationalism and developmentalism. On the other hand, the RPP, as the founder of the state, had to advocate the founding principles of the Turkish Republic, national unity, and secularism. Consequently, the political history of Turkish social democracy, from Inönü's left of center to today, includes many principles but not the core of social democracy, the labor movement. The history of the center left is the history of an attempt to form social democracy without labor.

The Nationalist and Islamist Right

The party of Turkish nationalism was the Nationalist Action Party (Milliyetçi Hareket Partisi [NAP]).[29] The leader of the party from 1965 to 1996 was Alparslan Türkeş, a former colonel who played an active role in the coup d'état of May 27, 1960. The party was unable to attract popular support during 1960s and 1970s, yet it was instrumental in terrorizing the country during the violent political era of the 1970s, with its anticommunist paramilitary organization (Ülkü Ocakları).

NAP maintained its extreme nationalist position through the 1990s, but after the death of Türkeş in 1996, Devlet Bahçeli was elected head of the party and pursued a more moderate nationalist stance. The votes of the party increased, and the party took second place in the 1999 elections. It became a coalition partner with the DLP of Bülent Ecevit and the MP of Mesut Yılmaz. But the economic crises of 2000 and 2001 also affected the NAP, much like the other coalition partners, and it failed to pass the 10% national thresholds in the 2002 elections. However, thanks to European obstructionism in accepting Turkey as a legitimate candidate country and to acts of violence by the Kurdistan Workers' Party (PKK), nationalism in Turkey was on the rise by the time of the 2007 elections, permitting the NAP to enter parliament with 14% of the votes cast.

As pointed out above, religion and politics were strictly separated in the early republican period; secularism was the rule of the game. The first party to explicitly challenge this rule was the National Order Party

(Milli Nizam Partisi) led by Necmettin Erbakan, a former engineering professor. The party was founded in 1970 but closed by the Constitutional Court on grounds that the party's activities threatened laicism. In 1972, the same cadre established a new party, the National Salvation Party (Milli Selamet Partisi [NSP]) and was permitted to compete, gaining 11% of the votes and 48 deputies in the 1973 elections. During the 1970s the party had a key position in the establishment of many of the coalition governments. However, the NSP was dissolved after the 1980 coup and the leaders of the party were tried by the military courts.

The Islamist political parties that were founded by Necmettin Erbakan and his group were called the National Outlook Movement. Three years after the dissolution of the NSP, the National Outlook founded the Welfare Party (Refah Partisi [WP]). The WP was, however, different in many respects from the previous NSP.[30] The NSP was a developmentalist party, functioning during a developmentalist era in Turkey with an emphasis on import substitution. Thus the party primarily aimed at attracting the support of small and medium-sized businesses. Moreover, a heavy industrialization campaign was at the center of Erbakan's addresses. However, after 1980, with the neo-liberal economic policies of the MP governments, social inequalities increased. Thus economic problems and primarily distribution problems became central and the new WP adapted itself to the new situation. It created a more egalitarian discourse, and through the 1990s, "Just Order" (Adil Düzen) became the main slogan of the party.

In the 1987 elections, the party failed to pass the 10% threshold. But in the 1991 elections, the Islamist and nationalist right parties established an alliance, and this alliance received 17% of the votes. An even greater increase in the votes of the party came in the 1994 municipal elections, when it took 19% of the valid votes and won the elections in many cities, including Istanbul and Ankara. One and a half years later, the WP received the highest votes in the 1995 elections with 21%. No party approached the WP to form a coalition government, but in June 1996 Erbakan established a coalition government with the True Path Party of Tansu Çiller. This government lasted only one year, during which time a secular media campaign against the government and the risk of a secularist military intervention increased the public discontent. In February 1997, at a meeting of the National Security Committee, the military issued resolutions to the government that aimed to suppress political Islam. The one-year period of government of political Islam was ended with this intervention and the WP was outlawed by the Constitutional Court.

In November 2000, a new party of the National Outlook, the Virtue Party, was also closed down by the Constitutional Court. The National Outlook Movement founded yet another new party after this decision, the Felicity Party (Saadet Partisi). However, members of the Virtue

Party who had been discontent with its policies did not join the Felicity Party but instead founded its own new party, the JDP, with Recep Tayyip Erdoğan as its leader.[31] The JDP won the 2002 elections and was still governing Turkey in mid-2009.

TURKEY'S NEW POLITICAL ERA: THE JUSTICE AND DEVELOPMENT PARTY TODAY

The JDP has been the ruling party of Turkey since the 2002 national elections, only one year after its founding in August 2001. Many party officers, including Erdoğan, had held office in the political parties of Erbakan's National Outlook Movement, but as noted the founders of the JDP had come together first as an internal opposition group of reformers in the last congress of the Virtue Party. The JDP renounced being the continuation of the National Outlook.

In the 2002 November national elections, the JDP received 34% of the total votes and 363 of the possible 550 seats in the National Assembly. Except the RPP, all other political parties failed to pass the 10% national election threshold. The head of the party, Tayyip Erdoğan, was barred from being a deputy by a court decision in 1998 and was thus unable to lead the government until 2003, when the ban was lifted and he became a member of parliament and premier after by elections.

After 2004, the cleavage between the secular segments of society and the JDP increased, as did the political tension. Thus Turkey entered a political crisis in the 2007 presidential elections. After several mass meetings and a semi-intervention of the military by an electronic declaration, the crisis deepened. The Erdoğan administration set new elections in an effort to achieve a victory that would overcome the chaotic political environment. This time the JDP took 47% of the total votes and again formed a single-party government. The political tension did not decrease, and quarrels on political issues continued. In March 2008, the Court of Appeals Chief Prosecutor Abdurrahman Yalçınkaya proceeded to seek to ban the JDP in Constitutional Court. The prosecutor accused the JDP of being the focal point for political activities against secularism. After the trials, the court did not ban the JDP, but deprived it of half of its allotted state financial aid on the grounds of its activities against secularism.

The post-1980 era had been a restructuring period for the Turkish economy and society. After 1980, the crisis of former import substituting industrialization was replaced by the neo-liberal policies of the successive governments. This transformation changed the distribution policies to the disadvantage of the masses, thus creating a new and large social stratum consisting of the losers of neo-liberal globalization. Prior to its dissolution in 1997, the WP's primary social base had clearly been the "losers of the neo-liberal restructuring process."[32] On the other hand, the WP established a cross-class alliance between this "poor and marginalized strata" and a new entrepreneurial class that was called Islamic capitalists.[33] However, this social alliance was not enough to make the party a single-party government. After the indirect military intervention of 1997 and the ban on the WP, this cross-class alliance was destroyed. The JDP restructured this alliance and moreover expanded it, and it enlarged its support in small and middle-scale business. Thus with the JDP the new entrepreneurial class of Islamic capitalists began to grow.

The political attitudes of the JDP supporters are in some ways different from those of other parties' electorates. The supporters of the JDP primarily define themselves as religious, rightist, and conservative.[34] As a catch-all party, the JDP has integrated those political attitudes into the economic and democratic demands of its supporters. The party's success at merging these political attitudes and its current political approach come from its ideological elasticity. The JDP defines itself as "conservative democrat;"[35] it does not try to establish a new definition of democracy or create a new type of it, but claims to open a new path under this label.[36] The party summarizes the necessity of such a path as normalizing politics, putting politics on a realist base, creating an autonomous conservative party, and constructing a catch-all political approach.[37] Thus, with an indigenous conservative democrat identity, the party tries to synthesize the historical experiment of universal conservatism and the indigenous values of Turkish political life. This method has allowed the party to expand its electoral base.

Consequently, the JDP is the party of ex-Islamists, but it is not an Islamic party.[38] It is also different from traditional Turkish center-right parties in many respects. The main difference comes from its conception of society-state relations. The center-right parties in Turkey historically have been the carriers of the social periphery's demands and have tried to carry those demands to the political center. However, the JDP defines itself as having the goal of making the social center (politically peripheral) the political center.[39] On the other hand, the founders of the party see the difficulty in continuing Islamic politics in Turkey, as manifested in their revision of the National Outlook's political discourse by accepting the current conservative democrat conception. The JDP experiment is a new phase in a hundred years of struggle between the secularist elites and the traditionalist masses in Turkey.

CONCLUSIONS

As many students of Turkish politics are acutely aware, the average life of a standard party in Turkey is much shorter than that of its counterpart in the western world. There is a high turnover in terms of their political vitality. With the exception of the RPP,[40] most parties have either been banned from politics via military interventions or through the verdict of a court or have become dormant through the democratic process. Yet two major tracks or schools of thought persevere. The first track is the one that aims to protect the state from the subject and from other states, while the other claims to protect the individual from the state.

However, this dichotomy has been rather unstable and porous. Liberal claims have hardly ever been able to survive the tests of power. Even the most liberal parties in the Turkish setting, if not faced with an existential political and or physical threat, have tended to be survivalist and Machiavellian. Once in power they tend to renounce their liberal tenets, if not explicitly, then implicitly. They gradually consubstantiate themselves with the state and claim to be its guardians. Rather than strengthening Turkish democracy, they construct a discourse asserting guardianship and seeking legitimacy in the eyes of the military and civilian bureaucracy.

In western cases, class formation, class structure, class politics, and class representation have crucial roles in the development of political parties and democracy, but in the Turkish experiment, class-based organizations were legally banned until the second half of the 20th century. The ruling elite suppressed labor organizations, labor parties, and labor politics until the 1960s. Under those circumstances, populism and solidaristic corporatism gained prominence in the political and social life of the country. Political parties are no exception to this rule.[41]

Conclusion to the Set: Origins of the Project, Summary by Region, Party Dedemocratization

Kay Lawson

INTRODUCTION

The purpose of this Conclusion is three-fold: to explain the genesis of *Political Parties and Democracy* and how it developed over time, to provide a brief summary, and to consider what significance this set of studies may have for future comparative work on political parties. In the first part I seek to show how the work of others spurred this project along, as I became acquainted over the years with what had been written and aware of what so obviously had not. I review the parties' literature but do so by intertwining the bibliographical with the personal. I explain how the first led me to devote my own energies to the comparative study of political parties as agencies of democracy, seeking the help of scholars who were experts on their own nations' parties and the context in which they had evolved, and how this present work, consisting of 46 chapters and 8 introductions, written entirely by indigenous authors, is, for me, the culmination of that effort.

In the second section I turn to the task of providing a brief summary of what these scholars have to say in this set of studies about the relationship between parties and democracies in their own countries, region by region. In the final section, I consider what broader lessons can be drawn from this collection and stress the need for comparative party scholars to move in new directions. I provide an extended framework of analysis that others may wish to question, corroborate, or extend yet further.

THE BEGINNING

When I began my graduate studies at the University of California in Berkeley nearly half a century ago, I had transferred to political science from a different undergraduate major, far removed. My first graduate course was a seminar on Comparative Politics and my first two assignments were to write a book review of *Political Parties* by Maurice Duverger and then a paper on the politics of Malta.[1] Although I had taken a few political science courses, I had never studied parties other than our own and had scarcely heard of Malta. I remember sitting in the library reading Duverger. At first I was not impressed. Almost all the examples were French, and the work did not seem seriously comparative to me. But after a while I could see that the book was offering ways to understand parties as possibly representative organizations, not just as machines that competed for power. Bearing that in mind when I moved to my second task, I found exploring the politics of a tiny quasi-nation interesting and doable.[2] Combining the study of parties and of comparative politics made political science possible for me. I decided to stay with it.

Almost all the work I did from then on was, although of course I did not know it, in preparation for this present work. I wrote my Master's thesis on the parties of France; taught U.S. Politics, U.S. Parties, and the Politics of Europe; wrote *Political Parties and Democracy in the United States*; joined a research project studying West African political systems; added courses on Soviet, Asian and African political systems to my teaching repertoire; and wrote *The Comparative Study of Political Parties*, using French, Guinean, and U.S. parties as cases.[3]

During this early period I read widely about parties, becoming more and more interested in their potential as agencies of democracy. It intrigued me that only parties, among all institutions, always claimed they would use power, as elected officials, to act on behalf of the people (or some of them), as representatives of their interests. Pressure groups promised pressure, judges promised to act without bias. But parties promised to act *with* bias, *inside* the other two branches of U.S. government. This was true wherever parties competed for office and competing for office was (and is) what makes an organization a party. But I also saw that although party leaders always claimed to represent citizens and to serve as agencies of democracy, they did not always do so, and when they did, it often seemed they did so only because it was the only way to get and hang on to what they really wanted: the job of ruling.[4] Parties and democracy did not necessarily always live together in perfect harmony. Far from it.

So what was the real connection between parties and democracy? This was the question that came to underlie all my work and guided most of my reading. It was a question that required thinking about parties as organizations with their own identities. Having started with Duverger helped. He considered how parties were organized (who did what), their characteristics as separate entities (origins, members, ideologies), and how they were shaped by constitutions and laws. The categories he developed are still pertinent. His best known contribution, explaining how electoral systems shaped party systems, was possible because he was able to focus on the parties within the systems and the people within the parties—he understood how certain electoral systems might encourage the weak to continue to compete against all odds and others might force them out before they had a chance to make their case.

But beyond suggesting strongly that the French Socialist model was the most democratic form of party organization, Duverger was not deeply interested in either comparative study of the genre or in parties' relationship to democracy. To find authors focussed more directly on such matters, especially the latter, I had to go back some 30-40 years, to Roberto Michels and Mosei Ostrogorski. What I found in their work was to the point, but it wasn't pretty. Michels believed that inexorable forces propel oligarchs back into power despite efforts to establish democratic procedures within parties and thereby in governments.[5] Even social democratic parties became instruments for bureaucratizing, institutionalizing, and ultimately dominating the masses. Ostrogorski was even harsher: for him, behind the façade of internal party democracy there were always "faceless wirepullers" who never gave up real control even for a moment.[6] Another powerful writer from the same era whose work touched on the representative role of parties was Max Weber. Weber was slightly more optimistic about parties' role in democracy but ultimately dismissive: party activists who saw politics as a vocation, and worked within the realm of the possible, could achieve important reforms, but then so could charismatic independent leaders if so inclined. The path to good governance lay in the quality of bureaucracy, i.e., in the organization of the state, and would not come from external political bodies.[7]

I was encouraged to discover a more recent author with a more positive outlook, the U.S. scholar Elmer E. Schattschneider (who is quoted by more authors in this collection of studies than any other), who valued parties as agencies that created democracy—and recreated it every day. True, he qualified his praise very carefully and very conservatively, and he never worried much about internal party democracy. But he was convinced that an alert electorate, recognizing the nature and impact of policies made by elected politicians, could and did use parties as agencies capable of effecting positive change on their own behalf.[8] V. O. Key, another important writer about parties (and pressure groups) in that era, acknowledged the ability of parties (and groups) to perform the crucial function of democratic linkage between citizen and state. Using the metaphor of the "transmission belt," and recognizing the positive role minor parties fulminating on the outer wings of the system could play, he reassured us that democracies produced "responsible electorates."[9] When Schattschneider and Key began to fade from the scene, Frank Sorauf picked up where they left off and continued to focus on the relationship between parties and democracy from 1964 through 1988.[10] All three authors, however, wrote only about U.S. parties, and their work received scant attention outside the United States, especially in the aftermath of World War II.

The origins of this war, festering and thriving within a putative democracy, were shocking to parties' scholars, especially those focussing on European parties. Now it was clear that parties could be instruments of dedemocratization as well as of democracy. They could exploit deepset discontents in order to sabotage democratic governance and create cruel systems of totalitarian rule. They needed to be watched.

Not surprisingly, this post-war shift put a damper on cheerful assumptions about the role of parties as agencies of democracy. What began to matter to many parties scholars now was understanding the political organization of discontent: how parties appealed to voters on one side or the other of deep-set cleavages, and what the results were for the stability of party systems and governments. In this perspective, "democratic governance" often seemed to mean little more than nontotalitarian rule. The focus was now less on how parties helped create and maintain democracy and more on whether or not they were ideologically moderate, limited in number, and capable of aggregating interests in ways that channeled dissent without endangering the polity.[11] A natural corollary was to emphasize what happened in elections, examining not how well individual parties articulated interests and once in office carried out the wishes of those who had elected them, but rather how many there were and how ideological. What mattered was, above all, political stability.

However unfortunate it may have been in some respects, the change in perspective was certainly understandable in the context of the times (although I don't remember thinking that at the time). Furthermore, it had the salutary effect of stimulating interest in the comparative study of parties. To understand how party systems did or did not serve as bulwarks against totalitarian rule, more cases were needed. During this post-war era, two edited books appearing almost simultaneously in the late 1960s made important contributions to the comparative study of parties. The first, edited by Lipset and Rokkan, stuck to the focus on cleavages, but included chapters on parties in Japan, Brazil, and West Africa.[12] In their introductory chapter the editors introduced the idea that parties form around three kinds of cleavages and become "frozen" in the roles they give themselves at the moment of origin. Most of the cases focused on the crucial cleavage of workers vs. employers (i.e., on social class).

The second book, edited by La Palombara and Weiner, unfairly less well remembered now, was somewhat more daring.[13] Breaking the grip of post-war fears of exploitable divisions that would lead to a return of totalitarianism, the editors placed less emphasis on cleavages per se, and more on the role parties played in the quest for democratization. They sought to explain how parties began and developed, how parties themselves were changing, and what role parties were playing in crises of political development and in the making of policies. The chapters came from around the world, still placing greater emphasis on the United States and Europe, but also examining party systems in Africa, the Middle East, and Asia as well. Some chapters used case studies while others made broader (less nation-linked) generalizations, sometimes exciting ones.[14]

In 1976, Giovanni Sartori brought us back to the focus on party systems with an emphasis on European examples. Parties were to be seen as the building blocks of party systems and the important question was what combination of kinds of parties within a system would lead to good governance and stability. Types of systems were characterized by number of parties, ideological distance between them, and relative degree of success (percent of votes, percent of seats). Well distinguished from one another, the types have remained useful tools for 40 years, only recently replaced, in some respects, by the work of Markku Lakso and Rein Taagepera, whose formula for counting how many parties are actually "effective" within a system is used by several authors in this set of studies.[15]

Note the three new words that have sneaked into our discussion: "degree of success." And note too that success was now being defined solely in terms of gaining power (or determining who does so). Although Sartori's work was based on limited observations, seeing party success as the winning of elections was very much in tune with the times. The 1970s were, after all, the era of a double revolution in political science, one that was to make the study of elections overwhelmingly attractive. At first it was called the behavioral revolution, because its scholarly militants declared it was time to move away from the excessive emphasis on the study of institutions to the study of individual behavior in politics. But of course it was also a revolution in methodology: survey research and statistical analysis of the answers collected permitted the study of the individual in politics *and* the quantification of political data as never before. Very rapidly, or so it seemed at the time, we learned a great deal more about the beliefs and motivations of individual voters. We learned about party realignment, meaning the realignment of voters, behind parties. We learned a bit about party activists as individuals, although little about what they could do and did do collectively, within parties, within rules, within national contexts. Indeed, through the new tools we learned very little about parties as organizations, and only indirectly anything at all about their link to democratic governance.

Some of us watched it all with a combination of approval and dismay, unprepared to do this new kind of study ourselves, but fascinated to see individual citizens become a more serious subject of study. I gave it a try, taking some post-Ph.D. course work in statistics, and, on my first sabbatical, dutifully gathering 100 interviews of party activists and leaders in France, asking each the same questions. But when writing up the results, I was puzzled by what to do with all the insights I had gleaned from these interviews that fit nowhere in the new scheme of study. And soon I learned how very small the number 100 had become, and also how common it was for those who had the resources to gather data banks (data banks!) weighty enough to achieve serious statistical respectability to treat citizens as little more than integers, mere numbers to be tweaked until they yielded up truths that were, all too often, disappointingly familiar, narrow, and of limited importance. Was it for this that I had struggled to understand what a standard deviation was?

Of course the grapes were not all sour and one could not simply walk away pretending that they were. Nor were they out of reach: one could draw on the quantified findings of others, using them in one's own books and edited volumes, and use them to lend support to comparative observations about parties as organizations and even about the relationship between parties and democracy—one thinks particularly (but not only) of the work of Stefano Bartolini, David Farrell, Piero Ignazi, Kenneth Janda, Richard Katz, Peter Mair, Alan Ware, and Harmon Zeigler, some of whom quickly proved adept as well at gathering the new kinds of data themselves.[16]

But throughout this time and indeed even now, party success continued to be defined as winning. Even as the new literature on democratization began to emerge in comparative studies, the prevailing view of parties remained that a party succeeds when it wins an election and takes power in government. What it did with that power, however nefarious, was not seen as taking away from the fact that it had succeeded. Those among us who tried to argue that a successful party was one that created democratic linkage between citizen and state, found it hard to make ourselves heard, very hard.[17] After all, who could deny that winning and succeeding were all but synonymous terms?

Yet surely it was important that at least some of us should stand back and take a larger view, particularly since the new methods were themselves revealing that parties everywhere, including the winners, were falling into greater and greater disrepute. If no one outside of academia really liked them very much, wasn't that a rather significant sign of failure for an organization basing its very right to exist on its ability to represent the interests of its supporters? Wasn't it reason enough to continue to ask just how good a job parties were doing in linking citizens to state?

And then there was the other nagging question: when we did talk about parties why did we so often write as if the only ones that mattered were in the United States or Europe and the only authors who could give us a clue about parties outside the west were westerners?

The articles and books I produced in mid-career were all based in some way on those two nagging questions. My first edited book grew out of my desire to find a better way to examine and name what parties actually did for (or to) citizens when they won office. Since they had to win votes, they had to establish ties to voters, but if those ties were not always consistent with democratic theory, then what kind of ties were they? I found four ways parties linked citizens to the state: they provided *participatory* arenas where citizens could help choose candidates and devise programs, they were *responsive* once in office, they offered *clientelistic* benefits to supporters, or they worked as *coercive* agencies of the state, keeping citizens acquiescent to power. To see if these were useful categories with wide applicability, I sought collaborators outside the United States, including indigenous authors writing about non-western cases. This double focus—linkage and indigeneity—guided all my work editing books in the 1980's, 1990's and early 2000's. It led me to put together and publish *Political Parties and Linkage* in 1980, followed by *When Parties Fail* (with Peter Merkl) in 1988, and then *How Political Parties Respond: Interest Aggregation Revisited* (with Thomas Poguntke) in 2004.[18] In the 1990's I agreed to organize a workgroup on political parties for the Committee on Political Sociology (CPS, a research committee affiliated both to the International Political Science Association and to the International Sociological Association); in 1998 I became its chair while continuing to lead the workgroup. My work with CPS put me in touch with younger party scholars, as well as with many of the more senior European ones whose work I had long admired but whom I had never met, and also with a wider range of non-western scholars. Taking leave from teaching in San Francisco every spring in order to teach courses on political parties in Paris helped as well. My French improved ("incredibly," as one charmingly gaellic insult/compliment had it) and so did my understanding of French politics, but yet more important was the opportunity to observe and appreciate an alternative way of viewing the world of politics, thereby learning how great the distance between such alternatives could be.[19]

During all these activities I was steadily gaining a deeper understanding of the importance of knowing the historical, socioeconomic and institutional context in which parties form and act in order to understand the relationship between parties and democracy—and also how difficult doing the job right could be. A short list of the many factors involved would clearly include the institutional structure of the state, meaning not only the constitution but also the electoral system and other laws directly influencing the opportunities for parties to form and make their case; the key points in the political history of the development of the parties, including but not limited to the outcome of elections; the issues that troubled and often divided the electorate, including ethnic and religious divisions but also the distribution of wealth and the provision of social services; the relationship of the nation and sometimes of the parties themselves to foreign powers and to the growing globalization of the economy. Where dictators were in power it would be essential to understand their relationship to parties and not simply assume that multipartyism necessarily curbs oppressive authoritarian rule. It was important to study party programs but also the extent to which they were ever carried out. Questions of party discipline were crucial, but so were questions of feasibility. And of course we needed to know the nature of supporters, how active they were, and how they too would change over time. Both quantitative and qualitative information would have to be gathered—we needed to know the numbers, but also the meanings lurking behind them, and what their shelf-life was: after all, what chance is there that what is true today will be true tomorrow? How good can predictions be, and why? And for some key matters, quantification would not be necessary or possible.

Facing the importance of doing justice to the complexity of context, I became still more certain of the usefulness of case studies written by indigenous authors. It was during this time that I began to develop the series Parties in Context, an idea that appealed to sympathetic editors at Praeger Publishers.[20] I edited one of the books, then found the editors for the others and worked closely with them all.[21] By century's end, several books had appeared, but the job was far from done; it was then that the idea for this present work evolved. I began talking to others about it, but the time I could give so mammoth a project was limited. I still had other promises to keep. Peter Merkl had persuaded me we should edit *When Parties Prosper*, a sequel to *When Parties Fail* that I saw would permit us (working with our contributors) to make clearer the distinction between electoral success (prospering) and party success as agency of democratic rule (providing participatory or responsive linkage). In addition, I had just become one of the two co-editors of the *International Political Science Review*, the journal of the International Political Science Association, a job that gave me invaluable new contacts throughout international political science, but also consumed many hours of my time.[22]

It was only two years ago that I could at last give this present work the time it deserved. By then I had the necessary network in place. Where I couldn't find the kind of party specialists I needed myself, I could rely on my six volume co-editors. They helped find the authors and worked with me to suggest revisions to first drafts (and sometimes to second and third ones). Although the first and final work has been mine alone, a great deal of what happened in between could not have happened at all without the assistance of Baogang He, Saad Eddin Ibrahim, Anatoly Kulik, Jorge Lanzaro, Marian Simms and Luc Sindjoun.[23]

SUMMARIZING BY REGION

Inasmuch as the volume co-editors (myself included) have provided summaries of each volume, here I seek simply to highlight some of the more striking differences among the regions, offering what may be seen as a summary of summaries. Since every region is rich in party diversity, every sentence I write should be taken as a generalization, not a truth with no exceptions, and of course what I find most striking may not always be what most interests or intrigues the reader of these five books.

Comparatively speaking, the parties of North America have strong histories as agencies of democracy. They were created for the purpose, they emerged in times of national liberation, their elected representatives worked in office to fine tune the promises of government by the people, and they listened when the citizens used the vote to tell them they were going the wrong way. Yet in recent years parties in the United States and Canada have been growing steadily weaker as agencies of democracy. Canadians are ever less partisan, ever less committed to party on ideological grounds, and ever less willing to vote. They are more likely than before to seek organizations that allow opportunities for meaningful citizen participation, yet parties now offer considerably fewer opportunities for members to participate. In the United States the situation is further advanced; parties' elected representatives have, especially within the states, devised a host of laws making it steadily more difficult for new parties to form and compete on a level playing field. During campaigns they work "in service" to the candidates who have won nomination largely by their own efforts, helping to gather and funnel immense sums of money to pay for exorbitant campaign costs they make no serious effort to abate when in office. The indebtedness of elected representatives to donors can be paid off only by resisting necessary reforms and passing requested legislation. Recent efforts to increase the role of smaller contributions have had only limited success, while limitations on campaign spending by corporations have been removed by judicial edict. Popular discontent with both parties grows ever stronger. Dedemocratization seems seriously on the march.[24]

The seven authors writing about Latin American parties make it clear that there has been remarkable progress toward democratization by party on that continent in recent years, even as serious obstacles make it difficult for parties to continue or complete the job. They take three different approaches to explain this situation. Two chapters stress particular difficulties: Argentina is plagued by institutional *departidization,* whereas Peru is marked by the continuing institutional weakness of parties in the post-Fujimori era. Three others show that in the recent moves to democratization the parties have been uncertain players: in Bolivia, social movements have the central role; in Mexico, right wing parties have moved much further toward democratization than left wing parties, still excluded from power; and in Chile two minority alliances, neither of them considered representative of more recent trends in the concerns of Chilean voters, have divided power and alternated in office.[25] And finally, two authors discuss strong competitive democracies that nonetheless have ever stronger presidential control over the parties: Brazil and Uruguay. All seven nations have emerged from long eras of colonial rule, and are now resisting neo-colonial exploitation as well as seeking to lessen their vulnerability to military takeover. Antidemocratic forces, both from within and from without (and sometimes in collusion with one another) remain powerful, but important changes have been made and further progress toward sustainable party democracy now appears to depend at least as much on internal as on external factors.

Volume II covers the parties of Europe and ten chapters analyze how the relationship between parties and democracy is in a state of flux. The seven chapters devoted to the parties of Western Europe show persistent decline in parties' role as agencies of democracy. In France the decline began with the weakening of the legislature, the central arena for representative party democracy, immediately after World War II when the Fourth Republic was established. The parties' struggle to regain their footing has been characterized by a shift to personalized presidential politics in which winning is everything. In Italy an overly fragmented party system that had led to legislative stalemate was followed by parties that took it upon themselves, often by corrupt means, to shift power to crowd-pleasing personalities that feel no qualms in using that power for the benefit of the few. As the game is recognized but the grip on power remains apparently secure, parties are now widely seen as a liability for democracy in that country. In Germany, Spain, the United Kingdom, Norway, and Denmark the shift to lower turnout, reduced partisanship, greater public distrust and disinterest as the parties become more powerful partners of the state and less concerned or able to fulfill their roles as agencies of democratic linkage may be more recent and less advanced (especially in Scandinavia) but the gradual transformation is nonetheless apparent to the native authors who present these cases.

The situation is dramatically different in Eastern Europe, where tremendous progress has been made toward democratization in the past two decades, but now seems stalled. Parties in Poland, Hungary and the Czech Republic are all laboring in the post-liberation era under socioeconomic conditions that make it all but impossible to realize dreams of party democracy as a way to improve standards of living. Time has proved that competitive elections are one thing, but effective democratic governance is another. By campaigning demagogically and fanning ideological conflict, rather than addressing their nations' problems pragmatically and honestly, the parties earn a share of the blame from all three East European authors.

In the post-Soviet region, Russia stands as a case apart, with little hope at present of democratization by party or other means. After Russia adopted its new constitution in 1993, the entire process of shaping parties has been aimed, says Anatoly Kulik, at transforming them into a tool to secure the survival and self-reproduction of the Putin regime. In the absence of any resistance from civic society, the party factions in the Duma are now nothing more than a rubber stamp for decisions made by the closed circle at the top of power.

Although Ukraine, Moldova and Georgia are alike in that all suffer from their soviet legacy, socioeconomic weakness, and public distrust of parties, there are differences among them. The situation of parties in these nations is far less dire than in Russia, but nevertheless in Ukraine we see stalemated struggles for power within both the parties and the government, Moldova suffers from the absence of a past democratic experience, and Georgia is described as having had a merely "botanical revolution" establishing democratic institutions with little or no democratic content; there the party, state and business seem inextricably linked and the borders between them are, we are told, ill-defined or nonexistent.

In Asia, China is also a case apart, having only one meaningful party. The Communist Party of China remains firmly committed to the maintenance of authoritarian rule yet is nonetheless making some surprising moves toward limited internal party democracy. It is important to recognize but not exaggerate these changes: within the party there are still no guarantees of gender equality, no democratic control of party funding, and no internal elections to choose candidates. Moreover, limitations on individual freedoms, including internet access, remain severe. Three other nations in Asia do have multiparty systems and have taken recent steps toward greater democracy. In Japan, even the Liberal Democratic Party now makes stronger appeals to ordinary citizens (insufficient, however, to maintain control of the government in the most recent elections); in Malaysia, opposition parties are winning more seats and even control of some state governments; and in South Korea a more decentralized nomination system makes it easier to form new parties. The fifth nation, India, long praised for early and important steps toward democratization, is in fact failing to advance and even backsliding: its party system is still clientelistic and now there is increased dynastic control of parties by families.

All five African nations discussed are moving slowly and with difficulty toward competitive multiparty systems. Nigeria has moved from internal military to civilian rule but the military remains very strong, as do identity cleavages. Serious movement forward is seen as unlikely until the nation finds its own "Afro-centric paradigm" of how to achieve democracy and development and adopts legislation guaranteeing political, civic, and socioeconomic rights. South Africa has moved from the institutionalization of discrimination to constitutionally ordained political equality but has a very strong dominant party which has not yet been capable of finding solutions to domestic problems put in place by its troubled past, exacerbated today by a ferocious medical plague and an unfriendly global economy. Namibia has moved from external military rule to independence but is also ruled by a very strong dominant party and Cameroon, independent thirty years longer, nonetheless still has a dominant party. Kenya's multipartyism is marred by deep divisiveness and its ethnic-based parties were leading players in the surprising outburst of violence in early 2008 that left over 1,500 people dead and an estimated 500,000 displaced from their homes, a tragedy that makes painfully clear the need to provide serious enforcement of the new law that provides a basic minimum of standards to which all political parties must adhere. What all five nations have in common is a complex history, a changing present and at least a hint of hope for a more positive future for parties and democracy. Considering the odds lain down by their colonial and post-colonial histories, the progress made in these African party systems is encouraging to the authors who write about them. What they tell us about context tells us not only why this is so, but guides our response, reminding us that although our goals may be universal, our standards for judging success must be relative to reality.

In Oceania Australia, New Zealand, Samoa, Fiji, and the Solomon Islands all have a legacy of British rule, with independence achieved only very recently in the smallest island states. Ethnic diversity and conflict have impeded democratization by party in Australia, New Zealand, the Solomon Islands and Fiji. Fiji, Samoa, and the Solomon Islands have had varying degrees of success in combining traditional kinship systems with British systems; shifting to a party system inevitably means an effort by outsiders to share or take power, and a battle by traditional leaders to retain what they had. In Fiji a minimally stable system of governance has yet to be achieved; for the Solomons and Samoa private calculations still outweigh ideological debate in the quest for power via competitive parties—the argument is made that ideological party politics is a desirable basis for principled democratic governance. Australia and New Zealand differ sharply in their ability to combine outright imposition of the British system with democratization by party, especially where democratization must mean fair treatment of large minority populations; the record of New Zealand in this respect is encouraging.

Thirteen of the 22 Arab states have no true parties at all. The volume co-editor, Saad Eddin Ibrahim, points out that the six covered here—Egypt, Algeria, Tunisia, Morocco, Mauritania and Lebanon—have common threads but great contextual differences. In most a similar path has been followed: a national liberation movement has established single party rule; the state moves to some form of multipartyism in order to channel dissent and gain international aid; the state remains dominant and is backed by the military; the parties lack internal democracy, organizational/institutional capacity to govern, disciplined membership, autonomous resources and functional links with civil society groups. The individual chapters show great differences in 1) the manipulative techniques of the true holders of power (see in particular the chapter on Egypt for a full description of how President Mubarak maintains his control), 2) the responsibility the parties themselves bear for failure so far to democratize; and 3) the role of ethnic and/or religious division in complicating the quest for democratization (nowhere more pronounced than in Lebanon). Two neighboring states with strong Arab influences, Israel and Turkey, are also placed in this volume, at the end. Turkish democracy is weak and the parties receive little credit for its existence: "Rather than strengthening Turkish democracy, they construct a discourse asserting guardianship and seeking legitimacy in the eyes of the military and civilian bureaucracy." The Israeli picture is more mixed: the parties have achieved some success as representative agencies and have upheld the nation's democratic institutional infrastructure, but they have failed to adjust to the changing mores of the electorate.

Although it is useful to organize and then summarize these 46 studies by region, we should not exaggerate the importance of regions per se in the comparative study of parties. Obviously, socioeconomic and cultural conditions vary enormously within regions and a nation may find its almost-twin well outside regional boundaries. Regional histories of widespread armed conflict and the concomitant spread of particular religions are perhaps the contextual factors most profitably studied at the level of the region. Did imperialists—from another part of the globe or from the same area—conquer and subject the region (or a large part of it) to centuries of colonial control, accompanied by oppression and poverty? Did eventual liberation from colonial rule lead to the establishment of new forms of authoritarian rule backed or overtly exercised by military force, itself sustained by external aid? Was religious conversion part and parcel of conquest and subsequent control? If so, has the dominance of one religion carried over into the present, and if so, how does it contribute to or hold back the progress of democratization? Or has the dominant religion separated itself from the state—or been ostracized by it? The answers to these questions may reveal region-wide differences with great significance for the possibility of democratic party governance. Yet they will also reveal exceptions: not every liberated state falls into the hands of military rule, even when that is the fate of most new nations within a region. Minority religions manage to survive even in regions heavily dominated by one. Democracy falters in regions where it has long seemed securely established.

LEARNING FROM THE WHOLE: PARTIES AND DEDEMOCRATIZATION

The value of *Political Parties and Democracy* is, in any case, not to be found in a brief summary at any geographic level. Indeed, our purpose in putting together this collection has been to move in the opposite direction: to privilege specificity, to look for the multitude of ways the fates of parties and democracy are intertwined. If we wish to learn all that it has to offer, each study must be considered in its own right.

Yet such comprehensive learning may not be the goal of every reader. Some will focus on specific parties, and many will be looking for new ideas or methods that apply to parties everywhere. It is my purpose now to point out ways this collection addresses those expectations.

First, this collection of studies provides a broadly comparative base in which those interested in studying only specific parties may anchor their work. Considering the wide variety of contextual factors that have influenced party development in these nations makes it easier to recognize comparable influences elsewhere, or note what happens when they are absent. Observing the effects of semi-hidden corruption, shifting loyalties, and organizational decay abroad, we may question more closely what is really going on at home, wherever home may be. Noting the constancy of change helps us avoid the hubris of final answers. Finally, those who are familiar with a wide range of cases will be better able to discuss the significance of their own findings with other party scholars, and more confident in prescribing to governments.

Second, *Political Parties and Democracy* demonstrates the value of consulting indigenous authors. When I began this work I felt some concern that indigenous scholars might be inclined to gloss over problems within their nations and present too patriotic a picture of party reality. I was mistaken to harbor such doubts even for a moment. The authors have without exception been ready to name the many shortcomings of parties as agencies of democracy or democratization. This may be so because they are less worried than external scholars about "protecting their sources"—*they* are their sources. But I think it is also because they feel the pain of these shortcomings personally, not only in their private lives but as citizens. Where the truth is grim, they understand the way forward must lead through honest presentation and explanation. In that respect, all are true patriots. And the study of parties becomes not only more comprehensive, but also more unequivocally honest. Thanks to them, this collection tells us exactly how parties work in one particular nation after another to enhance or inhibit democratization. If we are interested in only one, we can be sure the indigenous author will treat it as the central, special and different one that it is. We learn the importance of factors that outside scholars might well overlook, or misunderstand. As corollary advantages, those who are not natives of the nations whose parties they wish to study may bring a new appreciation to their study of the work of scholars who have lived within that system, and scholars everywhere may try harder to place their work in the world of international political science.

Third, by paying attention to so many and such varied cases, *Political Parties and Democracy* compels us to acknowledge and learn from complexity. Categories like dictatorship, tribal system, and democracy open up to reveal profound internal differences that affect what parties can do. Some dictators show remarkable ingenuity in finding new ways to hold embryonic parties hostage to their will—and others do not. Traditional chiefs and tribal leaders convert to ruling by party via reliance on their own strong reputations for probity, *or* by ethnic infighting, *or* by clientelistic or other forms of corruption, *or* by military conquest. Electorates in more established democracies combine ever greater discontent with parties with ever greater susceptibility to campaigning that manipulates them to vote contrary to their own most compelling interests. Party law ranges from minimally regulatory to totalitarian, from carefully enforced to blithely ignored. External forces shape domestic welfare and consequent political response. Recognizing this variety and volatility in 46 systems we learn to search for it in others. Certainly we can no longer pretend to understand the genus *political parties* by focusing so heavily on the parties that are best known and most studied in the west.

Finally, a careful reading of *Political Parties and Democracy* reveals that the process of dedemocratization is at work in one way or another in every nation studied.[26] Sometimes parties are its victims; sometimes they are its perpetrators. Sometimes the process is brutal; sometimes it is gradual, semi-concealed, and seemingly trivial in nature. Either way, these studies strongly suggest that if we care about the relationship between parties and democracy, it is time to begin to study more directly than hitherto the relationship between parties and dedemocratization. Tools to do so can fairly readily be found, as I attempt to show in these final pages.

One way to begin is by reconsidering and developing the concept of linkage. Participatory, responsive, clientelistic and coercive linkage are useful concepts for considering all the ways parties link citizens to the state. However, the studies in *Political Parties and Democracy* make it clear that parties provide other kinds of linkage as well. At least two additions are required: *revolutionary linkage* and *market linkage*.[27]

Revolutionary linkage occurs during the era of liberation, when overthrow of the autocratic state has not yet taken place, and no parties representing the interests of the citizens are allowed to compete for office. Those who find such rule intolerable join parties that have been outlawed or forced to go underground, or form new, embryonic parties. At such time the linkage the party provides is not to a state per se, but to an imagined one, one that is personified by its own elite. Linkage to an acceptable state is the dream, but linkage to a charismatic leader and his entourage may be the only presently available reward for joining the battle for liberty.

Market linkage is linkage for sale. In one sense it is not new: once in power parties in government have always favored those who helped them to office and been rewarded for doing so. What makes market linkage different today is the overwhelming power of advertising and the consequent need for vast sums of money to win votes. In this form of linkage, parties link groups to the state by collecting funds and waging campaigns on behalf of candidates selected by those groups; they seek to place their patrons' candidates in office and thus become indispensable partners in power. Ordinary citizens are encouraged to believe they will be the beneficiaries of responsive linkage, but their hopes and needs will be attended to, if at all, only after those of the patrons have been met. Their only hope in a system where market linkage is well entrenched is to form well-financed mass movements, that is, to become patrons themselves.[28]

Considering all six forms of linkage provided by party will be useful in the further study of dedemocratization. However, we need a broader framework for the identification and study of parties and dedemocratization, one that incorporates what we have learned so far and gives us tools for moving further. Table 1 identifies three forms of dedemocratizing behavior by political parties. *Proactive* parties work actively to weaken the decision-making powers of the party base. The cartel parties of Katz and Mair are proactive: they actively seek to free themselves from accountability to a democratic electorate. So are parties that offer clientelistic, coercive, or market linkage. Parties that overtly sponsor or support legislation or judicial decisions, that eliminate regulations protecting rights of political participation, are also proactive agents of dedemocratization.

Parties that are *complicit* in dedemocratization aid those who proactively seek its accomplishment. Complicity takes three forms: unconscious, venal, and ideological. *Unconscious* complicity takes place when party supporters accept proposals that lead to dedemocratization without recognizing what they are doing. For example, elected representatives may vote for a law they have too hastily decided does nothing more than simplify an overly complex electoral system, not recognizing that the implementation of one of its clauses will lead to the effective disenfranchisement of a portion of the population. *Venal* complicity describes the behavior of parties (or party leaders) that accept roles and rewards for themselves from the rich and the powerful and in exchange engage in no actions contrary to the wishes of those who grant them, regardless of the wishes or needs of those who vote for them. Parties working hand in glove with dictatorships are examples; so are parties in pseudo-democracies, such as the parties of Russia at the present time. *Ideological* complicity takes place when a party rejects fundamental precepts of representation and accountability on principle. Extremist and racist parties preaching the exclusion of minority populations can be, without ever winning office, ideologically complicit in dedemocratization.

Finally, *retreative* parties may serve dedemocratization. Electoral defeat may be so severe that quitting seems entirely reasonable, but nonetheless the decision may remove a democratic player from the game. Parties that strive to eliminate dictatorship, briefly succeed, and

Table 1 Three Forms of Dedemocratization by Party

Behavior		*Examples of Behavior*
Proactive		1. Collude with other parties to eliminate competition
Complicit		2. Support elimination of regulations protecting participation
	Unconscious complicity	Fail to recognize anti-democratic implications of measures the party supports
	Venal complicity	Party leaders agree to support dedemocratizing measures in exchange for personal rewards
	Ideological complicity	Allow extremist, racist, or other strongly held beliefs to guide party decisions without regard for possible dedemocratizing effects
Retreative		Party supports democracy but 1. Disappears entirely after electoral defeat 2. Disappears entirely when outlawed after military coup 3. Disappears entirely when outlawed by democratically elected regime

then are summarily replaced by military coup, as in so many of the nations studied here, are themselves victims of a dedemocratization engineered by others. However, some parties in that predicament quit the struggle while others relaunch the battle for liberation from abroad or from underground (or both); in such cases, the former are, willy-nilly, agents of dedemocratization. The same pattern is sometimes found when a party hitherto operating democratically is nonetheless outlawed by a new regime democratically elected. These various possibilities are summarized in Table 1.

Note that in many cases of complicity and retreat, there may be extenuating circumstances that make the behavior seem less heinous; nevertheless, the effects are the same. Note as well that Table 1 does not seek to include all parties, nor other agencies of dedemocratization, nor all possible *examples* of the three types of party behavior that cause them to become or serve forces for dedemocratization. It simply attempts to name the *kinds* of behavior that parties engage in, in elections and in office, that contribute to dedemocratization, and to provide a few fairly obvious examples. The job of identifying and categorizing more examples—and possibly more kinds of dedemocratizing behavior by parties—remains to be done.[29]

In conclusion, parties are more than agents of positive linkage between citizens and state, and more than machines in pursuit of power at any cost. Contrary to democratic myth and electoral reductionism, they also serve as agents of dedemocratization. The time has come for us to broaden our understanding of the relationship between parties and democracy and to pay much more systematic attention to their capacity for anti-democratic behavior. Only when we recognize and study the threat they pose *to* democracy will we be able to take the next step and work to reclaim them as instruments *for* democracy.

Notes

INTRODUCTION, POLITICAL PARTIES AND DEMOCRACY: THREE STAGES OF POWER

1. Having only indigenous authors is a unique and important characteristic of *Political Parties and Democracy* and thus well worth mentioning. As the word "indigenous" has two senses, it is perhaps also worth mentioning that here it is used in its primary sense: "living in a particular area or environment; native" to describe all authors and all co-editors, none of whom lives outside the countries he or she writes about. Authors of specific chapters occasionally use the words "indigenous" and "native" in their secondary sense, to refer to specific ethnic groups. Both usages are correct, and the reader will find that the usage intended is always clear in context.

INTRODUCTION, POLITICAL PARTIES AND DEMOCRACY: THE ARAB WORLD

1. The Freedom in the World 2008 Survey contains reports on 193 countries and 15 related and disputed territories. Each country report begins with a section containing the following information: population, capital, political rights (numerical rating), civil liberties (numerical rating), status (Free, Partly Free, or Not Free), and a ten-year ratings timeline. "Freedom in the World 2008 Survey." Freedom House. http://www.freedomhouse.org/template.cfm?page=351&ana_page=342&year=2008 Web. Accessed 23 December 2009.

2. E. Burke, *Thoughts on the Cause of the Present Discontent*, 6th ed. (Dodsley, 1770).

3. See Arab Decision: Jordan\Political Parties. http://www.arabdecision.org/inst_brows_3_3_8_1_5_13.htm. Accessed 23 December 2009.

4. "Algeria," wrote Abbas in 1931, "is French soil, and we are French-men with the personal status of Muslims." Barbour, Nevill. "Variations of Arab National Feeling in French North Africa." *Middle East Journal*, Vol. 8, No. 3 (Summer, 1954), pp. 308–320. Middle East Institute. http://www.jstor.org/stable/4322615. Accessed 24 December 2009.

CHAPTER 1, POLITICAL PARTIES IN EGYPT: ALIVE, BUT NOT KICKING

1. Amr Hashim Rabie, "A Problem of Parties not the Electoral System," *Al-Ahram*, January 14, 2002.

2. Adel Abdel Hamid Al-Attar, "Why Do Egyptians Eschew Political Life?," *Al-Wafd*, August 11, 2004.

3. This financial relationship could in part explain the phenomenon of the proliferation and state approval of small and marginal parties. The existence of such parties substantiates the regime's claim of an active pluralistic party life. Most of these small parties are requesting an increase of state subventions and patronage.

4. See Tariq al-Bishri, *The Methodology of Looking into the Contemporary Political Systems of the Muslim World* (Cairo: Dar al-Shuruq, 2005).

5. "Experts: Small Parties Are for Décor," *Al-Masry Al-Yaum*, December 16, 2005.

6. Beside the Muslim Brothers, these two years witnessed the establishment of several movements, such as Kifaya, Youth for Change, Journalists for Change, Intellectuals for Change, and Artists for Change.

7. Muhammad Al-Gazzar, "Spontaneous Movements Threaten Political Parties," *Rose al-Yusuf*, June 11, 2005, 20–22. Also see Jameel Matar, "The Decline of the Egyptian Parties and the Revival of their Alternatives," *IslamOnline.net*, September 3, 2005 http://www.islamonline.net/servlet/Satellite?c=ArticleA_C&pagename=Zone-Arabic-News/NWALayout&cid=1172072065871 (Accessed January 2006).

8. Ibrahim al-Bayoumy Ghanim, "Arab Civil Society: Cooperation with Governments is Better," *IslamOnline.net*, June 10, 2003, http://www.islamonline.net/Arabic/politics/2003/06/article09.shtml (Accessed January 2006).

9. *Al-Masry Al-Yaum*, January 14, 2006.

10. *Al-Ahram*, April 7, 2006.

11. Abdel Ghaffar Shukr, "Organizational Problems for Political Parties in Egypt," paper presented to the Fourth Conference for Democracy Development, Political Parties in Egypt: the Present and the Future. May 1999.

12. Ibid.

13. Khalid Muhi al-Din Mubarak of the Leftist Tagamou, and Ibrahim Shukri of the Labor Party have spent more than 25 years as party heads; Mustafa Kamel Mourad of the Liberal Party, close to 20 years; Diaa al-Din Daoud of the Nasserite Party, 15 years.

14. Shukr, "Organizational Problems for Political Parties in Egypt," 93.

15. There are about 25 parties awaiting the Parties Committee's approval or a court decision. The Wasat and Karama are the most important and serious ones.

16. In the 2005 parliamentary elections, the Muslim Brothers garnered 1.9 million votes of 8 million who cast their votes.

17. See the complete text of the Muslim Brothers Reform Initiative, March 3, 2004, and their electoral program of 2005. For a critical discussion of the levels of the MB's commitments to these issues, see Nathan Brown, Amr Hamzawy, and Marina Ottaway, "Islamist Movements and the Democratic Process in the Arab World: Exploring the Gray Zones," *Carnegie Papers* 67 (March 2006).

18. Khayrat Al-Shater, "No Need to Be Afraid of Us," *The Guardian*, November 23, 2005.

19. Khayrat Al-Shater, "We Do Not Promote an Anti-Western Agenda," *IkhwanWeb.com*, March 14, 2006.

20. The Wasat Program, available at: http://www.alwasatparty.com.

CHAPTER 2, THE LEBANESE PARTISAN EXPERIENCE AND ITS IMPACT ON DEMOCRACY

1. Maurice Duverger, *Les partis politiques* (Paris: Colin, 1951), 466.

2. Moisei Ostrogorski, *La Démocratie et l'Organisation des Partis Politiques* (Paris: Calmann-Levy, 1903), 618–620.

3. Roberto Michels, *Les Partis Politiques (Essai sur les tendances oligarchiques des démocraties)* (Paris: Flammarion, 1914), 294–296.

4. Bahige B. Tabbarah, "Les Forces Politiques Actuelles au Liban," thesis dissertation, Faculté de Droit de Grenoble, 1954, 325.

5. Salem Al Jisr, *The Elections Lexicon (in Arabic)* (Beirut: 1968), 128, 17–18.

6. Jalal Khouri, "Comrade Sij'ân" [a heroic-comic play in Arabic] (Beirut: Mokhtarat, 1987).

7. CE No. 912 of April 22, 1967, *Recueil de droit administratif* (1967), 137.

8. Cour de Cassation, *Chambre administrative* 75 (May 30, 1952): 818.

9. *Official Gazette* 8, February 20, 1992.

10. State Consultative Council, *Judicial Bulletin*, Decree No. 264, July 5, 1971, 756.

11. Nations Unies, CCPR/42/Add. July 14, 1996.

12. Court of Cassation, *Judicial Bulletin* 74, March 5, 1974, 166, in Georges Assaf, "Le cadre juridique qui commande la vie des partis politiques au Liban," ed. Antoine Messarra, *Political Parties and Forces in Lebanon, Beirut* I (Lebanese Foundation for Permanent Civil Peace in cooperation with the Konrad Adenauer Foundation, Librairie Orientale), 109

13. Decree No. 135, 2003–2004 with a commentary by Tawfik Rashid Hindi, *al Nahar*, February 4, 2004

14. *An-Nahar*, July 22, 2005. See also Antoine Messarra and Paul Morcos, eds., *Judicial Monitoring in Lebanon, Beirut* 3 (Lebanese Foundation for Permanent Civil Peace in cooperation with MEPI, 2006), 48–53, 56–57.

15. See website of Carnegie Middle East Center in Beiruit: http://www.carnegie-mec.org/.

16. Antoine Messarra, *The General Theory of the Lebanese Constitutional System (Comparative Research in Power-Sharing System)* (Beirut: Librairie Orientale, 2005), particularly chapter 2, "The Regulation of Relations between Religion and Politics to Safeguard the Principle of Harmony Between Religion and the State," 361–444.

17. Antoine Messarra, "Separate Religious Sects in Lebanon," in *Political Parties*, ed. Messarra, 475–485.

18. Judith P. Harik, "Perceptions of Community and State among Lebanon's Druze Youth." *Middle East Journal*, Vol. 47, No. 1 (Winter, 1993), pp. 41-62. Middle East Institute. For additional information on the origins of the Junblati-Yazbaki division, see Kamal S. Salibi, *The Modern History of Lebanon* (London: Weidenfeld and Nicolson, 1965), pp. 9-11, and Faris Ishtai, *Al-Hizb al-Taqaddumi al-Ishtiraki wa dawruh fi al-siyasa al-Lubnaniyya, 1949-1975 (The Progressive Socialist Party and its role in Lebanese politics, 1949-1975)*, vol. 1 (Al-Mukhtarah: Al-Dar al-Taqaddumiyya, 1989), pp. 57–59

19. The Civil War in Lebanon came to an official end in 1990, although the Ta'if Accords were reached in 1989.

20. Farid el Khazen, "Political Parties in Postwar Lebanon: Parties in Search of Partisans," *The Middle East Journal* 4 (2003): 605.

21. Ibid.

22. Antoine Messarra, "Positions of Political Parties in Elections (1996): More Retreat and Results that Shake Lebanese Balance," in *Parliamentary Elections—1996 and the Crisis of Democracy in Lebanon* (Beirut: Lebanese Center for Policy Studies, 1997), 359–387.

23. Joseph Moghaizel in "Parties . . .," 45–46.

24. Nabil Khalifeh, "What Is Hizbullah," *An-Nahar*, Supplement, June 10, 2000. See also Al-Awit, "To Lebanonize Hizbullah," *An-Nahar*, Supplement, June 10, 2000.

25. Theme of the three-year program (2007–2010) titled "Monitoring Economic and Social Rights in Lebanon," undertaken by the Lebanese Foundation for Permanent Civil Peace. Among its goals is to contribute to the creation of a general social public opinion.

CHAPTER 3, POLITICAL PARTIES IN MAURITANIA: CHALLENGES AND HORIZONS

1. For more details on this era, see the publication of president Mokhtar Ould Daddah bu Karthala, *Mauritanie Contre Vents et Marees* (2003).

2. On the circumstances that led to granting independence, see the work by the last French governor in Mauritania C. Laigret: "La Naissance d'une Nation," *Imprimerie National NKIT* 104 (1970).

3. On the negotiations of the Roundtable, which resulted in pluralism, see the study by Philip Marchesin, "Origins et Evolution des Parties Politique," in *Politique Africaine*, 55 (1994)

4. Mauritania obtained its independence under extraordinary circumstances characterized by an Arab boycott. During the Ashtoura Summit, a meeting held in Lebanon in 1960, the Arab League made the decision to support the Moroccan claims to annex Mauritania on the grounds that Mauritania was basically a Moroccan territory. This contributed to reinforcing the Mauritanian presence in the African Francophone space at the expense of its Arab affiliation.

5. Concerning the link between banning political activities and the deterioration of the situation in the aftermath of the Sahara war, see the works of the Mauritanian-Sahrwai writer Ahmed Baba Meska, particularly his publication *The Spirit of the People* (Media Department of the Polisario, 1973).

6. See Mohamed Ould Mey, *Global Restructuring and Peripheral States: The Carrot and the Stick in Mauritania* (Littlefield Adams, 1996), p. 203, n. 23.

7. The statistics of Amnesty International point to 260 casualties in the barracks, while the figures of Conscience and Resistance and the Front for the Liberation of Mauritanian Blacks believe that the figures reached 520.

8. For a deeper understanding of the Mauritanian class society see Philippe de Marchesin, *Tribus, Ethies et Pouvoir* (Paris: Karthala, 1992).

9. It is important to point here to the prominent study undertaken by P. R. Baduel in which he traced the trajectory of these figures. The study is published in *The Arab and Mediterranean World* under the title of "Political Parties in Mauritania 1945–1993."

10. To be fair to these individuals, we have to note that Ould Taya was the first statesman in Mauritania who paid special attention to the Arabic language and opened many senior positions to Arabophones who had suffered exclusion and marginalization from senior state positions in favor of the Francophones.

11. The repercussions of the case of Ali Ould Dah, the officer who was arrested by the French judiciary during the period of training in 1999 and was smuggled out of the country by the Mauritanian intelligence in 2000, indicate the gravity of internationalizing the problems of human rights. See D. Zisenwino, "The Military Coup: Domestic and International Implications," *Policy Watch*, Washington Institute for Near East Politics, August 18, 2005.

12. The disagreement between Al Harateen reached its peak in 2003 after the regime of Asghir Ould Embarak froze the activities of the Slave Salvage Organization headed by engineer Bou Bakr Ould Masoud.

13. All the legal records of the Mauritanian parliament are available in the Registry of the National School for Administration in Nouakchott.

14. Ibid.

15. cf. Manuela Francisco and Nicola Pontara, *"Does corruption impact on firms' ability to conduct business in Mauritania? Evidence from investment climate survey data,"* World Bank, 2007, http://ideas.repec.org/p/wbk/wbrwps/4439.html.

16. The reports of the international investigator in the case of the faulty figures in the Mauritanian Central Bank available at: https://www.imf.org/external/np/loi/2006/mrt/031406.pdf.

17. See the study published by the researcher in *Le Calame* on March 10, 2006, "Israel and Mauritania: Naivete or Realism?"

18. See the reports of the Crisis Group on the Islamic danger in Mauritania and the trap of exaggeration, August 2004. http://www.crisisgroup.org/home/index.cfm?id=3347.

19. See the article by Logourmo, "On Stakes and Horizons," UFP (party publication), 2003.

20. The *fatwa* of the minister Aslamou Iuld Sid al-Musataf says that any mosque can be considered a harmful mosque if it allows the stripping of the quality of sacredness of the place and it is used for any other purpose. This *fatwa*, although based on an old precedent in the Islamic history, has been seen by FLAM as violating the principle of respect of worship places in the Mauritanian society.

21. See the comment of the political parties on these elections at: http://www.rfd-mauritanie.org/fr/home.jhtml.

22. See the speech of the American ambassador in Mali on relations between cavaliers of change and the salafi group at: www.consciencresistance.org/derive.dangereuse.htm.

23. The speech of President Ould Taya on the security situation in Segou in Mali on June 15, 2005, Documents of the Presidency.

24. It is not a coincidence that Colonel Mohamed Ould Abdelaziz is the paternal cousin of Colonel Eli Ould Mohamed Fal, the head of the Military Council for Justice and Democracy.

25. See http://www.rfd-mauritanie.org/fr/home.jhtml.

26. See "Sur l'usage du coup d'etat," *Le Monde Diplomatique*, November 2005.

27. Sidi Ould Cheikh Abdallahi suspended his political activities for 27 years and did not adopt any political or ideological positions.

28. For the results see the site of the Mauritanian Ministry of the Interior at: http://www.ipu.org/parline-f/reports/1207 E.htm.

29. On the results of the second round, see ibid.

30. The political deal covered the presidency of the National Assembly, the Ministries of Water and Energy, Regional Reform, and Rural Development as well as the State Ministry for the Arab Maghreb.

31. Sidi Ould Al Cheikh refused to appoint former ministers in the governments of Muawya. See *Al Elm* 5 (May 2007).

32. This government was headed by an independent candidate in the presidential elections of 2007 who obtained 15% of the vote.

33. See the site of the Ministry of the Interior at: http://www.interieur.gov.mr/mi/index.aspx.

34. Lieutenant General Saleh Weld Hanana is the leader of the Hatem Party, the cavaliers' military organization, and was the commander of several failed coups.

35. See site of the Mauritanian Islamists: http://www.partitawassoul.net referenced at http://www.arabparliaments.org/countries/bycountry.asp?pid=139&cid=11.

36. Ibrahima Sar, a former prisoner and leader of the movement, won 7.8% in the presidential elections.

37. Although Arabic has for a long time been the language of communications between the Muslim elites in the African West, colonialism contributed to the creation of other elites that found in their language an avenue for social mobility and communications with the whole world and the African states that do not speak Arabic. European languages have been used as vehicles to eliminate tribal seditions, particularly in the states south of the Sahara in which several languages are used.

38. Mauritanian parties face genuine problems with regard to the issue of language, particularly given the implicit desire of many Mauritanians to maintain Arabic as a mediating language. We believe that strengthening the municipalities and the rural groups and providing them with the resources to enhance education and culture will help the political parties find solutions for the language problems and create genuine organizational links between political institutions and citizens. In this regard, the unique experience of Belgium deserves to be taken into account by the Arab countries that include multiple ethnic groups. See M. Abdoul, "Les communes dans le processus democratique: la quête difficile d'un pouvoir local effectif en Mauritanie," *Africa Development* 21 (1996), pp. 75-92.

39. These small parties fragmented, although each had won a single seat in parliament.

40. See Catherine Belvaude, *"Libre Expression en Mauritanie:"* La Presse Francophone Independante 1991–1992 (Paris: l'Harmatan, 1995), pp. 175–179, concerning the problems of the media which persist to this today.

41. "Mauritanian General Defends Coup Despite International Pressure," AFP, August 10, 2008. See also http://afp.google.com/article/AleqM5hsu-MTr-zyAGz ORSCrC wBZPrdg.

42. "Mauritanian Junta Begins Talks on Post-Coup Elections," AFP, December 27, 2008. See also http://www.google.com/hostednews/afp/article/ALeqM5g D1bpdnjWe21DaT5p9WPhx4dZkGg.

CHAPTER 4, THE ROLE OF POLITICAL PARTIES IN ESTABLISHING MOROCCAN DEMOCRACY

1. The term "vibrant forces" refers to the youthful bloc within the Independence Party which later on broke off from it and formed the NUPF in addition to Mohamed Belhasan al Wazani's Shura and Independence Party. The latter is the main rival of the Independence Party and the Moroccan Worker's Federation.

2. The Independence Party, the NUPF and the Shura and Independence party.

3. One of the main leaders of the national movement. He led Moroccan opposition after being forced to leave the country in 1962. He was kidnapped in France on October 25, 1965 while attending the meetings of the Three Continents Conference.

4. Leader of the leftist wing of the Independence Party who spun off from the party and established the NUPF; he was appointed prime minister in 1958

5. In the Moroccan official discourse, this is called the revolution of the king and the people.

6. The notion of the constituent council involves the idea of transfer of sovereignty from the king to the nation or, at least, the opposite of the current arrangement, whereby the constitution gives the king effective priority.

7. El Mahdi Benbarka, *The Revolutionary Choice*, Publications of the Democratic Left, Casablanca, 1995.

8. Formed by the National Union of Popular Forces and the Independence party.

9. The party leadership was divided between two wings: The internal wing under Abdelraham Bouebeid and the external wing under a number of political refugees outside Morocco, particularly Abdelraham Al Youssefy and Mohamed Al Basry, known as al faqik, against whom execution sentences were issued for plotting armed activities and seeking to overthrow the Moroccan regime.

10. There are no ideological justifications for these divisions. The conflict was over leadership and control over the Moroccan Work Federation, the most important trade union in Morocco at the time. The NUPF under Abdullah Ibrahim, former prime minister of the late earlier government maintained his political presence on the legal level in alliance with the Moroccan Work Federation but the strict decision adopted by the party to boycott all elections to be held later in Morocco marginalized and weakened it to the extent that some of its leaders withdrew or joined other parties.

11. Bouebeid's victory in Salla was going to be regarded as the victory of one of the local landowners as this was the image the state wanted to project, while

his success in Aghadir which is located 800 km away from Salla was going to be a political vote and the choice of the party to which he is affiliated.

12. Reconciliatory alternation is the political outcome reached by King Hassan II after a long period of negotiations with the National Bloc comprising the SUPF, the Independence party, the Progress and Socialism party and the Popular Organization of Democratic Work. The NUPF joined the bloc in the beginning but soon announced its withdrawal because the bloc's demands did not meet its expectations. The term reconciliatory alternation has been used because governance is not based on popular majority vote but on the political reconciliation between the king and the bloc's leadership.

13. Chapter 59 of the constitution.

14. The parties under the framework of the National Bloc were uncomfortable with this step because they saw that the goal behind the formation of a second chamber (counselors council) is to weaken the first chamber (house of deputies) and obstruct the process of proposing bills, particularly since the constitution gives the two chambers balanced powers although the house of deputies is elected by direct vote.

15. The two teams of the Socialist Union and Independence in parliament seek through the control petition to justify the deficiency of the constitutional stipulations which prevailed before the pre 1992 constitutional amendments and their failure to cope with new political requirements. According to Mohamed Al Yazeghy, the secretary general of the Socialist Union, the king summoned the leadership of the bloc for direct negotiations.

16. Moroccan politicians regard the 1972 constitution is a major retreat in comparison to the two previous constitutions (1962 and 1970). This is attributed to the fact that the constitution was drafted during the period of the two failed coups in addition to the aggravation of the confrontation between the palace and the opposition.

17. Most notably, the power to ratify budgets of local government on the local level and coordinate between regional departments of central administration.

18. Despite the fact that in a number of speeches King Mohamed VI called upon the political parties to open up to young people and democratize their structures.

19. The Socialist Union party held its sixth conference after 12 years (from 1989 to 2001) although its basic law stipulates the need to organize a conference every four years.

20. A study conducted by an independent Moroccan institution that year on the demand of the International Republican Institute found that the Justice and Development party ranks third in terms of voting intentions. Of the Moroccans who participated in the poll 27% said they were certain that they would not participate in voting; 7% said they would while 12% said they might not participate. When those saying they would boycott the elections were asked who they would vote for if the elections were to take place the following day, 47% said they would vote for the Justice and Development party

21. Founder of the Islamic Youth organization, the first organization that appeared in Morocco in 1969. In the past Abdelkarim worked with the leftists particularly inside the Moroccan Work Federation before becoming an Islamist activist.

22. The Guidance Council.

23. One of the former leaders who split off from the Justice and Charity organization and criticized other members for running the organization in an autocratic manner.

24. According to the national press the ministry of interior was not comfortable with the appointment of Mustafa al Ramid in this position

CHAPTER 5, TUNISIAN POLITICAL PARTIES, DEMOCRATIZATION, AND THE DILEMMA OF THE POLITICAL REGIME

1. Neo Destour means the New Free Constitutional Party, one of the two parties that emerged when the Free Constitutional Party broke into two parts. It is now the leading nationalist party. "Its activities," says Benjamin Rivlin, "sparked by the exuberance of youth, eclipsed those of the Old Destour" ("The Tunisian Nationalist Movement: Four Decades of Revolution," *Middle East Journal*, 6:2 (Spring 1952), pp. 167–193).

2. A small guerrilla force opened fire on the police station and military barracks in the town of Gafsa, calling the town's inhabitants to join them. None did, and the uprising was suppressed by Tunisian security forces.

3. For example, Ahmad El-Mistiri.

4. Sadok Chaabane, *Ben Ali on the Road to Pluralism in Tunisia* (Washington, D.C.: American Educational Trust, 1997). El-Sayyed Ahmed Ibrahim (of the Reform Movement), many years after undergoing this experience, commented: "Pluralism in the country has taken a purely symbolic ineffective characteristic, and its entrance to parliament was in effect its exodus from society." *The New Path* 20 (March 2001).

5. The first draft document of the first conference of the Reform Movement, presented by El-Sayyed Muhammad Harmal in the opening session. *The New Path*, March 2001, 5. Mahfouz Muhammad. *The New Path* 9 (December 1993).

6. http://tunisiawatch.rsfblog.org/archive/2007/07/index.html (no longer accessible).

CHAPTER 6, DEMOCRATIC TRANSFORMATION IN ALGERIA: THE ROLE OF THE PARTIES

1. Several publications addressed this issue including: Mohamed Harbi, ed., *Le FLN Mirage et Realitè, des Origins á la Prise du Pouvoir* (Naqd/enal, 1993); Abbas Farhat, ed., *Autopsie d'Une Guerre* (Paris: Garner, 1980); *L'Independence Confisquèe* (Paris: Flammarion, 1984); *Le Movement Revolutionnaire en Algèrie* (Alger: Barka).

2. The Algerian revolution took place on November 1, 1954, and on August 20, 1956, the first congress of revolutionary leaders (Sumam congress) was held. The conferees formed the structures of the revolution, including the National Council of the Algerian revolution and the coordination and work committee. On September 19, 1958, the committee of coordination and work became the transitional government of the revolution, and on January 18, 1960, the National Council established the army command for national liberation under Colonel Houari Boumédiène.

3. Ben Bellah is the first president of independent Algeria and is one of the historic figures of the liberation revolution. He took Boumédiène's position

when the latter disagreed with the transitional government and three years after assuming the presidency, Boumédiène overthrew him and placed him under house arrest. Chadli Bendjedid took over in 1978 following the death of Boumédiène and freed Ben Bellah and many other political prisoners. For more details about the alliance between Boumédiène and Ben Bellah see Saad Dahleb, *Pour l'Indèpendance de l'Algerie, Mission Accomplish* (Alger: Dahleb, 1990).

4. See the role of the military institution under Boumédiène and in choosing his successor in Abdelkader Yefsah, *La Question du Pouvoir en Algèrie* (1990).

5. Chadli Bendjedid was elected president on February 7, 1978, in presidential elections in which he was the only candidate. He resigned on January 11, 1992, following the first multiparty legislative elections in which the Salvation Front was the winner in December 1992.

6. The Islamic Salvation Front is an Islamist party that rose after the constitutional amendments of February 23, 1989, allowing the formation of political parties. Abbas Medani is one of its important leaders and Ali Belhaj was his deputy. The party adopted a hard-line discourse toward the regime on one side and its adversaries of political opposition, including other Islamists, on the other. It was able to mobilize many supporters on the political and social scene, relying on the conditions of congestion and frustration, the desire for change, and the natural affinity with the religious discourse among the Algerian people. It was dissolved in March 1992 and many of its members were put in prison. Its leaders and supporters were divided between resignation, opposition from abroad, armed work, compliance with the regime, and individual and media opposition.

7. The Salvation Front produced many passive signals on the level of discourse and practice, which scared off many political forces both locally and internationally. It offered them pretexts to strike against it using even undemocratic means. In addition, it included within it a strong radical trend that carried out, before the legislative elections under El Tayeb El Afghani, a military operation against a military squad near the valley on the Algerian-Tunisian border in which many soldiers were killed.

8. See the memoirs of General Khaled Nezar, Dar El Shehab, Algiers, 1999. Nezar, the former minister of defense and member of the State Council, states in his memoirs that he is the one who chose Lamin Zerwal and ended the tasks of the State Council prematurely. Zerwal took the constitutional oath in December 1994 and stated that the military had taken power for a transitional stage, only when all other options were exhausted. In November 1994, the first pluralist presidential elections were held and Zerwal won. Upon the escalation of the crisis during this period of time Zerwal organized presidential elections in 1999 in which Boutaflika was victorious and then voluntarily disappeared from the scene.

9. These include Ait Ahmed, a well-known political figure; Ahmed Taleb El Ibrahimy, a prominent politician; Mauloud Hamrouche, former prime minister; Youssel Al Khatib, chief of the fourth province during the liberation revolution; Abdullah Gaballah, head of the Islamist Renaissance Movement; Mokdad Safi, former prime minister. However, they all withdrew one day before the elections and accused the authorities of having predetermined the results of the elections in favor of Boutaflika. The constitutional council prevented Sheikh Mahfouz Nehnah from participating in the presidential elections of 1999 under the pretext

that he did not have a certificate indicating his participation in the Algerian revolution, despite the fact that he had prepared a file including testimony from revolutionary figures in his favor.

10. When Zerwal decided to restore the election process through the organization of pluralist presidential elections, he needed other candidates in addition to himself. When the active political parties (including the three fronts) decided to boycott the elections, four candidates including Sheikh Nehnah participated as candidates of the Peaceful Society Movement. He surprised everyone by mobilizing a large popular base that supported him in collecting nomination signatures. His great success should have qualified him for the second round at least, but the decision makers, who had not expected these results, falsified the elections. Sheikh Nehnah, known for his moderation and reason, refused to repeat the experiment of violent protest against this oppressive act against him, given the critical situation in the country.

11. The NLF's opposition and coordination with its two rival parties (the Socialist Front and the Salvation Front) is interpreted as part of Bendjedid's new orientation that rejected the option of canceling the legislative elections of 1991. It also represents an internal trend within the Liberation Front that rejected the military institution's control of the country's affairs. However, this opposition did not last for long. Abdelhamid Mehry, leader of the opposition trend in the Liberation Front, was overthrown after the 1995 presidential elections within a controversial political process, which the mass media dubbed "the scientific coup." Thereafter, the party went back to supporting the regime.

12. The regime is keen on controlling some of these organizations, such as the Algerian Federation for Trade Unions, more than political parties.

13. Djilali Sari, *Le Désastre Dèmographique* (Alger: Ed Sned, 1982) and Charles-Robert Ageron, *Les Algeriens Musulmans et la France* (Paris: Ed Puf, 1919). Many studies addressed the history of the national movement, including: Abulkassem Saad Abdullah, *The Algerian National Movement* (Beirut: Al Gharb al Islami Publishing House, 2000); Yehia Bouziz, *Political Ideologies of the National Movement through Algerian Documents* (Algiers: University Publications Department, 1990); Yehia Bouziz, *The Political History of Algeria from the Beginning till 1962* (Beirut: al Gharb al Islami Publishing House, 1997); Mahfoudh Kaddache, *Histoire du Nationalisme Algerien* 2 (Alger: Ed Enal).

14. See Ali Ben Mohamed, *The Liberation Front after Boumèdiénne, Facts and Documents of Dar Al Umman* (Algiers, 1998); Kamal Bouchama, *Le FLN a-t-il-Jamais eu le Pouvoir* (Algiers: Maarifa Edition, 1995).

15. See the study Nasser Gaby, "The Middle Classes and Politics between the Distortions of the Past and the Challenges of the Future," in *Democracy* (Cairo: Al Ahram Center for Political and Strategic Studies, 2004).

16. A few studies addressed political parties in Algèria during this period of time, including the study by Ramadan Redjala, "L'Opposition en Algèrie depuis 1962," in *Le PRS—CNDR, Le FFS* (Alger: Ed Rahma, 1988).

17. For more understanding of the social transformations and the political situation during this period of time, see Abdel Nasser Gaby, *Algeria from the Trade Union Movement to the Socialist Movements* (Algiers: National Institute for Work, 2001); *Elections: the State and Society* (Algiers: Al Qassba for Publishing, 1999).

18. Some publications addressed the ethnic dimension in the political issue in the region including Ahmed Ben No'man, *The National Identity: Facts and Faults*

(Algeria: Dar Al Umma); Ahmed Ben No'man, *France and the Berber Argument: Backgrounds, Goals, Means, Alternatives* (Algeria: Dar Al Umma); Azzeldine Layachi, "Ethnicitè et Politique en Algèrie entre l'Exclusion et le Particuliarité Berbere,"*Revue Naqd* 19–20 and 27–54.

19. The tribal region witnessed a severe crisis in 2001–2002 after a young man was killed in the headquarters of the police authorities. A new tribal trend titled Al Oroush rose and imposed itself on the existing political parties and civil organizations in the region. The political parties shied from entering the elections at this stage in solidarity with the rising trend and the protestors. The participation of citizens in the elections was very limited, stripping them of legitimacy. Yet the NLF won the elections and most of the seats.

20. These are mostly independent candidates or dissenters who turned to small parties when they were unable or did not wish to collect the necessary signatures from citizens, which is a requirement for the formation of independent lists. To achieve their political ambitions, they relied on their money and tribal weight.

21. See Mahfouz Nehnah, *The Algeria Aspired for the Missing Equation: Islam, Nationalism, and Democracy* (Alger: Al Nabaa Publishing House, 1999).

22. Ait Ahmed wrote his memoirs in French. See Hocine Ait Ahmed, *Memoire d'un Combatant, l'Esprit d'Independance 1942–1952* (Algiers: Bouchene, 1990).

CHAPTER 7, INSTITUTIONAL INCENTIVE AND ATTITUDINAL DETERRENTS: PARTIES AND DEMOCRACY IN ISRAEL

1. E. E. Schattschneider, *Party Government* (New York: Holt, Rinehart and Winston, 1942), 1.

2. Ingrid van Biezen, "How Political Parties Shape Democracy," Center for the Study of Democracy. University of California, Irvine, 2004. Available at: http://escholarship.org/uc/item/17p1m0dx.

3. Kay Lawson, ed., *Political Parties and Linkage: A Comparative Perspective* (New Haven, Conn.: Yale University Press, 1980).

4. Paul Webb, "Political Parties and Democratic Discontent: A Call for Research," in *Power to People: The Report of Power, an Independent Inquiry into Britain's Democracy* (London: Power Inquiry, 2006). Available at: http://www.power inquiry.org/report/index.php.

5. Lawson, *Political Parties and Linkage.*

6. Benjamin Akzin, "The Role of Parties in Israeli Democracy," *Journal of Politics* 17 (1955): 509–533.

7. Asher Arian, *The Second Republic: Politics in Israel* (Chatham: Chatham House, 1998), 111.

8. Yael Yishai, "Israel's Right Wing Jewish Proletariat," *Jewish Journal of Sociology* 24 (1982): 87–97.

9. Arian, *Second Republic*, 133.

10. Dan Avnon, ed., *The Parties' Law in Israel: Between Legal Framework and Democratic Norms* (Jerusalem: Ha-Makhon, 1993). Ariel Ben Dor, "Parties in Israel: Between Law and Politics," *San Diego International Law Journal* 1 (2000), 115–128.

11. Menachem Hofnung, "Public Financing, Party Membership and Internal Party Competition," *European Journal of Political Research* 29 (1996): 73–86; "The

Public Purse and the Private Campaign: Political Finance in Israel," *Journal of Law and Society* 1 (1996): 132–148.

12. On the details of democratizing the selection process see Shlomit Barnea, and Gideon Rahat, "Reforming Candidate Selection Methods: A Three Level Approach," *Party Politics* 13 (2007): 375–394.

13. Asher Arian et al., *Between State and Civil Society: The Democracy Index* (Jerusalem: Israel Democracy Institute, 2008), 33.

14. Peter Medding, *Mapai in Israel* (Cambridge: Cambridge University Press, 1972), 8.

15. Yael Yishai, "Israel's Shas: Party Prosperity and Dubious Democracy," in *When Parties Prosper: The Uses of Electoral Success*, ed. Kay Lawson and Peter H. Merkl (Boulder, Colo.: Lynne Rienner, 2007), 231–248.

16. Etta Bick, "Sectarian Party Politics in Israel: The Case of Yisrael Ba'Aliya, the Russian Immigrant Party," in *Israel at the Polls 1996*, ed. Daniel J. Elazar and Shmuel Sandler (London: Frank Cass, 1998), 121–145.

17. Vladimir (Zeev) Khanin, "The Revival of 'Russian' Politics in Israel: The Case of the 2006 Elections," *Israel Affairs* 13 (2007): 346–367.

18. Ibid., 365.

19. Ian Lustick, *Arabs in the Jewish State: Israel's Control of a National Minority* (Austin: University of Texas Press, 1980).

20. According to a press report, Arabs constitute some 20% of Kadima, subject to courting by the runners in the approaching primaries. *Haaretz*, August 3, 2008.

21. Ilana Kaufman and Rachel Israeli, "The Odd Group Out: The Arab Palestinian Vote in the 1996 Elections," in *The Elections in Israel 1996*, ed. Asher Arian and Michal Shamir (Albany: State University of New York Press, 1999), 85–116.

22. Hillel Frisch, "Stability Amidst Flux: The Arab Parties Come of Age in the 2006 General Elections," *Israel Affairs* 13 (2007): 368–383.

23. Eliezer Don-Yihyeh, "Stability and Change in a Camp Party: The NRP and the Young Revolt," *State, Government, and International Relations* 14 (1980): 25–52 (in Hebrew); Asher Cohen, "The Religious Parties in the 2006 Elections," *Israel Affairs* 13 (2007): 325–345.

24. Emanuel Sivan, "Enclave Culture," *Alpayim* 4 (1991): 45–98 (in Hebrew).

25. Tamar Herman and Ephriam Ya'ar, "Shas Dovishness, Image and Reality," in *Shas and the Challenge to Israelism*, ed. Yoav Peled (Tel Aviv: Ramot, 2001), 343–389.

26. Cohen, "The Religious Parties in the 2006 Election."

27. Ibid., 330.

28. Central Bureau of Statistics, "Religiosity in Israel, Social Survey Results 2002–2004," Press release, April 6, 2006.

29. Asher Cohen and Bernard Susser, *Israel and the Politics of Jewish Identity* (Baltimore: Johns Hopkins University Press, 2000).

30. Yael Yishai, "Interest Parties: The Thin Line Between Groups and Parties in the Israeli Electoral Process," in *How Political Parties Work: Perspectives from Within*, ed. Kay Lawson (Westport, Conn.: Praeger, 1994), 197–225.

31. Esther Hertzog, "Women's Parties in Israel: Their Unrecognized Significance and Potential," *Middle East Journal* 59 (2005): 437–452.

32. Bernard Susser, "The Retirees' (Ginla'im) Party: An Escapist Phenomenon?," *Israel Affairs* 13 (2007): 187–192.

33. Russell J. Dalton and Steven A. Weldon, "Public Images of Political Parties: A Necessary Evil?," *West European Politics* 28 (2005): 931–951; Russell J. Dalton, "The Decline of Party Identification," in *Parties without Partisans: Political Change in Advanced Industrial Democracies*, ed. Russell J. Dalton and Martin P. Wattenberg (Oxford: Oxford University Press, 2000), 19–37.

34. Richard Gunther and Larry Diamond, "Types and Functions of Parties," in *Political Parties and Democracy*, ed. L. Diamond and R. Gunter (Baltimore: Johns Hopkins University Press, 2001), 3-39; Kay Lawson and Peter H. Merkl, eds., *When Parties Fail* (Princeton, N.J.: Princeton University Press, 1988); Philip Schmitter, "The Changing Politics of Organized Interests," *Western European Politics* 31 (2008): 195–210.

35. Ingrid van Biezen and Petr Kopecky, "The State and the Parties: Public Funding, Public Regulation, and Party Patronage in Contemporary Democracies," *Party Politics* 13 (2007): 235–254.

36. Ingrid van Beizen, "State Intervention in Party Politics: The Public Funding and Regulation of Political Parties," *European Review* 16 (2008): 21–35.

37. Asher Arian, Nir Atmor, and Yael Hadar, *Auditing Israeli Democracy. Changes in Israel's Political Party System: Dealignment or Realignment? The 2006 Democracy Index* (Jerusalem: Israel Democracy Institute, 2007).

38. Ibid., 59.

39. Ibid., 80.

40. Ibid., 81.

41. Ibid., 85.

42. Ibid., 90.

43. Richard S. Katz, *Democracy and Elections* (Oxford: Oxford University Press, 1997).

44. Elin Allern and Karen Pedersen, "The Impact of Party Organizational Changes on Democracy," *West European Politics* 30 (2007), 68–92.

45. Dalton and Weldon, "Public Images of Political Parties."

46. Russell J. Dalton, *Democratic Challenges, Democratic Choices: The Erosion of Political Support in Advanced Democratic Industrial Democracies* (Oxford: Oxford University Press, 2004).

47. Arian et al., *Between State and Civil Society*, 56.

48. Ibid., 57.

49. A. Schedler, "Anti-Political-Establishment Parties," *Party Politics* 3 (1996): 291–312.

50. Ehud Sprinzak, *The Ascendance of Israel's Radical Right* (New York: Oxford University Press, 1991).

51. Ami Pedahzur, *Defending Democracy. The Israeli Response to Jewish Extremism and Violence* (Manchester: Manchester University Press, 2002), 51.

52. Ibid., 55.

53. Eric Belanger, "Antipartyism and Third-Party Vote Choice: A Comparison of Canada, Britain, and Australia," *Comparative Political Studies* 37 (2004): 1054–1078. See also Hans Daalder, "A Crisis of Party?," *Scandinavian Political Studies* 15 (1992): 269–288.

54. The center parties were: Telem, Yahad, Ometz, the Third Way, Center Party.

55. Reuven Hazan, "Kadima and the Centre: Convergence in the Israeli Party System," *Israel Affairs* 13 (2007): 266–288.

56. Quoted by Ephraim Torgovnik, "A Movement for Change in a Stable System," in *The Elections in Israel 1977*, ed. Asher Arian (Jerusalem: Jerusalem Academic Press, 1980), 87.

57. Ephrat Knoller, "Change (Shinui) in the Centre," *Israel Affairs* 10 (2004): 73–97.

58. World Value Survey available at: http://www.worldvaluessurvey.org.

59. Gideon Rahat and Tamir Sheafer, "The Personalization(s) of Politics: Israel, 1949–2003," *Political Communication* 24 (2007): 65–80.

60. Arian, *Second Republic*, 42.

CHAPTER 8, THE QUEST FOR PARTY DEMOCRACY IN TURKEY: UNEQUAL TO THE POWER OF HISTORICAL CONTINUITY?

1. Antonio Gramsci, *Selections from the Prison Notebooks*, ed. Quintin Hoare and Geoffrey Nowell Smith (New York: International Publishers, 1971), 151.

2. For the classical example of this literature, see Tarık Zafer Tunaya, *Türkiye'de Siyasal Partiler* (Istanbul: Hürriyet Vakfı Yayınları, 1984).

3. For examples of such works see Ersin Onulduran, *Political Development and Political Parties in Turkey* (Ankara: University of Ankara Faculty of Political Science, 1974) and Suna Kili, *1960–1975 Döneminde Cumhuriyet Halk Partisinde Gelişmeler: Siyaset Bilimi Açısından Bir Inceleme* (Istanbul: Boğaziçi Üniversitesi Yayınları, 1976).

4. In recent years several works in this line have become available. See Ümit Cizre, ed., *Secular and Islamic Politics in Turkey: The Making of the Justice and Development Party* (New York: Routledge, 2008); Berna Turam, *Between Islam and the State: The Politics of Engagement* (Stanford, Calif.: Stanford University Press, 2007); Esra Özyürek, *Nostalgia for the Modern: State Secularism and Everyday Politics in Turkey* (Durham, N.C.: Duke University Press, 2006).

5. For such an attempt, see Vali Nasr, "The Rise of Muslim Democracy," *Journal of Democracy* 16 (2005), 13–27.

6. For detailed information and official documents see Tunaya, *Türkiye'de Siyasal Partiler*, 1: 504–508.

7. For secessionist minority organizations see ibid., 501–611.

8. The early formation of the CUP came in 1889 by military medicine students. During the 1890s and 1900s the organization had several congresses. For the CUP, see Feroz Ahmad, *The Young Turks: The Committee of Union and Progress in Turkish Politics, 1908–1914* (Oxford: Clarendon Press, 1969); M. Şükrü Hanioğlu, *The Young Turks in Opposition* (New York: Oxford University Press, 1995).

9. These generals did not use their surnames. Surnames were not required in Turkey until 1934. The title "pasha" is equivalent to "general."

10. For the ideological priorities of the Entente Liberal, see Tunaya, *Türkiye'de Siyasal Partiler*, 1: 267–269.

11. For a detailed biography of Atatürk in English see Andrew Mango, *Atatürk: The Biography of the Founder of Modern Turkey* (New York: Overlook Press, 1999).

12. For the Progressive Republican Party see Feroz Ahmad, "The Progressive Republican Party 1924–1925," in *Political Parties and Democracy in Turkey*, ed. Metin Heper and Jacob M. Landau (London: I. B. Tauris, 1991), 65–82.

13. Erik J. Zürcher, *Turkey: A Modern History* (New York: I. B. Tauris, 1994), 179–181.

14. For the establishment of the single-party regime, see Mete Tunçay, *Türkiye Cumhuriyeti'nde Tek Parti Yönetiminin Kurulması* (Istanbul: Tarih Vakfı Yurt Yayınları, 1999).

15. For the Free Republican Party, see Walter F. Weiker, "The Free Party 1930," in *Political Parties and Democracy in Turkey*, ed. Heper and Landau, 83–98.

16. For the story of the transition to a multiparty system, see Kemal Karpat, *Turkey's Politics: The Transition to a Multi-Party System* (Princeton, N.J.: Princeton University Press, 1959); John M. Vander Lippe, *The Politics of Turkish Democracy: Ismet Inönü and the Formation of the Multi-Party System, 1938–1950* (Albany: State University of New York Press, 2005).

17. Feroz Ahmad, *The Turkish Experiment in Democracy, 1950–1975* (Boulder, Colo.: Westview Press, 1977), 123.

18. Zürcher, *Turkey: A Modern History*, 219.

19. Ibid., 221.

20. Ahmad, *The Turkish Experiment*, 125.

21. In this period, there were other political parties than the RPP and the DP, but the sum of the votes of these two parties constituted about 90% of the total votes.

22. For the military in Turkish politics see Ümit Cizre, "Ideology, Context and Interest: The Turkish Military," in *The Cambridge History of Turkey*, ed. Resat Kasaba (Cambridge: Cambridge University Press, 2007), 301–332.

23. For the JP, see Avner Levi, "The Justice Party, 1961–1980," in *Political Parties and Democracy in Turkey*, ed. Heper and Landau, 134–151.

24. For the MP, see Üstün Ergüder, "The Motherland Party, 1983–1989," in *Political Parties and Democracy in Turkey*, ed. Heper and Landau, 152–169.

25. For the True Path Party, see Feride Acar, "The True Path Party, 1983–1989," in *Political Parties and Democracy in Turkey*, ed. Heper and Landau, 188–201.

26. For a theoretical and historical analysis of problems of social democracy in Turkey, see E. Fuat Keyman and Ziya Öniş, "Globalization and Social Democracy in the European Periphery: Paradoxes of the Turkish Experience," *Globalization* 4 (2007): 211–228.

27. For the Social Democratic Populist Party, see Andrew Mango, "Social Democratic Populist Party, 1983–1989," in *Political Parties and Democracy in Turkey*, ed. Heper and Landau, 170–187.

28. For Ecevit's DLP, see Suat Kınıkoğlu, "The Democratic Left Party: Kapıkulu Politics, Par Excellence," in *Political Parties in Turkey*, ed. Barry Rubin and Metin Heper (London: Frank Cass, 2002), 4–24.

29. For the NAP, see Alev Cınar and Burak Arıkan, "The Nationalist Action Party: Representing the State, the Nation or the Nationalists?," in *Political Parties in Turkey*, ed. Rubin and Heper, 25–40.

30. For differences between the National Salvation Party and the Welfare Party, see Haldun Gülalp, "Political Islam in Turkey: The Rise and Fall of the Refah Party," *Muslim World* 89 (1999): 26–32.

31. Recep Tayyip Erdoğan was the former mayor of the city of Istanbul.

32. Ziya Öniş, "The Political Economy of Islamic Resurgence in Turkey: The Rise of the Welfare Party in Perspective," *Third World Quarterly* 18 (1997): 763.

33. Ibid.

34. Ertan Aydın and İbrahim Durmuş, "The Social Bases of the Justice and Development Party," in *Secular and Islamic Politics in Turkey: The Making of the Justice and Development Party*, ed. Ümit Cizre (New York: Routledge, 2008), 218.

35. For the term Conservative Democrat see Yalçın Akdoğan, "Muhafazakar Demokrasi," available at: www.akparti.org.tr

36. Ibid.

37. Ibid.

38. Yalçın Akdoğan, "Adalet ve Kalkınma Partisi," in *İslamcılık: Modern Türkiye'de Siyasal Düşünce*, ed. Yasin Aktay (İstanbul: iletişim yay, 2005), 630.

39. Ibid., 625.

40. The RPP was also closed down after the 1980 coup d'état, but it was reopened in 1992.

41. The author expresses his gratitude to Dr. Mensur Akgün for his contribution to this chapter. Without his cooperation and help, this work would not be possible.

CONCLUSION TO THE SET: ORIGINS OF THE PROJECT, SUMMARY BY REGION, PARTY DEDEMOCRATIZATION

1. Maurice Duverger, *Political Parties* (Paris: Armand Colin, 1959)

2. See Yunus Emre's apt quotation, in this volume, from Antonio Gramsci, *Selections from the Prison Notebooks*, eds. Quintin Hoare and Geoffrey Nowell Smith (New York: International Publishers, 1971), p. 151.

3. Kay Lawson, *Political Parties and Democracy in the United States* (New York: Scribner's, 1968); Kay Lawson, *The Comparative Study of Political Parties* (New York: St. Martin's, 1976). The research project was led by David Apter, my dissertation chair, and gave me my first window into the study of African parties.

4. Michel Offerlé, *Les Partis Politiques* (Paris: Presses Universitaires de France, 1987).

5. Robert Michels, *Political Parties: A Sociological Study of the Oligarchical Tendencies of Modern Democracy*, trans. Eden and Cedar Paul (New York: Dover Publications, 1959, first publication 1915). Readers of Michels will have no trouble recognizing the applicability of "the iron law of oligarchy" to the forces of dedemocratization at work today.

6. Moisei Ostrogorski, *La Democratie et l'organisation des partis politiques* (Paris: Calmann-Levy, 1903).

7. Max Weber, *From Max Weber, Essays in Sociology*, eds. H. H. Gerth and.C. Wright Mills (New York: Oxford University Press, 1958).

8. Elmer E. Schattschneider, *Party Government* (New York: Farrar and Rinehart, 1942). *See also The Semi-Sovereign People* (New York: Wadsworth, 1975). Schattschneider was one of the authors of *Toward a More Responsible Two-Party System*, published as a supplement to the *American Political Science Review*, XLIV, September 1950. The Report. widely read and cited, stressed the excessive decentralization of the two major American parties as the principal cause of insufficient accountability and proposed numerous reforms. Although cogent arguments were made, the Report's insistence that the main remedy would be to concentrate power at the top of two parties, and only two, made it unconvincing to me as an argument for democratization.

9. V. O. Key, *Politics, Parties and Pressure Groups*, 5th ed. (New York: Thomas Y. Crowell, 1964).

10. Frank J. Sorauf, *Political Parties in the American Systems* (Boston: Little, Brown, 1964), followed by *Party Politics in America* (Boston: Little, Brown, six editions, 1968, 1972, 1976, 1980, 1984, and 1988). Sorauf's turn to campaign finance, e.g., *Money in American Elections*, Glenview, IL (Scott, Foresman, 1988), demonstrated a continuing concern with the possibility of effective party democracy in the United States.

11. Gabriel Almond and Sidney Verba, *The Civic Culture: Political Attitudes and Democracy in Five Nations,* (Boston: Little, Brown, 1963). This cautious approach, suspicious of "excessive" participation, infused many textbooks in comparative politics over the next twenty years. One of the first books to break the pattern was by Mark Kesselman and Joel Krieger, eds., *European Politics in Transition* (D. C. Heath, Lexington, MA, 1986), followed by Mark Kesselman, Joel Krieger, and William A. Joseph, eds., *Comparative Politics at the Crossroads* (Boston: Houghton Mifflin, 1992) now retitled *Introduction to Comparative Politics* and in its fifth edition, 2010. In 1985 I made my own attempt to introduce a more broadly comparative text with greater emphasis on democratic principles, *The Human Polity: A Comparative Introduction to Political Science* (Boston: Houghton Mifflin, now in a fifth edition).

12. Seymour M. Lipset and Stein Rokkan, "Cleavage Structures, Party Systems, and Voter Alignments: An Introduction," in Seymour M. Lipset and Stein Rokkan, eds., *Party Systems and Voter Alignments: Cross-National Perspectives* (New York: The Free Press, 1967), pp. 1–64.

13. Joseph La Palombara and Myron Weiner, eds., *Political Parties and Political Development* (Princeton, N.J.: Princeton University Press, 1966). See also Harry Eckstein and David E. Apter, eds., *Comparative Politics: A Reader* (New York: The Free Press, 1963) for early efforts to give more serious attention to parties in the developing world.

14. See for example Otto Kirchheimer's explanation of the emergence of the catch-all party in "The Transformation of the Western Parrty Systems," in La Palombara and Weiner, pp. 177–200.

15. Giovanni Sartori, *Parties and Party Systems* (Cambridge: Cambridge University Press, 1976); Markku Lakso and Rein Taagepera, "Effective Number of Parties: A Measure with Application to West Europe," *Comparative Political Studies*, 12, 1979, pp. 3–27.

16. Stefano Bartolini: *The Political Mobilization of the European Left, 1860-1980: The Class Cleavage* (Cambridge: Cambridge University Press, 2000); David Farrell, *Electoral Systems: A Comparative Introduction* (New York: Palgrave Macmillan, 2001); Piero Ignazi, *Extreme Right Parties in Western Europe* (New York: Oxford University Press 2003); Kenneth Janda, *Political Parties: A Cross-National Survey* (New York: The Free Press, 1980); Richard S. Katz and Peter Mair, eds., *How Parties Organize: Change and Adaptation in Party Organizations in Western* Democracies (London: Sage, 1994); Alan Ware, ed., *Political Parties: Electoral Change and Structural Response* (New York: Blackwell, 1987); Alan Ware, *Political Parties and Party Systems* (Oxford: Oxford University Press, 1996); Harmon Zeigler, *Political Parties in Industrial Democracies: Imagining the Masses* (Itasca, IL: Peacock, 1993). For the strongest work among these authors on the relationship between parties and democracy see in particular Richard Katz and Peter Mair,

"Changing Models of Party Organization and Party Democracy: The Emergence of the Cartel Party, *Party Politics*, 1, 1995, pp. 5–28; Alan Ware, *Citizens, Parties and the State* (Princeton, N.J.: Princeton University Press, 1987); and Harmon Zeigler, *Political Parties in Industrial Democracies*. For the strongest and bravest plunge into quantification, see Kenneth Janda, *Political Parties*. For more recent examples of work on parties that asks crucial questions regarding democratic successs, see Florence Faucher-King, *Changing Parties: An Anthropology of British Party* Conferences (New York: Palgrave, 2005) and Laura Morales, *Joining Political Organisations: Institutions, Mobilisation and Participation in Western Democracies* (Colchester: ECPR Press, 2009).

17. I was proud to be one of the founding members of the Committee for Party Renewal, under the leadership of James MacGregor Burns. We had many interesting meetings, but very little national impact. I was one of three colleagues forming a California chapter that managed to put together a lawsuit challenging state party law making it unconstitutionally difficult to form new parties. Although the case went all the way to the U.S. Supreme Court and our side won, with a unanimous decision written by Thurgood Marshall, California simply wrote new law that was even more restrictive. See Kay Lawson, "Eu, Secretary of State of California, et al., v. San Francisco County Democratic Central Committee et al.," *Comparative State Politics Newsletter*, 10:3, 1989.

18. Kay Lawson, ed, *Political Parties and Linkage: A Comparative* Perspective (New Haven: Yale University Press, 1980); Kay Lawson and Peter Merkl, eds. *When Parties Fail: Emerging Alternative Organizations* (Princeton: Princeton University Press, 1988); Kay Lawson and Thomas Poguntke, eds., *How Political Parties Respond: Interest Aggregation Revisited* (New York: Routledge, 2004.)

19. For an excellent recent examination of that alternative, see Jean Leca, "Comparative, Arab, and European Studies: Still a French Exceptionalism?" *International Political Science Review*, 30:5, 2009, pp. 487–500.

20. I owe Praeger editor James Sabin great thanks for guiding me through the publication of the first books and Praeger editor Hilary Claggett every bit as much for the idea that the final planned books could be combined in a set, and for staying with me while I worked my way forward toward that goal. Praeger editor Elizabeth Potenza has been the editor on duty throughout the two years of actual preparation, and her patience and assistance have been invaluable. The excellent work of Ruth Einstein in helping with copyediting chores that went far beyond the normal ones of books written completely within English-speaking nations must also be warmly acknowledged. Final readings by Mark Kesselman, Dale Marshall, and Jo An Chace led me to make important improvements in the concluding chapter. Throughout the project, as in all the others of my scholarly career, no one has helped me more than my husband, William Lawson, who has steadfastly told me "yes you can." I owe him far too much to say.

21. Kay Lawson, ed., *How Political Parties Work: Perspectives from Within* (Westport: Praeger, 1994); Piero Ignazi and Colette Ysmal, *The Organization of Political Parties in Southern Europe* (Westport, CT: Praeger, 1998); Kay Lawson, Andrea Rommele, and Georgi Karasimeonov, *Cleavages, Parties and Voters: Studies from Bulgaria, the Czech Republic, Hungary, Poland and Romania* (Westport, CT: Praeger, 1999); Subrata K. Mitra, Mike Enskat, and Clemens Spies, eds., *Political Parties in*

South Asia (Westport, CT: Praeger, 2004). Anatoly Kulik and Susanna Pshizova, ed., *Political Parties in Post-Soviet Space: Russia, Belraus, Ukraine, Moldova, and the Baltics* (Westport, CT: Praeger, 2005).

22. Kay Lawson and Peter H. Merkl, eds., *When Parties Prosper: The Uses of Electoral Success* (Boulder, Colorado: Lynne Rienner Publishers, 2007).

23. I must also thank Byung-Kook Kim, who took the first steps toward volume co-editorship of the Asian section and helped me convince his very able successor, Baogang He, to take over when he himself was summoned to an important post in the Korean government.

24. It is now sometimes argued that at least in the United States interest groups and other social movements may be replacing parties as agencies of democracy by providing arenas for participation and sometimes achieving responsive policy outcomes. However, meeting the demands of non-elected representatives of groups with limited memberships can itself be seen as a form of dedemocratization and in any case such groups are not institutionalized as part of the decision-making process in the same way that parties are. Even when incorporated into advisory agencies, they remain vulnerable to the decisions of the parties' elected and appointed representatives in government. For continuation of this argument, See Mildred Schwartz and Kay Lawson, "Political Parties: Social Bases, Organization and Environment," in Thomas Janowski, Robert B. Alford, Alexander M. Hicks and Mildred Schwartz, eds., *The Handbook of Political Sociology* (Cambridge: Cambridge University Press, 2006), and Kay Lawson and Mildred Schwartz, "Parties, Interest Groups and Movements: Shall Change be Midwife to Truth?" Subrata K. Mitra, Clemens Spies and Malte Pehl, eds., *Political Sociology: State of the Art* (Openladen, German: Barbara Budrich Publishers, 2010). For its extension to the international level, see Kay Lawson, "Introduction: Parties and NGOs in the Quest for Global Democracy, in Kay Lawson, ed., special issue on "Towards Global Democracy? The Role of Parties and NGOs in International Politics," *International Political Science Review*, 23:2, 2006 and Kay Lawson, "The International Role of Political Parties" in Richard Katz and William Crotty, eds., *A Handbook on Political Parties* (London, U.K., 2006).

25. The most recent presidential election in Chile is a case in point, having placed in power Sebastian Pinera, a leader of the same political parties that provided support to the Pinochet dictatorship from 1973 to 1990. (New York Times.com/aponline/2010/01/18/world/AP-LT-Chile-Election.html). The parties in both alliances have moved toward the center—but not, it is contended, to the present.

26. A review of the section "Sumarizing by Region" in this chapter (pp. 197–201) will remind the reader of some of the examples of dedemocratization associated with parties that have been presented in *Political Parties and Democracy*.

27. For other contemporary adaptations of linkage theory see Andrea Rommele, David M. Farrell, and Piero Ignazi, eds., *Political Parties and Political Systems: The Concept of Linkage Revisited* (Westport, CT: Praeger. 2005).

28. Cf. The fund raising drives of the various grass roots movements organized to support or oppose the campaign and presidency of Barack Obama in the United States.

29. "Political Parties in the Service of Dedemocratization" is my working title for an article to be devoted exclusively to this subject. I invite readers of the present work to submit examples (which will be acknowledged if used) to klawson@sfsu.edu.

Contributors

GENERAL EDITOR

KAY LAWSON is Professor Emerita of political science at San Francisco State University. She was a visiting professor at the University of Paris, Sorbonne, 1992–2000, and coeditor of the *International Political Science Review*, 2000–2009. She is general editor of two series: "Political Parties in Context" (Praeger) and "Perspectives in Comparative Politics" (Palgrave). She is the author of numerous books and articles on political parties including *The Comparative Study of Political Parties* (1976) and editor of many others including *Political Parties and Linkage* (1980), *When Parties Fail* (1988), and *When Parties Prosper* (2007), the last two with Peter Merkl. Her textbook, *The Human Polity: A Comparative Introduction to Political Science*, is now in its fifth edition. In 2003 she received the Samuel J. Eldersfeld Career Achievement award of the section on Political Organizations and Parties of the American Political Science Association.

VOLUME I: THE AMERICAS

JAMES BICKERTON is professor of political science at Saint Francis Xavier University in Nova Scotia, Canada. Recent publications include coeditorship of *Canadian Politics*, 5th ed. (2009), coauthorship of "Regions" in Danielle Caramani, ed., *Comparative Politics* (2008), and *Freedom, Equality, Community: The Political Philosophy of Six Influential*

Canadians (2006). His research interests include federalism, nationalism, and regionalism, as well as Canadian party and electoral politics.

DIANA DWYRE is professor of political science at California State University, Chico. She is coauthor with Victoria Farrar-Myers of *Legislative Labyrinth: Congress and Campaign Finance Reform* (2001) and *Limits and Loopholes: The Quest for Money, Free Speech and Fair Elections* (2008), as well as author of many journal articles and book chapters on political parties and political finance. She was the William Steiger American Political Science Association Congressional Fellow in 1998 and the Australian National University Fulbright Distinguished Chair in American Political Science in 2009–2010.

ALFREDO JOIGNANT is professor and researcher of the Instituto de Políticas Públicas Expansiva UDP, Diego Portales University in Chile, and past president of the Chilean Political Science Association (1998–2000). He is the author of several articles on political parties, political competence, and political socialization in the *Revue française de science politique*. His work currently focuses on the political sociology of elites and the politics of memory.

JORGE LANZARO is professor at the Instituto de Ciencia Política, Universidad de la República (Uruguay), of which he was founder and director. Among his latest publications: "A Social Democratic Government in Latin America," in Steven Levitsky and Kenneth Roberts, eds., *Latin America's Left Turn* (Cambridge University Press, forthcoming); "Uruguayan Parties: Transition within Transition," in Kay Lawson and Peter Merkl, eds., *When Political Parties Prosper*; "La 'tercera ola' de las izquierdas en América Latina," in *Las izquierdas latinoamericanas* (Madrid: Pablo Iglesias); and *Tipos de Presidencialismo y Coaliciones Políticas en América Latina* (Buenos Aires: Clacso).

FERNANDO MAYORGA is professor and director of CESU-UMSS, Saint Simon University in Cochabamba, Bolivia. He is the author of *Encrucijadas. Essays about Democracy and State Reform in Bolivia* (Gente Común 2007) and *The Antiglobalization Movement in Bolivia* (Plural/UNRISD 2008) as well as multiple book chapters and articles about neo-populism, parties, and political discourse.

ANA MARÍA MUSTAPIC is an associate professor in the Department of Political Science and International Studies of the Torcuato Di Tella University in Buenos Aires. Her primary areas of research include Congress, political parties, and electoral systems. She has served as a consultant for the OAS, the UNDP, and the IDB on political reform. She is currently finishing a book on the micro foundations of party politics in Argentina.

JAIRO NICOLAU is professor in the Department of Political Science, Instituto Universitário de Pesquisas do Rio de Janeiro (IUPERJ), Brazil. He is author of *História do Voto no Brasil* (2002) and *Sistemas Eleitorais* (2004), and multiple book chapters and articles on political parties, electoral systems, and elections.

ESPERANZA PALMA is professor in the Department of Social Sciences, Universidad Autónoma Metropolitana-Cuajimalpa, in Mexico City. She is the author of *Las bases políticas de la alternancia en México: un estudio del PAN y el PRD durante la democratización* (México, UAM-A 2004) and author of multiple book chapters and articles on political parties during transitional processes in Latin America, particularly in Mexico, the so-called crisis of parties, and the perspectives of consolidation of the leftist parties in Mexico.

MARTIN TANAKA is Peruvian and took his PhD in political science from FLACSO Mexico. He is currently a senior researcher at the Institute of Peruvian Studies (IEP) and professor at the Catholic University of Peru. He is the author of numerous books, book chapters, and articles on political parties, democracy, and social movements, in Peru and in Latin America; published by the IEP, Cambridge and Stanford University Presses, Brookings Institution Press, and the University of London, among many others.

VOLUME II: EUROPE

ATTILA ÁGH is a professor of political science at the Budapest Corvinus University and director of the research center Together for Europe at the Hungarian Academy of Sciences. He has published books in the United Kingdom on the democratization of the east-central European region and has recently edited a series of books in English on the new member states of the European Union, focusing on governments, parties, and organized interests.

ELIN HAUGSGJERD ALLERN is postdoctoral fellow of political science at the University of Oslo, Norway. Her research interests include party organizational change, the relationship between parties and interest groups, and multilevel government and political parties. Her work has appeared in several edited volumes and journals, including *West European Politics* and *European Journal of Political Research*, as well as her book, *Political Parties and Interest Groups in Norway* (ECPR Press 2010).

JØRGEN ELKLIT is professor of political science at Aarhus University in Denmark. His main professional interests are local and national politics and elections in Denmark and elections and democratization in new democracies. His latest book is *Nye kommunalvalg? Kontinuitet og forandring ved valget i 2005* (New local elections? Continuity and change in the 2005 elections) (2007, coedited with Roger Buch).

CHRISTIAN ELMELUND-PRÆSTEKÆR is an assistant professor at the Department of Political Science, University of Southern Denmark. His most recent book is on negative campaigning in Danish elections (*Kammertoner og Unoder i valgkamp,* University Press of Southern Denmark 2009). He has published several articles on political communication, negative campaigning, agenda-setting, and party organization.

JUERGEN FALTER is professor of political science at the University of Mainz (Germany) and was president of the German Association of Political Science (2000–2003). He has published about 25 books and monographs, and over 200 articles on voting behavior, the Nazi electorate, political extremism, political attitudes, and methodological problems of the social sciences.

PIERO IGNAZI is professor of comparative politics at the faculty of political science of the University of Bologna, Bologna, Italy. His recent publications include *Political Parties and Political Systems: The Concept of Linkage Revisited* (Praeger 2005, coedited with A. Rommele and D. Farrell), *Extreme Right Parties in Western Europe* (Oxford University Press 2006*), and Partiti politici in Italia* (Il Mulino 2008).

ULRIK KJAER is professor of political science, University of Southern Denmark. His most recent book is on local political leadership (*Lokalt politisk lederskab,* with Rikke Berg, University Press of Southern Denmark 2007). He has published several articles and book chapters on political recruitment, elections, parliamentarians, local governments, and local party systems.

HIERONIM KUBIAK is professor of sociology at the Jagiellonian University and Andrzej Frycz Modrzewski Cracow University, Poland. Among his recent publications are: *Democracy and the Individual Will* (1997); *Parties, Party Systems and Cleavages in Poland: 1918–1989* (1999); *Reformers in PUWP* (2000); *Poland's Democratic Left Alliance: Beyond Postcommunist Succession* (2007); and *On the Threshold of the Post-Westphalia Era. A Theory of Nation* (2007).

LAURA MORALES is a research fellow at the Institute for Social Change of the University of Manchester. Her interests lie in the areas of political behavior, social capital, and political parties. She is the author of *Joining Political Organisations* (ECPR Press 2009) and of many book chapters and articles, among which is "European Integration and Spanish Parties: Elite Empowerment amidst Limited Adaptation" (with L. Ramiro), in Thomas Poguntke et al., eds., *The Europeanization of National Political Parties: Power and Organizational Adaptation* (London: Routledge 2007).

MIROSLAV NOVAK is the first professor of political science at the Charles University and rector of the CEVRO Institute, both in Prague. He has published regularly in French and in Czech, including *Systemy politickych stran* (Political Party Systems, 1997). He is—among other appointments—a member of the editorial boards of *La Revue internationale de politique compare, La Revue d'etudes politiques et constitutionelles est-europeennes,* and *l'Annuaire francais des relations internationals.*

LUIS RAMIRO is associate professor of political science at the University of Murcia, Spain. He is the author of many book chapters and articles on political parties, including "Euroscepticism and Political Parties in Spain" (with I. Llamazares and M. Gmez-Reino), in P. Taggart and A. Szcerbiak, eds., *Opposing Europe? The Comparative Party Politics of Euroscepticism* (Oxford University Press 2008) and "European Integration and Spanish Parties: Elite Empowerment amidst Limited Adaptation" (with L. Morales), in T. Poguntke et al., eds., *The Europeanization of National Political Parties: Power and Organizational Adaptation* (Routledge 2007).

NICOLAS SAUGER is senior research fellow at Sciences Po (Paris) and associate professor at the Ecole Polytechnique, France. He has coedited the special issue "France's Fifth Republic at Fifty" of *West European Politics* 32(2) (2009) and several book chapters on political parties, institutions, and methodological issues related to survey research.

PAUL WEBB is professor of politics at the University of Sussex. His research interests focus on representative democracy, particularly party and electoral politics. He is author or editor of numerous publications, including *The Modern British Party System* (Sage 2000), *Political Parties in Advanced Industrial Societies* (Oxford University Press 2002, with David Farrell and Ian Holliday), and *Party Politics in New Democracies* (Oxford University Press 2005, with Stephen White). He is currently coeditor of the journal *Party Politics.*

VOLUME III: POST-SOVIET AND ASIAN POLITICAL PARTIES

Post-Soviet

IGOR BOTAN is the executive director of the Association for Participatory Democracy, an independent center of analysis and consultation on the decision-making, political, electoral, and socioeconomic processes in the Republic of Moldova. He is the author of many articles on electoral and party system development in Moldova and is also the political analyst for Moldovan issues at Radio Free Europe/Romanian Service and at the Intelligence Unit of *The Economist*.

ANATOLY KULIK is senior research fellow in political science at the Russian Academy of Sciences and lecturer at State University—Higher School of Economics (Moscow). He writes widely on comparative party politics, political party development in post-Soviet Russia, and e-governance. Among his recent publications are: "Russian 'Mnogopartijnost' in the Light of Political Competition," in *Political Competition and Parties in Post-Soviet States*, edited by E. Meleshkina et al. (2009); "Russian Party System after Electoral Cycle 2007–2008: The End of the History?," in *The New Political Cycle: Agenda for Russia*, edited by O. Maliniva et al. (2008); and "To Prosper in Russia: Parties Deep in the Shadow of the President," in *When Parties Prosper: The Use of Electoral Success*, edited by Kay Lawson and Peter Merkl (2007).

ANDREY A. MELESHEVYCH is professor and dean of the School of Law, National University of Kyiv-Mohyla Academy in Ukraine. He is the author of *Party Systems in Post-Soviet Countries: A Comparative Study of Political Institutionalization in the Baltic States, Russia, and Ukraine* (2007) and multiple book chapters and articles on political parties, electoral law, and institution building in transitional countries.

GEORGE TARKHAN-MOURAVI is codirector of the Institute for Policy Studies (IPS) in Tbilisi, Georgia, and chairman of the board of directors, PASOS association of Eastern European think tanks based in Prague, Czech Republic. He has authored a number of publications on political developments and regional security in the Caucasus and the Black Sea region, interethnic relations, forced migration, human development, and democratic transition in Georgia.

Asia

BAOGANG HE received his MA from the People's University of China, Beijing, and PhD from ANU, Australia. He is chair in international studies at the School of Politics and International Studies, Deakin University, Melbourne, Australia, and author of four books, three edited books, and numerous refereed articles. His current research interests include deliberative democracy, Chinese democratization, and Chinese politics.

EDMUND TERENCE GOMEZ is an associate professor of political economy at the Faculty of Economics and Administration, University of Malaya, and recently (2005–2008) served as research coordinator at the United Nations Research Institute for Social Development (UNRISD) in Geneva. His many books include *Malaysia's Political Economy: Politics, Patronage and Profits* (1997), *The State of Malaysia: Ethnicity, Equity and Reform* (2004), *Politics in Malaysia: The Malay Dimension* (2007), and *The State, Development and Identity in Multi-ethnic Countries: Ethnicity, Equity and the Nation* (2008).

M. V. RAJEEV GOWDA is professor of economics and social sciences at the Indian Institute of Management Bangalore. He coedited *Judgments, Decisions, and Public Policy* (2002). He is also active in Indian politics. He has authored book chapters and articles on Indian political parties and also on e-democracy.

TAKASHI INOGUCHI is president of the University of Niigata Prefecture, professor emeritus of University of Tokyo, executive editor of the Japanese *Journal of Political Science*, and director of the AsiaBarometer project. He has published 80 books and numerous journal articles on Japan and international affairs. His current interests include political party systems, political cultures, and cross-national comparisons of norms and values through surveys. He is the coeditor of *Globalization, the State and Public Opinion* (with Ian Marsh, 2008) and "Demographic Change and Asian Dynamics: Social and Political Implications," *Asian Economic Policy Review* (June 2009).

HOON JAUNG is professor of political science at Chung-Ang University in Seoul, Korea. He is the author of *President Roh Moo Hyun and New Politics in South Korea* (2003) and numerous articles on party politics and democratization issues of Korea. He was Reagan-Fascell Fellow at the National Endowment for Democracy (Washington, D.C.) in 2005 and now serves as editor-in-chief for *Korean Legislative Studies*.

ESWARAN SRIDHARAN is the academic director of the University of Pennsylvania Institute for the Advanced Study of India (UPIASI), New Delhi. His research interests are in comparative party systems and coalition politics, political economy of development, and international relations of South Asia. He has written or edited five books, published over 40 journal articles and book chapters, and is the editor of *India Review* (Routledge).

VOLUME IV: AFRICA AND OCEANIA

Africa

ADEKUNLE AMUWO is professor of politics at the Howard College Campus, University of KwaZulu-Natal, Durban, and has recently completed a term as executive secretary of the African Association of Political Science (2004–2009). He is a widely published pan-African scholar and activist. Two recent works are *Constructing the Democratic Developmental State in Africa: A Case Study of Nigeria, 1960–2007* (2008) and a coedited book on *Civil Society, Governance and Regional Integration in Africa* (2009).

NICOLA DE JAGER holds a DPhil in political science from the University of Pretoria and is a lecturer at the political science department of the University of Stellenbosch in South Africa. She has published in peer-reviewed research publications and has consulted locally and internationally on issues of democratization, dominant party systems, political society, and civil society with a specific focus on South African and African politics.

LEAH KIMATHI holds a BED (Hons) from Moi University and an MA in history specializing in international relations from Kenyatta University. She also holds a fellowship in international philanthropy from Johns Hopkins University. A recipient of the Claude Ake Memorial Award in 2004, she has been involved in several research works in the area of the African state and has published in the same. She is programs coordinator with Africa Peace Point, a Pan-African conflict resolution organization, and a part-time lecturer at the Catholic University of Eastern Africa in Nairobi. She is currently a conflict mediator and researcher.

WILLIAM A. LINDEKE now serves as the senior research associate for democracy and governance at the Institute for Public Policy Research (IPPR) in Windhoek, Namibia. He was professor of political science at the University of Massachusetts Lowell (retired) and professor of political studies at the University of Namibia. He has authored or coauthored several book chapters and articles on Namibian politics and on SADC issues. He is co-national investigator for Round Four of the Afrobarometer in Namibia.

ANDRÉ DU PISANI is professor of political studies and former dean of faculty at the University of Namibia (UNAM) and is the director in Namibia of the Southern African Defence and Security Management Network (SADSEM). He is the author, editor, or coeditor of several books and numerous articles on Namibian politics and security issues in the SADC region.

LUC SINDJOUN is professor and head of the political science department at University of Yaoundé II (Cameroon). He is the author of several books, chapters, and articles on comparative politics, African politics, and international relations.

HERMAN TOUO is a lecturer at the University of Ngaoundéré, Cameroon. His PhD dissertation was titled "Les dynamiques d'ancrages du pluralisme partisan au Cameroun (1990–2006): l'economie des rapports entre pouvoir et opposition." He is also interested in youth movements, especially the impact of youth mobilization on democratic governance in Cameroon. He participated as 2002–2003 fellow on Understanding Exclusion, Creating Value: African Youth in a Global Age, a project initiated by the Africa Program of the Social Science Research Council (SSRC).

Oceania

ALUMITA L. DURUTALO is a lecturer in the Division of Politics and International Affairs at the University of the South Pacific, Fiji Islands. She obtained her PhD from the Australian National University in Canberra and specializes in party and electoral politics and customary and modern political leadership in the Pacific. Her numerous journal articles and book chapters include "Fiji: Party Politics in the Post-Independent Period" (Roland Rich et al., eds.).

RAYMOND MILLER is an associate professor and chair of the Department of Politics at the University of Auckland, where he specializes in political parties, representation, electoral systems and elections, and leadership. He has collaborated on a number of election studies, including *Proportional Representation on Trial* (2002) and *Voters' Veto* (2004). Recent publications include *Party Politics in New Zealand* (2005), *New Zealand Government and Politics* (2006), and *Political Leadership in New Zealand* (2006).

GORDON LEUA NANAU is a researcher at the Solomon Islands College of Higher Education (SICHE). In 2009 he completed his PhD at the School of International Development, University of East Anglia, U.K., with a doctoral dissertation on insecure globalization in the South Pacific. His research interests are in the areas of rural development, decentralization, conflicts and peace making, globalization, and international development. His chapter on "Intervention and Nation-Building in Solomon Islands: Local Perspectives'' appeared in *Interventionism and State-building in the Pacific: The Legitimacy of ''Cooperative Intervention''* (eds. Greg Fry and Tarcisius Tara Kabutaulaka, Manchester University Press, 2008).

MARIAN SIMMS is professor of political studies and Head of Social Sciences at Deakin University in Melbourne, Australia. She has published numerous articles and books including ''Australian and New Zealand Politics: Separate Paths but Path Dependent,'' *The Round Table,* 2006, and *From the Hustings to Harbour Views; Electoral Administration in New South Wales, 1856–2006* (University of NSW Press, 2006). Her next book, *Kevin07: The 2007 Australian Election,* is in press.

ISALEI SIOA is a senior lecturer in history and head of the social sciences department at the National University of Samoa. She has made contributions to the following books, *Lagaga: A Short History of Western Samoa, Tamaitai Samoa (Women of Samoa: Their Stories),* and has published articles in the *Journal of Arts Faculty,* National University of Samoa.

VOLUME V: THE ARAB WORLD

Arab World

MOHAMED OULD MOHAMED ABDERRAHMANE MOINE is a Professor of Diplomacy in the Ecole nationale d'administration of Nouakchott University in Mauritania. From 1992 to 2008, he occupied diplomatic and governmental positions in Belgium, Canada, and South Africa. He is the author of numerous articles on the subjects of human rights protection, international relations, and democratization.

MOKHTAR BENABDALLAOUI is professor of philosophy and head of the Department of Philosophy at Hassan II University, Casablanca, and director of the Center for Studies and Research in the Humanities.

SAAD EDDIN IBRAHIM is professor of sociology at the American University in Cairo, founding chairman of the Ibn Khaldun Center for Development Studies and founder of the Arab Organization for Human Rights. He is widely known for his work on electoral fraud in Egyptian elections, work that led to his arrest and conviction and a global outpouring of support from scholars, human rights organizations, and political leaders. Recently convicted a third time, he is now in exile. During 2008–2009 he served as professor of political sociology at Indiana University and as the Shawwaf Chair Professor at the Center of Middle East Studies at Harvard University. His numerous awards and publications are listed at http://www.eicds.org.

SALAHEDDINE JOURCHI is a journalist and the vice president of the Tunisian Human Rights League in Tunis.

ABDERRAZAK MAKRI is a medical doctor and holds an M.A. in Islamic law and a post-graduate degree in Management Sciences. He is a founding member of the Movement Society of Peace (MSP) in Algeria and is currently the vice-president of the Movement and an elected member of the Parliament in Algeria. Dr. Makri is the author of several publications, including *Islam and Democracy, Towards an Effective Citizenship*, which was developed by the Center for the Study of Islam and Democracy (CSID) and Street Law, Inc., and has been used as a training manual for NGO leaders and Imams throughout the Arab world.

ANTOINE NASRI MESSARRA is professor of political science at Lebanese University and Saint Joseph University, Beirut. He is president of the Lebanese Political Science Association and program coordinator of the Lebanese Foundation for Permanent Civil Peace.

EMAD EL-DIN SHAHIN is the Henry Luce Professor of Religion, Conflict and Peacebuilding at the University of Notre Dame. He was an associate professor of political science at the American University in Cairo and visiting associate professor of the Department of Government, Harvard University, while writing for this study. His recent works include *Political Ascent: Contemporary Islamic Movements in North Africa* (1997); coeditorship of *Struggling over Democracy in the Middle East and North Africa* (2009); and coauthorship of *Islam and Democracy* (2005, in Arabic).

Neighboring States

YUNUS EMRE is a Ph.D. candidate at Bogazici University, Istanbul, and a graduate assistant at Istanbul Kultur University. His research interests are European and Turkish politics, the economic and social history of modern Turkey, and 20th-century historiography.

YAEL YISHAI is Professor Emerita of political science at the University of Haifa, Israel. She is the author of several books including *Land of Paradoxes. Interest Politics in Israel* (SUNY, 1991) and multiple articles and book chapters on interest groups, civil society, and political parties in Israel. Her current research interests are in the processes leading to "antipolitics" and its outcomes.

Index

Tables indicated by *t*.